PRAISE FOR
IN THE LAND OF MEN

"Funny and shrewd. . . . Miller offers a keen and caustic take on the literary universe at a crossroads. . . . Her musings on the 'psychologically intimate' work of an editor are enlightening; her passages recounting blatant and insidious sexism are bracing; and her disclosures about her relationship with Wallace are cathartic. Miller's love for language and faith in the power of art deepen this finely composed, forthright, witty, and involving memoir of one woman's triumph in the competitive literary cosmos." —Donna Seaman, *Booklist*

"An incredible guide to a ridiculous era and its outrages. Many will praise Miller's ability to bring a time and place to life, but I would also like to add that this book is very, very funny." —Gary Shteyngart, author of *Lake Success*

"Miller recounts her years as 'improbable gatekeeper' and spins an elegy for the glory days of American magazines, with cameos by Norman Mailer, George Plimpton, and Dave Eggers. The star of the show, though, is David Foster Wallace, who . . . quickly became her greatest confidant. So began a long-distance love affair that defied definition. . . . What a treat to listen in." —*Vogue*

"*In the Land of Men* conjures the last-hurrah days of Manhattan magazine publishing . . . but it is full of contemporary resonance. With an easy intimacy and intellectual acuity, it's an engrossing story of innocence and influence. . . . [It is also] an intense, claustrophobic portrait of a complex relationship. . . . You get the sense that, as she wrote it, Miller was still having arguments in her head with Wallace. But this is what gives the book its energy and its wisdom." —*New Statesman*

"Adrienne Miller did not merely find herself in the midst of a bright, innovative, challenging, unforgettable moment in literary culture: she made it happen. It was easy to miss that then, given all the attention paid to the brilliant writers, mostly men, she discovered, nurtured, and endured. But now, with ferocious humor and honesty, she conjures once more that Narnia-like world of books before blogs and magazines, before the Internet—capturing all its giddy verve and all its frank injustices— with her own unmatchable taste and wit at the dead center, where it always belonged."   —John Hodgman, author of *Medallion Status*

"Miller delivers a beautifully written, fiercely honest account of finding her way—and her voice—in a male-dominated industry."
—*Washington Post*

"This cool, careful, enraged book about condescension has quiet humor . . . perfect pitch . . . and an unfashionable stoicism. . . . When finally the fuse that's been burning under her desk for nearly a decade of literary gatekeeping and risk-taking goes off, you don't even feel as if Miller is raising her voice, only saying what she means, editing out, as was her profession, whatever doesn't need to be there."
—Greil Marcus, *Los Angeles Review of Books*

"Bookworms, former English majors, and anyone tired of Old White Men novels will enjoy the blunt descriptions of petulant literary giants (John Updike), highbrow celebrities (Todd Solondz), and other behind-the-scenes figures."   —*A.V. Club*

"Riveting. . . . Reckons with power, and the dark truth about who gets to have it."   —*Esquire*

"Deftly evokes the spirit of a particular world at a particular time . . . presenting ample evidence of the power structures—some obvious, some not so visible—that bound it and all its problems together. . . . The most enjoyable quality of the book is its relentless cataloging of Wallace's inventively awful behavior, and of Miller's efforts to withstand the on-slaught. That Wallace was not a great guy is no surprise, but a lot of the detail here is fresh."   —*The New Republic*

"The jury's still out on whether or not one must ultimately choose between the perfection of the life or the perfection of the life's work. But, after taking an invigorating tour through Miller's bookish world, it is clear that the verdict still matters."   —*Arts Fuse*

"She makes magic on the page. . . . If you're a devotee of David Foster Wallace, you'll devour this memoir with pleasure. If not, you may enjoy the cultural scavenger hunt and appreciate how much Adrienne Miller makes you stretch."   —*Washington Independent Review of Books*

"Deftly brings to life the free-spending and freewheeling glossy magazine culture of the 1990s."   —*New York Times Book Review*

"An irresistible glimpse into the glory days of print magazines and the not-so-glorious behind-the-scenes moments."   —theSkimm

"A literary junkie's dream come true. . . . *In the Land of Men* is both tender and painful. It's power and mercy. If you love literature, novels, or anything that has to do with the written word, you will enjoy [this book]."   —Associated Press

"A story of coming of age in the last gasp of the golden era of magazine journalism, against the backdrop of a thoroughly male and insistently masculine literary landscape. . . . The most powerful thing that *In the Land of Men* does is make Wallace nothing more or less than a character in the story of Miller's life—a fascinating and indispensable one, but a character nonetheless."   —Literary Hub

"A deeply personal memoir by former *Esquire* editor Adrienne Miller, *In the Land of Men* recounts her coming-of-age career in a male-dominated magazine world and the cost of breaking in."   —*Parade*

"A sharp blend of memoir and cultural/literary history. . . . A good portion of her book centers on her difficult-to-define relationship with Wallace; her excerpts from phone conversations and voicemails and dates with him illustrate a personality that was undefinable yet brilliant. Miller exhibits a particular adroitness in her ability to recreate, with at times biting humor, various events and interactions in her career and relationships. . . . A refreshingly relatable memoir from a gifted, intellectual writer." —*Library Journal*

"Intimate. . . . Intriguing . . . will appeal to book nerds and fans of David Foster Wallace." —*Publishers Weekly*

"Movingly recounts the sexism she endured. . . . Miller's experience as a woman at a male-dominated magazine is unique." —*Kirkus Reviews*

"Adrienne Miller has written an homage not just to the heady last days of legacy publishing and the mercurial, madcap vicissitudes of 1990s New York; she has brought us eloquently back in time to a predigital, less mediated, more forgiving but also more brutally uncompromising era. *In the Land of Men* is about being the only woman in the room. But beyond that, it's about the magic of rooms themselves. It's a revisiting of life before the age of ubiquitous screens, when we shared physical space—sometimes uncomfortably and sometimes ecstatically—with our heroes and our nemeses alike. I was thrilled to make the trip."
—Meghan Daum, author of *The Problem with Everything*

"Adrienne Miller's voice is lucid and remorseful, and she's brought us a beautiful, painful book, a tender dissection of elusive subjects up to and including the passage of time and youth itself." —Jonathan Lethem, author of *The Feral Detective*

"*In the Land of Men* is the memoir I've been waiting for: a bold, incisive, and illuminating story of a woman whose devotion to language and literature comes at a hideous cost. It's Joanna Rakoff's *My Salinger Year* updated for the age of *She Said:* a literary New York now long past; an intimate, fiercely realist portrait of a mythic literary figure; and now, a tender reckoning with possession, power, and what Jia Tolentino called the 'Important, Inappropriate Literary Man.' A poised and superbly perceptive narration of the problems of working with men, and of loving them." —Eleanor Henderson, author of *Ten Thousand Saints*

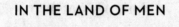

IN THE LAND OF MEN

Also by Adrienne Miller

FICTION
THE COAST OF AKRON

In the
LAND of
A MEMOIR
MEN

Adrienne Miller

ecco

An Imprint of HarperCollins*Publishers*

For Joe

A hardcover edition of this book was published in 2020 by Ecco, an imprint of HarperCollins Publishers.

FIRST ECCO PAPERBACK EDITION PUBLISHED 2021

Designed by Renata De Oliveira

Library of Congress Cataloging-in-Publication Data

Names: Miller, Adrienne, author.
Title: In the land of men : a memoir / Adrienne Miller.
Description: First edition. | New York : Ecco, 2020.
Identifiers: LCCN 2019028856 (print) | LCCN 2019028857 (ebook) | ISBN 9780062682413 (hardcover) | ISBN 9780062682420 (trade paperback) | ISBN 9780062682437 (ebook)
Subjects: LCSH: Miller, Adrienne. | Periodical editors—United States—Biography. | Women periodical editors—United States—Biography. | Esquire.
Classification: LCC PN149.9.M44 A3 2020 (print) | LCC PN149.9.M44 (ebook) | DDC 070.5/1092—dc23
LC record available at https://lccn.loc.gov/2019028856
LC ebook record available at https://lccn.loc.gov/2019028857

21 22 23 24 25 LSC 10 9 8 7 6 5 4 3 2 1

Author's Note

At twenty-five, I became the first female literary and fiction editor of *Esquire*. It was 1997 and *Esquire* had for decades been one of the country's most significant magazines; home to the writers who defined "masculinity" (if you will excuse the term) for the twentieth century: Ernest Hemingway, Norman Mailer, Raymond Carver, and the practitioners of New Journalism.

My mission was to help the magazine find its new voice. I understood that I was following in the footsteps of two legendary editors, Gordon Lish and Rust Hills, men of extraordinary vision and taste. Of course, I knew that I was, in every way, a baffling choice for the job: I was a woman, I was notably young, and I had had no sparkling editorial career behind me. But I was passionate about writers and writing, I was eager-eyed, and, I believed, I had taste.

During my tenure, I discovered many new writers, I worked with many giants. But it was with the formally audacious David Foster Wallace story "Adult World," which, according to David, every other magazine had rejected, that my journey—professional, personal, artistic—really began. David and I met in 1998. I was twenty-six and he was thirty-six. I had been at *Esquire* only a few months and was doing what I could to refurbish the magazine's moribund literary section. *Infinite Jest* had been published two years before and David was on his way to becoming the most influential and imitated American fiction writer since Hemingway.

I would acquire and edit four of David's stories for *Esquire*. I read his manuscripts, we were friends, we dated. After his suicide, my private approach to him, already well honed during his lifetime, became ever more entrenched; my preferred modes: "avoid," "shut down," and "avoid" some more. I couldn't talk about him, I couldn't read anything about him, and I couldn't read his work. I certainly couldn't write about him. God knows I never planned to, and couldn't have imagined a world in which I ever would.

What has changed in my thinking? So much has been bothering me in the eleven years since David's death. It's nothing new to suggest that as his persona has been processed by the culture industry he so loathed, the living man has faded from sight. Nearly everyone gets him wrong—but that's beside the point. Whether he's presented as a hero or a monster, he's been reduced to a darkly glamorous suicide doll. There are also significant lacunae in the public record of David's life and in the public record of his evolving thinking about his own work during the period of time we were friends.

With these thoughts in mind, I started writing about what it was like for me to know him, but also, crucially, about my own personal odyssey: a young woman trying to do good work and trying to get herself taken seriously in a world of men.

During my career, I would learn about the profoundly compromised men who make the art we venerate, and I would learn about protecting the egos of these men. I would learn about power. That was the world I lived in. Little did we know then that we were in the last days of a dying order. All empires collapse eventually, of course.

—AM, August 2019

1

In my office at *Esquire* was a hand-me-down frame, bequeathed from fiction editors of the past. It was made of chrome, complicatedly beat up, and held a piece the magazine had run in the eighties called "Who's Who in the Cosmos 1987." When I started my job as the magazine's literary and fiction editor, I found this frame lying on the floor underneath my desk.

The "Who's Who," published in the August 1987 summer fiction issue, was part of a special section that month called "The Literary Universe." It was one of those exercises in classification and pigeonholing that magazines have done since the beginning of time, a power chart of the era's so-called literary establishment. Cover stars from this issue: John Updike and William Styron. The "Who's Who" map, which looked kind of like a kid's outer space place mat, was a three-page gatefold with hundreds of floating, context-free names of various writers, editors, agents, critics, teachers, and publishers grouped in categories such as "Rising Stars," "Falling Stars," "Out of Orbit," "The Parallel Universe," and "Lost in Space." You get the drift. Or maybe you don't. Probably you shouldn't. With all due respect to the legendary *Esquire* fiction editor L. Rust Hills, who compiled the thing as a sort of reprise to a literary power chart the magazine published in 1963, I could never make heads or tails of it. I can guarantee that few *Esquire* readers of the eighties could, either.

One thing was clear: the place to be on the chart was "The Red-Hot Center." As Rust had written in his introduction, the persons located there were generating "enormous amounts of heat." The fiction writers placed within that particular red-hot sun (they are all dead now, the sun a graveyard) were Saul Bellow, John Updike, Raymond Carver, Elmore Leonard, and Norman Mailer. Toni Morrison, probably the most important living American novelist, was relegated to a moon in deep space, mentioned only in a roundup of her agency's clients. The red-hot center did contain the names of three women, but none of them were novelists and only one was a writer—a book critic; the other two were a literary agent and a socialite. And they are all still very much alive, these three, but that's no real surprise. The women always do seem to persevere in the end.

I never knew what to do with the frame. I loathed the literary star system and everything this chart represented, and there was no way I was ever going to hang it on my wall. But I could never quite bring myself to toss it, either. I tried to give it away, but I never found any takers, not even among the more seasoned *Esquire* veterans (meaning: Rust Hills, who never seemed to want to take credit for his own creation). So, during the years I had that office, the framed "Who's Who" existed in a kind of purgatory, lying faceup on the bottom shelf of a bookcase behind my desk, with books and submissions and whatnot stacked on top of it.

When I started the job in 1997, no single media outlet could presume the Literary Universe–wide authority *Esquire* had attempted to claim for itself a decade before. Was there anything vaguely resembling a red-hot center or even a general literary universe anymore? And if there was, was I now somehow, at age twenty-five, as *Esquire*'s literary editor, an improbable gatekeeper to it? (Or warden? Den mother, maybe?)

At the bottom of the page was a large catchall category called "On the Horizon," and included in it was a twenty-five-year-old novelist named David Foster Wallace, who had just published his first book. Eleven years after his Literary Universe cameo, David was in my office, sitting in the squat red velvet swivel chair across from my desk, with the frame in his lap.

"God, I *hate* this thing," he said.

David's hair was cut short underneath his blue bandanna, his complexion was turbulent, and he had, as my grandmother liked to say about any white person who'd been in the sun, good color. I considered him for a moment.

"You're looking very tan right now, David."

The brown-gold Wallace eyes gleamed deviously. I would edit four short stories of David's for *Esquire*. He was the fiction writer with whom I'd work the most frequently at the magazine.

"Well, I *am* half quadroon," he said.

David was using my purple-and-white plastic TRUMP TAJ MAHAL cup—which I'd acquired two years before on an ill-advised trip to Atlantic City and had brought to the office for reasons unknown—as his tobacco cuspidor. Patiently, he waited for me to figure out what a half quadroon was.

"Octoroon," I said finally.

"Touché," he replied.

I had been amazed, and not in an entirely good way, how David was able to recollect so many details about the Literary Universe chart—who was situated where; the names, for example, of the writers placed in the "Falling Stars" category, and the distinction between the "Rising Stars" grouping and David's own "On the Horizon." (The "Rising Stars" category had Julian Barnes, Richard Ford, and Louise Erdrich in it and was the far better place to be.) The truth was that I hadn't known much at all about the notorious history of the Literary Universe, which had been seemingly scrubbed from the *Esquire* institutional memory, or anything about what a toxic plum cake it had been in literary circles, before David told me about it. According to David, writers and editors had spent the summer of 1987 nattering away about the Literary Universe—everyone joined in the belief that the thing was shallow, cynical, and ridiculous . . . yet everyone knew exactly where, or if, he was placed on it. The most I'd ever heard, or would ever hear, from *anyone* about the Literary Universe was from David.

"How old were you when it came out?" he asked.

I did a quick calculation. Fifteen. Ninth grade.

"Jesus," he said.

He'd had a residency at a writers' colony in upstate New York when the issue was published and began describing how he had taken his august inclusion in the chart as an excuse to behave as badly as possible at the colony, and everywhere else.

"But do you know what's most depressing of all?" he asked. "How much I actually *cared* about this thing. All I could think was *When do I get to the red-hot center?*"

The dark little laugh.

I suppose if there *was* a red-hot center in the late nineties/early aughts, that center might as well have been David. There was a sense that David, more than any other living writer, was read competitively, his sui generis–ness unbearable to all. It was dangerous, having David around in the world then. Before he could be turned into something else entirely—first, a beloved tragic personage; then, a cultural hero; later, a cautionary tale; finally, a monster—he would need to be safely, tactfully dead. Blood is required of our heroes—and monsters.

"Why would you even *care* what some magazine says?" I asked.

David looked over at me, eyes bright behind his glasses.

"The good thing about *you*," he said, "is that *you* would never do anything like this."

"*Obviously* not," I sensibly replied.

He started fanning his T-shirt. "Is it exceptionally hot in here or is it just me?" he asked.

The visit to my office had been David's idea ("I can't detach from you just yet"), though he was being very weird about it: he didn't want anyone to see him, so we kept the door closed.

I asked him if he wanted me to open the door to let in some air.

"Eh," David said. "I'd be too self-conscious to talk to you if the door were open."

He discreetly expectorated into my TRUMP TAJ MAHAL cup and went into a quick story about a photo shoot for *Us* magazine (seriously, *Us* magazine?) he'd agreed to do with several other young writers in the eighties. By his account, the shoot had not gone well. Indeed, it had gone the opposite of "well."

"And do you want to know what good old Dave did before they even took the picture?" he asked. "I ran away. I just ran down the street, crying like an *infant*."

"Were you wasted?" I asked.

"I wish I *had* been."

Already, nothing David told me about himself came as a surprise—as Quentin Crisp said about why he gave up cleaning his apartment: after a certain point, the dirt can't get any worse. Have I ever known *anyone* who's talked about his past as much as David talked about his?

"Interesting," I said.

David stayed in my office for the rest of the afternoon, describing more about the excesses of his past. (That was David for you—always wading, no, cliff diving, into the blackest edges of himself, and us.) One of the conclusions I had reached about him, and perhaps the only one about which I would remain consistent, despite everything: his artistic triumph in the face of such tremendous psychological and emotional odds was a miracle for which we all must be forever grateful.

David said, "I hope no one ever writes about any of it."

But he knew perfectly well what was coming, and so did I. The bill would come due. The bill always comes due. We are always held accountable in the end.

"Oh, they will," I said.

A heavy pause.

"Ew," he said. "I am completely fucked."

He knew where our world was headed: Soon there would be no distinction left between the public and the private. Soon it would all be the same thing.

What is someone "like"? Is he "good"? Is he "bad"? Is she this way, or is she that? What is *wrong* with him? Who *does that*? All this thinking we do about other people—all of our talking and complaining, all of our fretting—is an attempt to understand the unexplained inconsistencies and paradoxes in their characters. How do you even begin to negotiate the disjunctions we all have? Almost no one makes any kind of logical, unified sense, and very few people fit together into an integrated whole. All we really have are projections of other people: impressions of character, phantasms of character—vague ideas that may or may not be connected to reality.

2

When I was young, I was always watching, always trying to piece together a version of the world from whatever smoke signals arrived to me. I didn't need people too much. It was, in my first memories, the bicentennial. The national gestalt was sort of a hokey, good-natured patriotism, and any child of four would certainly have been fascinated by the fire hydrants painted to resemble Revolutionary War–era VIPs such as Thomas Jefferson, George Washington, and Ben Franklin. Patchwork Holly Hobbie purses—empty, always and forever, for what was there to keep inside, other than perhaps a dandelion?—were all the rage, and let's not forget unisex plaid shirts with mother-of-pearl-esque snaps and jeans with embroidered back pockets. A child's hair, whether upon a male or female head, was to be styled in the gender-neutral no-muss-no-fuss bowl-cut manner.

Marysville, Ohio, is now pretty much a commuter suburb of Columbus, but when I was growing up there, it may as well have been rural Kansas in the thirties. It was a self-contained small town with a main street of Victorian-era buildings, and there was a department store, Weiss Brothers, which, enthrallingly, had a dumbwaiter that carried your money and goods from one floor to another. There were soybean farms and cornfields. There was a Goodyear plant that made conveyor belts and a then new Honda motorcycle plant. It was a town built on lawn pride—the Scotts Miracle-Gro corporate headquarters was also there—and in the summer the yards of our town's nicer homes, the ones with garden globe ornaments set upon grasses of supersaturated green, were redolent of lawn chemicals.

Our house was a tidy Cape Cod. A morning glory plant grew along a fence in the backyard, and for family photographs I'd pull a purple flower from the vine, posing with it behind an ear. I made humble bouquets of Queen Anne's lace, dandelions, and clover. I liked drawing flowers, small fragile ones. The wallpaper in my bedroom had bright blue blossoms on it, but I was already developing a sensibility and knew that I might have preferred something more delicate, something in wistful Frenchified pastels perhaps (not that I had any concept of Frenchified, much less France). But you don't have much of a determinative role as a child. No one asks your opinion about much, not even parents like mine.

When I could read, I was enthralled by a collection called *A Child's Book of Poems,* rapturously illustrated by Gyo Fujikawa, which introduced me to the wonders of Christina Rossetti, Eugene Field, and Edward Lear and the following unattributed limerick that fried my brain and kept it fried:

There was a young lady named Bright,
Who traveled much faster than light.
She started one day
In the relative way,
And returned on the previous night.

Other favorites: *T.A.* [*Transactional Analysis*] *for Tots (and Other Prinzes),* the book that gave us, for better or worse, the terms "warm fuzzies" and "cold pricklies"; and, of course, the big daddy of the day, Shel Silverstein. I had a lot more books than my parents did, come to think of it, and my mom's titles—*My Mother/My Self, Sybil, Zelda,* and *Personhood*—tended, like *T.A. for Tots,* to be exemplars of the seventies personality movement, the movement, sad to say, that paved the way for the noxious individualism of the current era. My father subscribed to *Foreign Affairs*—the battleship-gray type-only cover guaranteeing the solemnity of the enterprise—semiread back issues of which accumulated like so many silvery mushrooms on the bookshelves he, a high-level handyman, had built in our family room.

I suppose it's fair to say that my parents could be characterized, at least then, more accurately as *doers* rather than as *readers.* It is true that if I spent too much time lollygagging vacantly on the sofa, say, perhaps with a book, although probably not, my mother would suggest, "Why don't you get up and *do* something? *Move.*" In my family, when you said that you hadn't sat down all day, you said it with pride.

My parents were in their midtwenties when I was born. This was in no way notable, because the parents of everyone else I knew were the same age as mine, yet my mother and father just always felt younger than everyone else's, as if they were my peers almost. They drove his and hers Volkswagen bugs (his: green; hers: tan); they owned multiple tanning lamps; they drank gin martinis before and during dinner. They were of a permissive seventies mind-set, and it's certainly possible that we had too *few* hang-ups—social ones, I mean (we're actually very emotionally repressed). When I was five, my father told me that if I had been a boy, my name would have been Matthew. Matthew Miller. Sure. I mean, why not? Sounded good enough. Dependable old Matt Miller.

But what did that even mean, *if* I had been a boy? I would stand in front of a buckling full-length mirror in the small room downstairs where my mother stored Christmas ornaments and sewing supplies, looking at my reflection, trying to work out how I felt about this information. Sometimes, when studying my image in the mirror, I would feel a little pang of mourning for the other version of myself I had somehow . . . what? Killed? Because if *I* hadn't been *me,* would "Matt" be alive? Or was "Matt" my brother? My almost brother, I mean.

And still, decades later, if I meet some guy named Matt, I continue to think, *Hey, that's my name, too.* It's a strange thought to have and I never share it, of course. You can't just go around saying things that might alarm people. You have to be sensitive with others. There was always this dissonance about identity.

TEACHERS WOULD REMARK TO MY PARENTS OF MY QUIET INTELLIGENCE and generally obliging nature, but also of my dreaminess and of a punishing perfectionist streak then manifested in a near psychosis about checking my schoolwork over and over and over before the teacher would eventually pry it away from me. I'm sure I seemed docile enough, but it's possible there was something just a little bit sly about me, too. And, for better or worse, I lived nearly entirely in my head. But I guess I'd always had this idea that the mind must be allowed to investigate for itself, without interference. The mind must be free and agile—and incoercible.

Fog delays of an hour or two were routine at my school. In the mornings, fog would rise from the ground like an otherworldly presence, and everything—farmland, silos, roads, houses—was shrouded and reconfigured, the way that blizzards rearrange the world, or dreams, until the fog was burned away by the sun.

Do you want to know one of the problems with having read lots of books in your life? You're unsatisfied with descriptions that aren't metaphor.

My parents were always busy. Both were from Pennsylvania and had already moved a lot for my father's job as an engineer at Goodyear: first to company HQ in Akron, Ohio, then to Lincoln, Nebraska, now to Marysville, and eventually back to Akron again. There was no extended family anywhere close to us, and we were a harmonious, and dangerously self-sufficient, unit. My father, who looks—then, now, forever—unnervingly like George Washington (or Chevy Chase), was in grad school, too, working on an M.B.A., forever making the long, flat drive on Route 33 back and forth to Columbus. My mother taught at my Unitarian Universalist preschool—a place just crawling with fellow Silverstein fans, as you might well imagine—and later worked in our town as a case manager at a workshop that employed developmentally disabled adults with tasks such as sorting and packing small automotive parts.

Throughout my childhood and adolescence, my mother specialized in telling these long, slightly surreal stories about the clients at her workshops, tales that stalk me still. I would hang out with her at work sometimes, and occasionally she would take me along to client home visits—to group homes or to apartment buildings with dark, airless hallways. These were the first glimpses I ever had of truly marginalized people—people who then seemed to me, to steal a line from James Baldwin, in "the long, hard winter of life." Mostly I dreaded these trips; on them, I recall having all these nebulous semi-thoughts I knew I wasn't scheduled to have yet, sort-of thoughts about the idea of luck, about how merciless fate was and how so much of who you were was a mere accident of birth. But I think somewhat differently, and a bit more practically, about things now. I now understand that these were people who fought to lead productive lives, and I also see that they didn't need anyone's sympathy.

Even when I was young I was old, and I always had more of an interest in adults than I did in other children. I still have an exceptionally vivid image of the rather curious woman who drove my elementary school bus, yet I can't entirely recall the faces of any of the kids on the bus with me. This bus driver, who, in memory, was always chewing on a toothpick and who, even in deepest winter, would keep the fan over the dashboard blowing, was clearly someone who had been through some rough stuff (she was missing a pinkie). I've always enjoyed learning about the processes of how things are done, and I was interested to observe that, when driving over railroad tracks, she would stop the bus right in the middle of the tracks and *then* crank open the door to listen for a train. It had seemed to me then that the actual railroad track was perhaps not the ideal location from which to determine if a train was barreling toward you, but what did I know?

She kept a small transistor radio up in front with her and had it tuned to a Top 40 station. Confirmation that my story is a period piece, whether I like it or not (I do not): two of the era's big hits I'd hear most often on the bus were the Marvin Hamlisch reboot of Scott Joplin's "The Entertainer" and "Feels So Good" by flugelhornist and composer Chuck Mangione. But there was another song on that radio, one that got to me even more: "Games People Play," by a band with the superlatively noncatchy name of the Alan Parsons Project. It was an up-tempo tune in the somewhat cold prog-rock manner, but the lyrics ground me to pieces:

> *Where do we go from here*
> *Now that all of the children are growing up?*

The song was, in my interpretation, a howl from middle age: the dispossessed man, fearing irrelevance, fearing purposelessness, asking, *What do I do with myself in the world now?* I was just a little kid, but I can tell you that I really keenly felt this song.

Writers—or anyone who does anything "creative" (used loosely)—are always getting asked where they get their ideas, but that's never the right question. You always know everything, all the time. There are no new emotions; there are only new events. If I may quote Ingmar Bergman, and the following observation he gives to a character in his brilliant film *Fanny and Alexander:* "One can be old and a child at the same time." I knew that this "Games People Play" song was saying something I didn't particularly want to hear, but something I already understood about what it feels like to be a person in the world.

There is wisdom beyond knowledge.

Also: What if adult life was a game you couldn't win?

MY FATHER WAS PROMOTED TO A NEW JOB AT GOODYEAR HQ IN AKRON, and two days after my ninth birthday, we moved from the cornfields in the center of the state to the Rust Belt up north. The move happened in late winter, and it was colder in the new place, a little bit harder, and everything—people included—seemed slightly more beaten up. The sunsets, at first, before I finally started paying attention, didn't seem as striated or as luminous as they had back in the flatness of Marysville, and new categories of precipitation fell from the sullen, but possibly more interesting, northeast Ohio sky. Although I hadn't complained about it too much, I hadn't wanted to leave Marysville. I remember how unutterably sad it seemed to me, seeing, in March, Christmas decorations still up in the window of a local insurance office in my new town, Tallmadge—then a dry town, by the way, with the discouraging motto "City of Churches." Tallmadge was adjacent to Kent, home to Kent State, and I soon learned the names of the four young people murdered there by their government on May 4, 1970: Jeffrey Miller, Allison Krause, William Schroeder, Sandra Scheuer. I always kept these names close.

Soon after we moved, there was a fire at a house in our new neighborhood. The house, one street over, was, in my view, the best one around—a late seventies translation of a center hall colonial, and one night it burned to the ground. But why hadn't we heard any sirens? Had there been sirens? We awoke one morning to see, from our dining room window, the big white house we barely knew now lying in ghostly ruin.

My father, a cause-and-effect man, a realist, and, frankly, a cynic, was of the opinion that the fire was probably arson and an insurance scam—everyone in the house was absent that night (so we'd heard; we were the new people in the neighborhood, and we'd never met or seen the family), including the pets. This actually seemed to me a reassuring hypothesis, since it had to do with money.

But my mother, for reasons unknown, was certain that a curse had been placed on the house.

"A hex," she would say. "Gene, that house was *hexed*."

She kept this up for years. I never disbelieved the theory. Not to get too mystical about it, but I guess a part of me has always half thought that everything we see in front of us is a prop and that the true nature of the world is hidden from view. Sometimes there was a hint of some greater reality, but that hint was all you got.

After the fire, I would ride my bike over to the charred skeleton of the house. The house was still recognizably houselike, but the roof and windows were gone, and its walls were the purest black. The air around it was malignant; it rippled, it buzzed. Soon, the place was razed and a new house was built on the lot, but still, in imagination all these decades later, when I think of that street, I always see the ruins of the old house, not the new house built where it had stood. The old image displaces the new, and I can never see the current one straight.

My new elementary school was one of those flat brutalist-style institutional buildings with painted cinder block walls. When I started there, my mother and I met the principal, a prim older lady in a tweed suit, in her office.

"Do you have a lot of fog delays?" my mother asked.

The principal looked at my mother in bewilderment. "*Fog* delays?" she asked. "I've never *heard* of a *fog delay*."

I did not care for this lady, who, incidentally, the following year, would make an announcement over the PA system that she'd unilaterally decided to ban the Olivia Newton-John song "Physical" from being played at school. Too racy. No, I did not like the principal already, but while seated there I reminded myself of the correct spelling of the word "principal": "the principal is my pal." I'd read that somewhere.

"Adri told me that she wants a young and beautiful teacher," my mother said.

This had been just some dumb thing I'd said to my mother, and I was slightly mortified that she would repeat it there. (I mean, I didn't want the principal to think I was *that* shallow, though I was.) Also, I no longer wanted to be known by that babyish truncation "Adri." No, I hadn't been happy about leaving my home—moving in the middle of a school year was a disjuncture I've still never gotten over—but at least this new place seemed to offer the possibility of presenting myself anew.

"I have *just* the teacher for you," the principal said.

My new homeroom teacher, who had short black hair, styled in the layered bob made fashionable by Lady Di, was indeed young and glamorous. On my first day of school, I was given an assignment to prepare a short presentation in which I would introduce myself to the class. She explained that there would be a bulletin board, and on it I was to thumbtack photographs of my family and also index cards with whatever biographical information I wanted. I would have a few days to gather my pictures.

I found some Polaroids of my parents and my dog, ones my mother didn't mind if I punctured with a thumbtack, and I made my father take a picture of our new "contemporary"-style house. The house, by the way, was boxy, gray, and unadorned, and our new development had scrappy young silver maple trees all over the place. I prepared my index cards, writing in neat block letters:

MY FAVORITE COLOR IS LIGHT GREEN (PASTEL)

MY BEST FRIEND IS MY DOG SUSIE

WHEN I GROW UP I WANT TO BE A LAYWER

I think about her a lot, that earlier self with her gender-neutral plaid shirt, her adult handwriting, and her big "laywer" dreams. But I already knew that being a lawyer was not going to suit me. I already had this sense that I didn't really want to deal with worst-case situations or, frankly, with reality; what I wanted, really, was an *alternative* to reality.

During the presentation, I gestured to the photo of my new house and boasted that my new bedroom had not one but two closets.

A girl's hand went up. "Your house looks like a barn," she said.

I went back to my desk. The teacher said she had something important to tell us. She was going to start a new job in a few weeks.

"I'm leaving," she said, "to be a . . . *flight attendant.*"

Cries of distress issued from around the room. A girl with lots of freckles across her cheeks doubled over her desk, weeping torrents, rending her garments asunder, etc. She wasn't the only one. All the students in class looked as if they'd been hit in the face by a collective dodgeball. I attempted my own pantomime of distress—I sat at my desk and tried, and failed, to make myself cry—although I knew I did not deserve it, the feeling or the performance.

"But *why* would you want to get a new job?" asked a boy, also very bent out of shape. (This boy would, two years later, become my first "boyfriend," provisionally speaking.)

"Oh, I won't be far away. Just remember—look up," she said distantly, pointing a dazzlingly long nail, painted red, at the ceiling and the sky beyond, "and *that's* where I'll be."

This woman and I intersected for probably a total of three weeks of our lives, but I will admit that for years afterward, when I would look up to the unreal airplanes in the sky overhead, I would often half wonder if she, this once adored former teacher, was on one of them.

Teachers, it turned out, seemed to drop like flies in my new school. Not long after that, we lost another one. He was a music teacher, with the longish white hair of a mad scientist or a syphilitic nineteenth-century composer, and he would, in nearly every class, remind us, this group of unexceptional nine-year-olds at a public elementary school in northeast Ohio, that he had a Ph.D.; as evidence of his exquisite educational credentials, he would go up to the blackboard and write something, any old thing, demonstrating how terrible his handwriting was. And it really was. His claim, and one that has always stuck with me, was that the more formal education a person had, the worse the handwriting became. In his class, we sang beautiful and enigmatic songs about the Erie Canal and the Underground Railroad, and I was interested to learn that the lyrics to "Follow the Drinking Gourd" were a coded map for slaves escaping north. (It is also a fact that this teacher began many of his classes by playing a recording of the original Paul Lynde version of "Kids" from *Bye Bye Birdie*.)

For the length of time I had him as a teacher, he would refer to me as "the new person." As in: "*New person*, what do you think 'Low Bridge' is about?"; "*New person*, what is a 'whole note' worth?" Don't ask me why this man decided to zero in on me, but he sure did. After I sang a terrified surprise solo version of "Yellow Submarine" in front of the class—"terrified," "surprise," and "solo" because my performance partner, Mindy, was a no-show at school that day (but you've gotta do what you've gotta do)—the music teacher said, "*New person,* you never cease to amaze me."

One afternoon, he made his big announcement: he would be leaving, too.

The music teacher was perhaps not as adored by students as was the brunette Lady Di, yet a student in class was still curious enough to ask him why he was going away.

I still remember the teacher's response.

"Because *this*," he said, "is *not* the place to be, my friends."

3

who is responsible for our circumstances

Our destinies come at us in unlikely ways. We tend to over-dramatize our own agency; we like to attribute whatever success we've had to our own ingenuity, industry, brilliance, good looks, overall irresistibility, etc., but the truth is that luck is at least 80 percent of life and maybe even more than that. In Renaissance drama, Fortune is the principal force—the primary character—that shapes human lives. It is not impossible that free will is an invention of the novelist, who is in the interiority business.

When I was twenty-two, a week before my college graduation, I flew from Ohio to New York to interview for a job as an editorial assistant at the men's magazine *GQ*. Up until a few weeks before, I had been intending to go to grad school, like everyone else. In my view, literature class was the only place to be: there was no "right answer," there was no group consensus, you got to choose your own truth, and you got to grapple with one exemplary mind—the mind of the writer. And when you learned how to read novels, the actions in your own puny little life intensified and took on a very different sort of consequence.

I liked to read, and I liked to write, and grad school was a place in which both of those things could be blamelessly done. What harm could come of that?

A lot, evidently. A professor tried to discourage me from the plan.

"Whatever you do, *don't* become an academic," she said. It was a month before my graduation, and she and I were standing in a hallway in the English department. "You're too independent."

The "independent" bit did not seem meant as a compliment. The truth is that I was independent only insofar as I had approached my studies in a somewhat delusory fashion—until, that is, I started taking this professor's classes. She taught literature and women's studies, and I knew she was mine forever after two things happened: When she announced to the class, "Just so you know, you are all being trained to be middle managers." And when, during the following class, she walked up to the blackboard and wrote these words: "I CAN'T GO ON, I'LL GO ON."

She also added, there in the hallway, "Academia is a horror for women."

My professor, it turned out, had this friend, and this friend had a friend. The friend's friend was an editor at *GQ*. She suggested I call the *GQ* guy for what she somewhat extravagantly called career advice. Of course, I had no career. This was not a call I wanted to make.

Now, I'd known plenty of kids in college who'd worshipped at the altar of the glossy magazine, but I was not quite one of those. I considered myself too high-minded for the mainstream commercial magazine, and I wouldn't have been caught dead in high school with any periodicals other than my father's *Foreign Affairs*es and, of late, his *New Republic*s. But there was a catch. I was obsessed with, just completely infatuated by, fashion, and most of what I knew about fashion I had learned by reading fashion magazines—alone in my room at home. I actually hated that I cared so much about clothing and considered it a potentially soul-deforming weakness. I also knew that I was quite dangerously enticed by fashion magazines' conspicuous consumption angle. So maybe my relationship with the glossy magazine might have been more accurately called "love-hate."

I did make that call. Turned out the *GQ* editor's assistant had just quit. Would I like to be considered for the job? The interview date the editor gave me conflicted with my graduation, but I knew this was my one shot, and I took it.

SO NOW HERE I WAS, A MONTH LATER, IN NEW YORK CITY, MEETING WITH the editor, David Granger, at a bar in a restaurant at Grand Central Station.

He gave the bartender a wave. "My daughter here will have a chardonnay," he said.

Of course it probably would have been a more professional move for me to ask for a sparkling water, but no one had ever told me what was appropriate and what was not; no one had ever told me anything, really.

"Are you even old enough to drink?" Granger asked skeptically.

I assured him I was.

He asked where I was staying. I told him.

"Why *there*?" he asked, clearly of the mind that this very touristy theater district hotel was just about as uncool as it got and doubtlessly drawing all sorts of unwelcome conclusions about my class, sophistication level, gaucherie tolerance, etc.

"Because it has a revolving restaurant?" I said experimentally.

Granger was a soft-spoken, thoughtful guy in his late thirties with light brown hair and glasses. He had on a baggy suit and a tie with horizontal stripes. He asked why I liked *GQ*. Helpfully, it turned out that the stories I enjoyed most were the ones he had edited. Back at school, when I should have been studying for finals, I had instead crammed back issues of *GQ*. In those pre-Internet days, there was only one way to get a back issue of a magazine: go to the library. The periodicals at my college, it turned out, were kept in the chemistry library (I had not even known there *was* a chemistry library), and for the better part of a week, I'd sat with the chemistry nerds and studied old issues of *GQ* with the devotion of a Quranic scholar. The stories I liked best in the magazine were weird and had mystery and a beating heart. I ran little reading comprehension tests of them on myself and tried to remember everything I read.

As Granger and I spoke, it became apparent that I did have one thing going for me: I was able to talk about past issues of *GQ*. Later, he said that I got the job because I was the only person he'd interviewed who'd actually even bothered to open the magazine.

"Never underestimate how unprepared most people are," he would later observe, correctly.

But back in the chemistry library at school, I'd also noted that the magazine's representation of women was problematic at best. *GQ* barely published any female writers, and the only women it seemed to have space for were starlets, preferably in stages of dishabille, which is a more attractive way of saying that they were photographed seminude: nearly every time a woman showed up, the otherwise respectable joint became a strip club (although no nipples—leave that business to *Playboy*). I'd also come across an inane recent special issue about women, which had this exceptionally sexist (and remarkably type-heavy) cover line:

"Ah, Women. What do they want? What do they want from *us*? What do they fear? What makes them tick, makes them crazy, rocks their world—and why are they so damned angry? Here in the paranoid, PC Nineties, loving women has never been dicier. With this special issue, we search for some answers, and signs of hope that we can all get along."

Speaking of "I can't go on, I'll go on." Little did I know then that this would become the central concern of my career: dealing with men's magazines' judgments of women.

The job was to be not only Granger's assistant but also assistant to the literary editor and to an assistant managing editor. Before my *GQ* deep-dive, I will admit I hadn't known that the magazine even published fiction, so this was a surprising and welcome feature of the job. I also learned that the assistant managing editor at *GQ* had been a hallowed early editor at *Rolling Stone,* a detail also of particular interest to me. In one of my creative writing classes back at school, there'd been this one student who'd been scheming to get an internship at *Rolling Stone,* and I swear, *Rolling Stone* was *all* I heard about that semester.

In brief, this *Rolling Stone* striver at school was not exactly my ideal writer—think Charles Bukowski, but on paint thinner; he was utterly untainted by self-consciousness and had that special quality of implacable self-belief. This kid, who had long brown hair and wore Tevas (I can still picture his toes) had been playing some sort of vaudeville idea of a "writer" in the way that the girls never did: he had a sinister little hoop earring, was conspicuously dismissive of any story written by a woman, and would describe student stories that had no tone by their "tonalities." It was from him that I first heard that dread label "gonzo journalism."

We listened to every detail of this guy's *Rolling Stone* internship application saga: the composition of the cover letter, the possible story pitches, the names of the *RS* editors he'd boldly cold-called (I'd never heard that expression, either—"cold-calling"), etc. He dropped the names of *Rolling Stone* editors past and present as if they were marquesses of France or what have you. A well-known right-wing-leaning *RS* columnist, P. J. O'Rourke, had gone to my school in the sixties, and you can bet that this boy kept making a big point of that in class, too; if all else failed, this would be his "in."

My response in class to the guy's terminal name-dropping and everything else: eye rolls and lip gloss reapplications.

The interview with the other two *GQ* editors, and also the operative from human resources, took place the day after my meeting at the bar in Grand Central, at the old Condé Nast building at 350 Madison Avenue. There was an annular solar eclipse that day. The sky above Madison was pristine, and eclipse watchers were gathered on sidewalks, gazing heavenward with special dark glasses, or else looking down at the projection of the sun in homemade camera obscuras. I didn't experience the eclipse as a celestial phenomenon (hadn't even known about it until I saw all those people), and I can't tell you whether there was a slight breeze for those few moments when the moon passed overhead, or if everything felt a little bit colder, or if the sky grew slightly darker, because the eclipse was, to me, a human event.

That so many people had dropped whatever they were doing and had come outside for a few minutes to watch the sky seemed an expansive and noble thing to do. It also spoke to some profound need in the human soul: a desire for meaning, control, harmony. And for just that moment, when the sun went from disk to ring and everything was elegant and aligned, reality—that is, the world behind the illusion—opened its door and showed us what it was.

I found myself in a nearly exuberant mood when I entered the Condé Nast HQ: I was thinking about order and harmony; I was thinking about signs and symbols and omens—good ones. To expand on a metaphor I once heard, the Condé Nast building rose up like an avenging Valkyrie over the two humdrum men's clothing stores down below: a Brooks Brothers and a Paul Stuart—two elves of an earthen realm. I took in the scene in the building lobby with wonder. First impression: this place is some kind of cult . . .

and these cult members are *so* not the types to get derailed by the occurrence of a semi-rare annular eclipse.

As these women glided through the lobby, you noted the eerie confidence in the way they possessed their bodies, yet the overall effect was of stasis—they were static in the way that a photograph in a magazine is static. As I signed my name in the book at the front desk, I did a quick scan of the page and noted some names of individuals (public figures, you might even say) I'd actually heard of before—two fashion people and one literary one. Was this unutterably thrilling to me? Yes, it was. Indeed it was.

GQ editorial was on the sixth floor, and the atmosphere there was more low-key than whatever it was I had just experienced in the lobby. It was also much more "male." I met the other two editors in their offices, which were as nondescript and antiseptic as could be. The editors were both kindly men; the ex–*Rolling Stone* guy said nothing about *Rolling Stone,* and neither did I. I nodded benignly along as each man spoke of various awards *GQ* and its writers had won. Had I ever heard of any of these awards? I had not. I possessed nothing to offer these editors, or the place, other than some somewhat unhinged enthusiasm.

I got the job, but getting it probably didn't have all that much to do with me. It was absolutely a right-time-right-place-type situation. The fact: I was just wandering through life like everyone else. *So far,* I should say. The Robert Frost line "Yet knowing how way leads on to way" is the actual answer to how most human lives are led. (Mostly, you find that adult life largely comes down to a path of least resistance.) My purported career was handed to me on a platter, and that is the truth. But from here on out, everything would be up to me.

ON THURSDAY, MAY 19, 1994, THE DAY JACQUELINE ONASSIS DIED, MY parents drove my stuff and me from Ohio to New York, through the endlessness that is the state of Pennsylvania. I would begin my job the following Monday. We stayed at a hotel in Weehawken, New Jersey, not because the town was the site of Alexander Hamilton's fatal duel with Aaron Burr or anything like that, but because my father is a thrifty man. Across the Hudson River, Manhattan looked glittering and heroic. I loved my parents, but I couldn't get back to the city soon enough.

For the moment, there was an NYU dorm where I would be able to live throughout the summer. The clock was ticking, though, and I would have to find a real apartment of my own by the fall. My parents moved me in on Friday. Item: when you are a teenager or a very young adult, and when your parents are moving you into a new place, it will always be the hottest day in human history, and your dad will always be in the worst mood ever.

"God*damn*," said my father through clenched teeth, lifting another heap of garment bags from the Oldsmobile trunk, "you have so much *stuff*. I think you should ask yourself why you believe you need all of this."

I tried to convince my parents to take me to lunch at an upscale restaurant, but all I got out of them was a humble pizza, eaten in my room. Traffic concerns were on their minds; they hit the road for Ohio ASAP, and we didn't have what you'd call a sentimental goodbye. I met my new roommate, a premed student from South Korea. She wasn't confident with her English, but during our first chat it somehow got communicated that she was peculiarly fixated on finding a mysterious perfume. She had discovered the scent back home in Seoul but didn't know the name of it; the perfume, which had haunted her for years, was now half remembered, as if in a dream.

Well, naturally, there was only one solution:

"We should go to Barneys tomorrow," I said, "for *research*."

The old original Barneys, on Seventh Avenue and Seventeenth Street, was the most fantastically wonderful place in the world, and my new roommate and I spent a memorable Saturday afternoon together there in the cosmetics department, grinning frantically as we sprayed perfume onto our pulse points and onto each other's. After about an hour, the elusive scent actually *was* identified: Hanae Mori. Victorious, my roommate gave the bottle three wordless spritzes into the air. It *was* nice. She bought two. I bought one, because I'm always buying stuff. A couple of months later, when I had found my own place a few blocks away and was moving out of the dorm, I found a letter from my roommate on my pillow: "Dear Friend," she wrote, in the most elegant, painstaking handwriting. That letter was a physical work of art.

The following day, Sunday, the day before I started my job at *GQ,* I drifted around the Metropolitan Museum of Art. Somehow, I had never been to the Met before. During the last two summers in New York, when I wasn't operating the microfiche reader at work (I had an internship that involved copying grant information from microfiche files of philanthropic foundations' tax returns), my free time had been occupied with a guy whom I'll call Kevin. Kevin was older than I by nearly a decade, and he lived in deepest Brooklyn. He was a writer of sorts, an unwavering Harold Brodkey fan, a gifted visual artist, an outstanding impromptu chef (give him leftover chicken, some heavy cream, and a humble spice you'd never thought of before like paprika, and Kevin could produce a masterpiece), and the person who explained to me the provenance of the name Steely Dan. We all have that person in our lives.

But I hadn't spoken with Kevin in nearly a year, since I'd had what I'd briefly believed to be a medical emergency. In summary, I had fallen off a table at a nightclub, the Roxy, and thought I'd broken a rib. It's an embarrassing story, and there's not much else to it (and know that I had been, as usual, substance-free that night): I had gone out dancing with a friend from college; the theme song to *The Jeffersons* came on; to express my enthusiasm, I climbed up onto a high cocktail table, lost my footing, and fell on something bad (bench? boulder?). Whatever had happened, it hurt.

When I got back to my dorm early that morning, still in tears—or a new set in the same series—I called Kevin for advice.

"Go to the emergency room at Saint Vincent's," he said, and paused.

Saint Vincent's was the only hospital in the Village; throughout the years, it ministered to the victims of the Triangle Shirtwaist Factory fire, homeless people, AIDS patients, and 9/11 victims. Dylan Thomas died there. The hospital is gone now, lost to history and luxury condos.

"I have to get off the phone now," Kevin said. "I'm eating a muffin."

So that was Kevin. But so was this: before the Roxy incident, I had been thinking about taking a class in college on Vladimir Nabokov. I wanted Kevin's opinion about this intriguing Russian. If Kevin had said, *Nabokov sucks,* or *Nabokov? Never heard of him,* it is very possible that I would not have taken the class. But instead Kevin said, "If you like well-written prose, which you do, you will love Nabokov."

It seems important to keep reminding yourself that everything you say, no matter how minor the utterance seems to you, has the power to change someone's life. Some little throwaway comment, even one from sour old you, can have consequences that reverberate, for better or for worse, throughout a lifetime.

And so here I was, returning now to New York in mini-triumph, to begin a coveted job at this men's magazine I'd known nothing about until a month ago. And I was contentedly alone. Without a guy around, you could do great things that you'd always wanted to do, like go to the Met for an afternoon in lush late spring. Guys, I was starting to understand, took up a lot of time. There'd been Kevin, and there'd been some guys in college, but what was the point, really? The most important thing in the world is for the mind to be free. When the mind is allowed to investigate for itself, other freedoms follow—or at least they should.

I spent a couple of hours wandering around the eighteenth-century European galleries. I stood before paintings by François Boucher and Jean-Honoré Fragonard, wishing I could step into the pictures and idle with their frivolous youths and rosy cherubim, swing with them on their fabulous swings. The translation of myself into different mental states and worlds always came so easily for me. I loved the eighteenth century and revered everything about the period—the sumptuousness and the social theater of it, the dream of the Enlightenment and its goal of understanding the world through reason (there is a truth, said the Enlightenment, and an untruth)—and I'd always felt that in some weird, deep way I *got* this time already. George Orwell, who was otherwise right about pretty much everything, said while the past is always with you, it has no reality. I'm not so sure about that. It's hard to explain, but the past has always been so very present for me—it doesn't take too much for me to actually be *there*.

I had lunch alone at the marvelous old first-floor cafeteria in the Met, designed in the fifties by Dorothy Draper. There were dramatic columns and enormous golden birdcage chandeliers big enough to crawl inside. But why was I thinking of enclosures? Of my mental landscape then, it certainly must be true that I imagined that the self was a fundamentally private one, shaped in isolation, and maybe it was.

After lunch, I took myself on a walk north along Fifth Avenue and Central Park. Something was happening across the street, some sort of human commotion, at Eighty-Fifth Street. Although my usual instinct whenever I see a crowd is to get as far from it as possible, I found myself going toward this particular herd.

This, it turned out, was Jacqueline Onassis's building. When I was back in Ohio, packing, preparing myself for whatever this new life of mine in New York would be, cable news had been ghoulishly consumed with a 24/7 Jackie deathwatch. Now here I was with these formations of people, united in one brow of woe, and milling around on the sidewalk outside her apartment building. Placed around the long flower beds were tributes of the floral and Hallmark variety, cellophane offerings, the odd homemade trinket, stuffed animals. There were overheard comments ("she was my mother's favorite," as if Mrs. Onassis were a thing to be owned); there were midwestern-looking folks with, yes, fanny packs, standing with arms crossed in solemn consideration of those deli flowers.

The whole scene felt very creepy to me, but I couldn't have told you why that was then; it's hard to make these sorts of value judgments (one person's pathos is another person's crude sentimentality), but such public lamentations really did feel excessive. Did any of these sidewalk comminglers actually know the great woman? Well, no, of course not, so this communal distress must surely have contained a theatrical dimension—how can public grief over a celebrity death be about anything else other than yourself?

Or maybe that wasn't right. Maybe we use public grief as an excuse to express some of the private heartbreak we all live with, because we all know that pain is never overcome but is something that just sits there like a scab.

But there was another thing I didn't like about it: living a life onstage, as Jacqueline Onassis so spectacularly had, also meant having a death there. That seemed too great a price.

At the Eighty-Sixth and Lexington subway stop, I bought enough subway tokens to get me through my first week at work. I took the train downtown, to SoHo, and, with the money my parents had given me so that I might survive until my first paycheck, purchased luxury footwear: a pair of black Robert Clergerie platform boots and a pair of blue suede Prada wedges. Of the boots, the salesman said, "All of the top girls are wearing these"; of the wedges, another salesman at another store wrote on his business card: "Now 'Go Get 'Em' at *GQ*!! In a year from now, YOU will be on the cover!! (MY PREDICTION)."

I've always been fatally susceptible to any sales pitch agreeable to my self-image.

Whatever minuscule leftover parental sum I still had was spent on prepared foods at the old Balducci's, with its beautiful outsized green awnings, on Sixth Avenue and Ninth Street—yet another stop in what I somehow assumed would magically be the upward-mobility train. That was dinner. I made calls on the pay phone in the basement of my dorm: my parents, a couple of friends back home, and my professor who started the whole thing.

"You should start keeping a journal," she said. "You don't want to forget any of this."

"Oh, don't worry," I said. "I won't forget."

It always seemed to me that my parents existed mostly in the present tense: they didn't reminisce, they didn't "tell stories" (it was impolite to talk about oneself, yet they never told any stories about my childhood, either), and so it had always been up to me to remember everything. That was my job; I was always the family rememberer, the one who would watch, who would pay attention, who would try to put everything together. If I weren't watching watchfully—trying to be a reliable witness, trying to get to the bottom of things, trying to understand the story behind the story—then everything about us, and about me, would be lost.

Remember this, I've always said to myself. *Remember this, remember this, remember this.*

The prospect of my new job at *GQ* was so thrilling to me, but I also knew that my future was already narrowing: *magazines*. Magazines, magazines, magazines. Did doing one thing in the world mean a life of endless repetition? I didn't sleep that night before I started my job. How could I have? I had the world before me, but I was scared to death. I already knew that there was a problem with saying yes to a certain path: It meant a denial of everything else. It said that the life I've chosen is bigger than my imagination for what my life could be.

4

My morning began in a human resources conference room at the company. There were maybe four or five other people seated at a long table with me, also starting their jobs at Condé Nast this very day. Before us loomed an HR woman, asking if anyone had worked at the company before. One hand went up. That hand belonged to an older (in my perspective) woman in a smart blue pantsuit. She went through her professional history: she had worked at one magazine at the company; she had left the company for another magazine; she was now back at the company, working at a third magazine.

If she'd been a writer and if I'd been an editor, I might have suggested she try to jazz up her narrative a bit.

Yet what an interestingly equalizing experience it was, being at this table—magazine veterans such as this woman (the next time I saw her, she was struggling through the lobby on crutches) and newcomers such as myself, democratically coexisting. For all I knew, the woman in the pantsuit could have been starting a job as an editor in chief somewhere. As the HR lady went into her little recited speech about company policies and procedures, I thought: *Am I the youngest person here? Had to be, right?*

The HR meeting lasted an hour, and I was released to *GQ* editorial on the sixth floor. The *GQ* assistants had long white laminate desks in the hallways outside their editors' offices. My desk was outside two of my three bosses' offices and was likewise mere feet from the editor in chief's corner office. All three of my bosses stood before my desk as I got settled into my black swivel chair. I twirled around in a three-sixty.

"It's so *big*," I said, meaning my workspace.

"It'll get smaller," replied all three in sober unison.

Helpfully, my predecessor had left a printed list of job duties at my desk. As I read through the pages, it occurred to me that I had no idea what my new job actually involved. It was with a sense of real discovery that I learned I would answer phones, sort and open mail, draw up contracts, help manage editors' and writers' schedules, make writers' travel arrangements, communicate with writers (whatever that meant), help writers research and report stories, process expense reports, make photocopies of the gossip pages in the mornings, and make photocopies in general. At the bottom of the memo was a note about how to handle the short-story submissions described by the grave, ugly word "unsolicited."

Then came an even graver and uglier term for those manuscripts: the "slush pile."

The slush pile was to be tackled if and only if there was nothing else left to do. In general, the slush stories were to be responded to with a form rejection letter. Maybe one slush story out of a hundred could be passed on to the literary editor, and probably not even that many.

Granger took me on a tour of the office, offering a log line about each group. First was the art department. The room was dark, illuminated by desk lamps and the ambient glow from desktop computers. Many of the art department people had headphones on; most wore jeans; none bothered to look up as we did our walk-through. On their computer screens were prototypes of pages in the magazine, and no matter what stage of my career I was in, no matter how much I liked or disliked the content of the magazines I worked for, watching these pages materialize on-screen always seemed a feat of alchemy.

Pinned onto a bulletin board on a wall by the entrance were more mock-ups of pages in later design stages. The real text of these stories hadn't been input yet and dummy copy was used as a place-holder. One page was filled with wild Dadaesque poetry; another with Edward Lear–type nonsense rhymes. Some clever unknown art department functionary had really spent some time on these.

"Pretty funny," I said to Granger.

"Yes," he replied grimly. "Unfortunately, the dummy copy is often better than many of the actual stories we run."

Back to the office tour. Had I ever used a fax machine before? I had not. Had I ever *seen* a fax machine before? I had not. We popped into the fashion closet, which was, quite literally, a closet. But what were these people in there actually *doing*? It was explained. They sorted and organized clothing samples for photo shoots, they removed clothes from hangers, they put clothes back onto hangers, they steamed, ironed, and lint-rolled clothes, they packed up clothes and had them returned via messenger to designers' showrooms.

ME: "That's a *job*?"
HIM: "Those jobs are very hard to get."

On to the copy and fact-checking departments now. The copy editors (the unsung heroes of every media outlet) were going about the very serious business of making the writers sound better than they actually were; the fact-checking department seemed a little more fun. Fact-checkers are the ensurers of editorial standards and are always the smartest and most hilarious people at every magazine (they're also always great about helping when you have a question you're too mortified to ask anyone else). Hanging out in research departments, I would also discover, was a great way to kill time when that well-known phenomenon of afternoon editorial torpor (in Joyce Johnson's nice formulation from her Beat-era memoir, *Minor Characters*) had set in.

Question: If the fact-checkers did the reporting, and the copy department did the rewriting, what did the *writers* do?

Unclear.

Now I would be introduced to the editor in chief of the magazine, Art Cooper, the man who had single-handedly created the brand we know, for better or worse, as *GQ*. He had been at the magazine for eleven years when I went to work there. This was already a great run for any editor in chief. This was also a problem.

There never was anyone else like Art. He wouldn't exist today. He couldn't. A midcentury boulevardier with sensibilities entirely unbuttressed by irony, Art adored Frank, Dean, Sammy, and the Great American Songbook; in his office, he smoked miraculous quantities of cigarettes; he enjoyed multiple lunchtime and non-lunchtime martinis; he had an actual catchphrase: "Heads are gonna roll!" He was a king. Like all kings, he was terrifying.

Into his corner office we went. There behind his enormous desk he sat. Art was smoking a cigarette and reading, his glasses set truculently low on his nose.

"*Well,*" he said in a rich, booming baritone. "We've been *waiting* for you."

Art was wearing a chalk-striped suit with peak lapels. His beard was sparse, and he was rotund like a king who feasts on foie gras during times of famine.

On the yellowish walls of his office were jazzy expressionist paintings by the artist Richard Merkin, and on his desk, in a glass-top display case, was an extraordinary collection of gleaming fountain pens that probably weighed fifty pounds each. They looked like expensive little lacquered missiles, and I imagined the pleasure that could be had by signing my name with them, as floridly as you please, on whatever correspondence I might have with whatever writers with whom I'd soon be communicating.

"And how is he treating you?" Art asked. He looked from me to Granger.

This was a perfectly pleasant thing to say, but every encounter with Art, innocuous or not, always felt like standing in the path of a high-pressure hose. My mind became an abandoned amusement park. I had a complete language breakdown—nothing was there.

"Great?" I said comprehensively.

Art blinked at me for a moment through his glasses and turned his attention to Granger. I took the hint and scampered back to my big/little desk.

Short history lesson: *GQ*, founded in 1931, had essentially been a men's clothing catalog—male models modeling turgidly, entranced by the odd prop—until Art Cooper became editor in chief in the eighties. Art transformed *GQ* into a truly significant magazine, molding the editorial content after *Esquire*'s in its glory years, but now, the tables were turned—*GQ* was the big fat success story, and *Esquire* was as thin as a pamphlet.

Yet when *GQ* editors talked about *Esquire*, I would come to note a complex succession of grievances coming from every which way. It was, I learned, like the Sharks and the Jets, and, like the Sharks and the Jets, it was hard to remember who was who. *Esquire*, created in 1933, had perhaps been, for a period in the sixties, the greatest general-interest magazine of all time. Under the editorship of the legendary Harold Hayes, *Esquire* had been at the forefront of the New Journalism movement, which brought novelistic techniques to nonfiction writing. *Esquire* published genre-defining pieces by Norman Mailer, Tom Wolfe, and John Sack; two early exemplars of this kind of journalism: "Frank Sinatra Has a Cold," by Gay Talese (who, sad to say, in 2016 would remark that he had not been influenced by one female writer, not one), and "Twirling at Ole Miss," by Terry Southern. A later classic of the New Journalism: "What Do You Think of Ted Williams Now?," by Richard Ben Cramer. And, of course, the greatest New Journalist of them all: Michael Herr and his reporting from Vietnam.

One of Art's favorite parlor games involved guessing when *Esquire* would go, as he'd so vibrantly say, "belly-up." The sense was that *Esquire* was then still running on the fumes of its three-decades-old prestige.

To the side of my computer, rising like the Grand Tetons, was the slush pile. Short-story submissions had not been removed from their manila envelopes for weeks, maybe a month—who was to say? I sliced open a few envelopes with my letter opener.

Amazingly, a couple of the cover letters didn't even get the name of the literary editor right. Maybe the prospective authors ought to at least have had a quick peek at the masthead before sending in a submission? Just a thought. But this also seemed to me not an encouraging sign, like perhaps even aspiring fiction writers were not overly familiar with the literary component, such as it was, of the magazine. (Even *I'd* known the names of the current *Esquire* fiction editors when I was in college: Rust Hills and Will Blythe.) In the Sharks-Jets death match, *Esquire,* not *GQ,* was the clear fiction category winner. Example: *GQ* received around fifteen to twenty unsolicited fiction submissions a day and maybe five to ten submissions from agents; *Esquire,* as I would learn, received about three times that.

Granger emerged from Art's office. We continued on our tour. He introduced me to some other editors—mostly they were men, but there were some women, too, and most of them seemed to have a limited interest in meeting the new girl. The *new person*. Which was fine; I got where they were coming from. I had entered a rich and complex caste system, an elaborate theater, really, and I supposed that I would be required to participate in it.

I met the other editorial assistants—all young women, and all of us joined, I would soon come to appreciate, in varying agonizing attempts to be taken seriously. Finally, I was introduced to the assistant who was charged with the task of taking me out to lunch.

"Just make sure you order wine," said Granger avuncularly, as he handed me off to her and exited stage left.

This young woman took one long scan of me, from root to branch and back again, and said, "When I heard that you were from a state school in Ohio, I figured you'd be this gigantic hick. For the last couple of weeks, everyone here has been like, 'Who is *this* going to be?'"

This comment bothered me less than it probably should have. (But yet: Do you have to include what other people think about you in your own understanding of yourself?)

Granger had made a reservation for us, the other assistant and me, at a French restaurant in an elegant town house on the Upper East Side. I'd never set foot in a town house before. The restaurant was quiet, had low ceilings and attractive up-lighting. It was elegant and civilized, and Chopin would have been the soundtrack had there been a soundtrack. The other assistant and I followed instructions and ordered wine. I still wasn't much of a wine drinker (my go-to wine product at school: Boone's Farm Strawberry Hill, beverage of kings and up-and-coming queens, too). I ordered a glass of chardonnay.

"So why didn't you go out of state for college?" asked the other assistant.

I thought about this for a moment. "Because I wasn't aware of any other possibilities," I said.

I had gone to my university because I'd won an academic

award in high school and had gone to a summer camp there; thus it was the only college I actually knew anything about. (Although I hadn't gotten the memo then that the experience of being a student there would feel like being trapped inside a Red Hot Chili Peppers video for four years.) And it was, insanely, the only college I applied to. I had considered myself a bad-attitude high schooler—although in actual fact, I was cheerful, sane, and high achieving—and was deeply irritated by the surreal nightmare of the college application process, which seemed to me corrupt, reductive, brand-name obsessed, antihuman, and profoundly insulting to me as a citizen of this, our Arcadian republic. I would opt out of the game, I decided. I had believed then that this refusal, or whatever it was, was brave and freethinking of me. The truth: I was lazy. And also self-defeating.

But at the same time, everything, and I mean *everything,* in my life afterward would have been different if I hadn't gone to school there.

Of course, wouldn't you just know it—this other assistant had graduated from a highly prestigious college. Interestingly, there would always be a discernible power dynamic at play in all my interactions with her; indeed, I was already beginning to sense something chilling about adult life in New York: you may, through no fault of your own, find that you are expected to reflexively defer to those who attended sophisticated academies, in the way that you will also be expected to defer to people who've got a ton of money or power.

I ordered a starter and an entrée, both goat cheese oriented. The other assistant, who was a few years older than I, definitely did talk quite a lot about her school—understandable, though, I guessed, given that those years were clearly more of a life high point than her present reality as a disgruntled editorial assistant. Truism: there is no bitterness like the bitterness of the editorial assistant who has been on the job for three years.

She had a warning for me: "It's very hard to move from assistant to non-assistant."

She was a potentially corrupting influence, and I would have to keep my eye on her. Actually, we ended up becoming friendly, and she always had some good office gossip. Most of that gossip at lunch centered around Art, as you'd expect. He was our king, after all.

Did I know that Art had been the editor of *Penthouse*? I did not (*creepy*). Had I perhaps already gotten to witness the hilarious scene that occurred when Art would summon one of his *GQ* editors to his office, and how that editor would run wildly down the hallway to him, like some decapitated chicken of myth? Did I know that, on high-summer days, Art was known to wear a seersucker suit, a straw boater hat, and an actual gold pocket watch on a chain? ("The Fourth of July float has landed" was the email that would go cruelly around on those seersucker mornings. But I would have to wait for that.) I would soon observe that Art was immune from the opinions of grubs like us. An editor in chief is the king of his little kingdom, and the king can enact his own fantasies. It's good to be the king, mostly—he doesn't have to know how he's seen, at least not by the likes of us. But from Art, I would also come to understand that power is not absolute. This was a valuable early lesson for me: you're always just a part of things, even when you want to be the whole.

After lunch, the other assistant and I parted, and I stopped in at a Chemical Bank branch on Madison Avenue to open my very first checking and savings accounts. I arrived back at my desk two and a half hours after I left it, and this seemed to be . . . OK?

I had no external email. The real mail came twice daily, morning and afternoon, and those arrivals more or less set the psychic clock for the assistants' days. One of my other bosses, the former *Rolling Stone* guy, was listed on some publicity databases as both the travel editor and the grooming editor, and he probably got more mail than just about anyone else in editorial.

Now, what sort of wizard could possibly be an expert in both travel *and* grooming, you ask? (A "grooming" editor being the men's magazine equivalent of what is euphemistically called a "beauty" editor at a women's magazine; these jobs involve the sorting and organizing of nearly indistinguishable bottles of lotion and/or packages of cosmetics.) Well, I'm not certain this gentleman did have much expertise in the travel and grooming categories, but he had something better—he was a genuine character. There were still some of those around.

This editor was known to bebop down the hallway, snapping his fingers and humming to a tune he alone heard; he'd sometimes say "dig it" to introduce a point; he'd sometimes start his days, upon the morning's first flick of the light switch, by invoking Dorothy Parker and proclaiming to me, to no one, to the universe, "Ah, what fresh hell is this?" He was also a repository of information about sixties pop culture—most of which was interesting and, I believed, accurate *enough,* although it did sound fishy when he told me that Brian Epstein, the amazing, heartbreaking Beatles impresario whom I'd always felt so much for, was the inspiration behind the lyric "he blew his mind out in a car" from "A Day in the Life."

"Yeah, but wasn't Brian Epstein still *alive* when *Sgt. Pepper's* came out?" I had asked, since I did not know when to keep my smart, smart mouth shut, or when to open it.

At my desk, I intercepted a call from a woman with a forbidding British accent, calling on behalf of something called Cunard. She wanted to speak about a product, or maybe an event, or even possibly a location, which I spelled phonetically on my message slip as "The Queue Eee Two (?)." I hoped that that befuddled "(?)" would exonerate me at least somewhat.

Had there been an Internet then, I might have done a quick search and come up with the answer: the *QE2,* the *Queen Elizabeth 2* luxury cruise line. But there was no Internet at work to ask;

we were on our own. (This would have been an ideally capricious question to ask a fact-checker, but I didn't know about that option yet, either.) It had not been explained to me that calls from travel and grooming publicists were not always *necessarily* meant to be passed along. Editorial assistants are required to be discerning about the messages from their call sheets they choose to convey to their bosses. It is often the only exercise of creativity the editorial assistant possesses.

So what else did I do that first afternoon? Glaring at me on my desk was a troublesome expense report, awaiting the arrival of the new girl (the *new person*), from a recently killed story. I'd never heard that term before—a "killed" story. Definition? Patiently, it was explained: the story came in, and it sucked; edits were submitted to the author and the edits went unheeded; the story still sucked; there was another round of edits, and again the edits went unheeded; therefore, the story continued sucking. Hence, the arrival of the guillotine, swift and merciless.

But this particular situation had to be handled with extreme delicacy—there was some relationship between the author of the killed story and an important contributor to the magazine, and the important contributor needed to be kept happy, or at least placated somewhat. I noted the existence of webs of influence and power, and it occurred to me that things could go disastrously wrong with a story, despite the initial good intentions of everyone involved.

I was asked to make some photocopies of something. The copy machine was attractively located across the hallway from the ladies' room, which *GQ* shared with the ad/sales department for *Mademoiselle* (now defunct). Sylvia Plath, that brilliant possessor of one of the most devouring imaginations of the twentieth century (the other being David Foster Wallace), had worked at *Mademoiselle* in 1953 as a college student—she won an internship there—and her unhappy tour of duty at the magazine inspired *The Bell Jar*. From what I could tell from my frequent perch by the copy machine, some of the *Mademoiselle* ad/sales women who used the bathroom as a regrouping area seemed to exist in similar emotional states themselves. We men's magazine gals were a tough bunch, though. We had to be.

When I got to the copier, I found an unpleasant, but unsurprising (I'm always having trouble with electronic equipment), ERROR message on the screen. I was too stubborn and too afraid to ask any other assistant for help, so I called an in-house copier doctor, whose number was posted up by the machine. The copier doctor arrived immediately. He was probably in his forties, had white hair and a young face, and, like all doctors at the time, wore a pager attached to a belt loop.

He crouched down to the floor and opened a door on the machine, started rooting around in there.

"Got a real bad paper jam," he said in the direction of the machine. "Real bad one."

I told him I didn't really know what I was doing. I told him I had just moved from Ohio.

He glanced up at me. "Fresh off the boat, huh?"

But saying you're from Ohio does not even count as information. Everyone is from Ohio, it turns out. And, as data, it's just not that interesting—saying you were from Ohio was like saying you were a seven on the pH scale, a neutral solution. An everyman, as it were. You were the peak of the bell curve, a golf ball driven straight and square down the middle of the fairway, the leaden mean. Saying you were from Ohio was basically like saying your name was Matt Miller. You were just good enough.

"You play volleyball?" the copier doctor asked.

Without looking at his work, he did a series of complex maneuvers that could be understood by only the copier professional.

"God, *no*," I said.

"You look like a volleyball player," he replied, peering back into the copy machine. His toolkit was placed on the floor next to him. "You must get that all the time."

"Actually, no," I said. Basketball. *That* was what I got all the time. The tall girl's unfortunate fate. *Are you a basketball player? Hey, how's the weather up there? Did you play basketball in school?* No, sir, I do not and did not play basketball.

From within the ladies' room came the sudden thunder of a flushing toilet.

The copier doctor stood. "You want to get lunch sometime?" he asked.

I didn't really see what possible professional reason there could have been for having lunch with this man. It would seem a bit strange, maybe? But on the other hand, everyone here seemed to have lunch all the time. Lunching seemed to be *what they did*.

I had been raised with an iron fist of egalitarianism—I enjoyed telling people (somewhat smugly, looking back on it) that I came from a line of old-school FDR progressives—and also this guy seemed kind of weird, and I liked kind of weird (although with an emphasis on "kind of") . . . and so, partially to be contrary, I said, "Sure."

"Next week?" the copier doctor asked.

"Sure."

From my parents, I'd received as a graduation gift (selected by me) a pricey Filofax organizer, and I'd spent an embarrassingly large amount of time these past few weeks fantasizing about what cosmopolitan NYC happenings I'd fill it up with. I now had something to write down. Poignant to think that a Filofax was an actual status symbol to a certain (very specific) demographic back then. More innocent days; days of paper, days of ink. For years, my hands were blotted with ink stains, supplied by fountain pens of a lesser kingdom than Art Cooper's.

"I'll pick you up here," the copier doctor said.

"Here" being the copy machine.

At the end of the day, as I waited in the lobby for the elevator, the most senior member of the art department—English, dapper, droll—passed by and did a gallant thing.

"So how *was* your first day?" he asked.

I already knew what a hierarchy-obsessed world I now found myself in, and this guy was disarming for bothering to talk to me at all.

"Harrowing," I said.

I didn't know why I said that. I just liked the word, I guess, and sometimes when you hear yourself speaking, you may not even really know why you're saying what you're saying. Sometimes your brain doesn't actually sync up with your lips, to expand on a Laurie Anderson lyric.

I put my headphones on and walked forty blocks back to my dorm. On my red Sony Walkman, a holdover from adolescence (the device was about the size of a toaster), I listened to a tape of Mozart's Piano Concerto no. 23, the Adagio movement, over and over again. Only Mozart could supply what I needed that evening.

If we all have one Jamesian moment that defines us, mine happened when I was thirteen and saw the Milos Forman film *Amadeus*. It was the single experience that opened the curtain for me in every way. I was a child before I saw the movie at a somewhat shabby but still glorious second-run theater in east Akron called the Linda, and afterward I was a proto-adult, with a body still in middle school, doing dumb things like making deep-fried dough-nuts from Pillsbury dinner rolls for extra credit in home ec class, but now with a brain haunted by capricious eighteenth-century entities, the Enlightenment, rage, retribution, passion, and art. I inhabited a liminal world that year, somewhere between reality and unreality. Art wants its own perfection, and if I have any kind of religion, it is an appreciation of mastery, and it started then.

I made my father take me to see *Amadeus* eight times. He

would drop me off at the Linda for evening shows and for Sunday matinees. I would watch it alone. I remember every detail about the theater: the smell of damp, ancient popcorn; how cold it always was; the velvet seats; the globular sconces on the blue fabric-covered walls. *Amadeus* was a release into a different world. It had starfish tentacles, as David Wallace used to say, that took me everywhere; my interest in it proliferated and changed, and I now had a project—many projects—to undertake. I was now ravenous for information. I wanted understanding. I wanted to understand. I made my father drive me to the Akron Public Library every Saturday, where I read everything the great playwright and *Amadeus* screenwriter Peter Shaffer had published: *The Royal Hunt of the Sun,* anyone? *Lettice and Lovage?* (Let me add here that Shaffer is probably as great as Harold Pinter, not to mention Michael Frayn and David Hare, and probably even approaches Tom Stoppard–zone greatness, though he hasn't gotten his due—but literary reputations are wrong and unfair, often.) I discovered that I loved reading plays because I loved reading written dialogue. Because what *was* a play—and what, really, was *human life*—other than a series of verbal conflicts?

And I thought: *Maybe* I *could write some plays someday.* But I had no idea how to go about that—how did you even do anything artistic? The idea seemed about as unattainable as getting myself to Jupiter.

In the library, I read about Mozart and learned that he considered himself a man of the theater above and beyond everything else, and that at the time of his early death he was considering writing an opera based on *Faust,* and I learned about Mozart's sister and about the Kingdom of Back, the fantasy world they created together where everything went backward; I read about the classical style, the best of all possible styles, which led me into the highly pleasurable topic of eighteenth-century decorative arts, which led me to Boucher and Fragonard (although both were too froufrou to be officially considered of the rigorous classical style), which led me to the French Revolution and to *A Tale of Two Cities,* and I fell wildly in love with Sydney Carton, but I was still only thirteen and was then, of course, stalked by nighttime dreams of the guillotine.

But then came the tempering influence of Thomas Jefferson, another enduring obsession, and I had to know everything about the founding generation of Americans (with a special emphasis on crabby Jefferson frenemy John Adams). I revised my handwriting to look like what I believed to be some sort of eighteenth-century style, because everything ought to be regarded as an art form and should be as splendid as you can make it, even and especially your handwriting. Although I was not a promising pupil, and although my piano teacher always gave a shrug and a lethargic "good enough" at the end of each of my lessons, I committed myself to piano practice with a renewed vigor. I started taking violin lessons, too.

Obscurely, at thirteen, I knew that I had been exposed to some new kind of knowledge. My life at school—it just kind of gave reality to us. And who wanted *that*? I needed to have a place at civilization's table. What you had to do, it seemed to me, was to teach yourself, so you'd know enough to create your own story.

5

In the midcentury, 40 percent of the nation's tires were made in Akron. When I was growing up there, Akron was pretty much a one-industry town, and nearly all the parents of the kids I knew worked for the venerable tire companies: Goodyear, Goodrich, and General Tire. Here's something I learned early on: corporations, for better or worse, run your life. Everything you had, and everything you were, you owed to the company. You bought a house thanks to the largesse of the corporation, you bought a car thanks to the corporation, you raised a family thanks to the corporation. You depended on the company for everything. If you weren't part of the company, what were you?

The villain of my northeast Ohio childhood was the late Sir James Goldsmith, the British billionaire and corporate raider, and allegedly Oliver Stone's inspiration for the character Sir Larry

Wildman in *Wall Street*. Goldsmith (sneeringly referred to as "Sir Jimmy" in the Akron of my youth) owned nearly 12 percent of Goodyear's stock and in 1986 attempted a hostile takeover of the company. This takeover bid was Akron's 9/11, an act of war on us. The whole thing was shocking and terrifying, and during that terrible fall of 1986, I made my father completely nuts by asking him over and over again if he was going to lose his job. He said he wouldn't, but the truth is that we all believed we'd be ruined.

The people of Akron stood up to Sir Jimmy and fought back: they protested and petitioned, they put up signs in their yards that said SAVE GOODYEAR, they, hilariously, sent bags of rubber bands to Goldsmith's town house in Manhattan (merry fate being what it is, the man who wanted to take over the great rubber company apparently had a rubber-band phobia). Ultimately, the company bought Goldsmith off; the takeover bid failed, and Goodyear survived and adapted, but went into massive debt. After Sir Jimmy, things were never the same in northeast Ohio. Many people lost their jobs, lives were destroyed, and the forces of rage, revenge, and nihilism were set in motion. At my school from then on, bubbling poisonously away underneath everything like contaminated quicksand, was the whispered word "layoffs."

It was then that I became for the first time aware of the concept of class stratification—there was now a discernible split between the kids with parents who had the nerdy white-collar jobs at the tire companies and the ones whose parents had the manufacturing jobs. The kids with the science-y-job fathers and mothers (the engineers, statisticians, chemists) tended, like me, to have come from elsewhere, and everything usually felt more secure—psychically, I mean. The men and women with the manufacturing jobs were generally from the big, extended stay-put families, but they were the ones running scared.

It just so happens that I'm friendly now with a man who considers Sir James Goldsmith his personal mentor. This guy really loved Goldsmith. He has actually described Goldsmith as "a sweet man," and when he speaks of Goldsmith's human warmth, his wit and generosity, plus his daunting backgammon skills, it will always inevitably occur to me that we never have anywhere near even a partial perspective on anyone.

Yet on the other hand, when thinking in a sentimental way about kings, it is dangerously easy to forget about their power—about the severed heads upon which they walk.

THE COPY MACHINE MAN AND I WENT TO LUNCH AT A RESTAURANT AT Grand Central. As he talked about his mother, his job, and his commute—he had a notable Long Island–area accent—it occurred to me that he might actually have believed we were on kind of a date. The whole thing felt kind of date-y, to be honest. I didn't feel too comfortable with that. He also paid for the meal, which was OK, I guessed. I had no money, of course. I had spent it on footwear. And I wouldn't have any money until my first paycheck, and that was still a few days away.

After lunch, we walked down the wind tunnel of Vanderbilt Avenue and crossed onto Madison, back to the office building. During my first week at *GQ,* I had become accustomed to the sight of phalanxes of Condé Nast ladies, bare-legged if in a skirt (less fashionable women still wore nude pantyhose back then, if you can believe), waiting for their hired Big Apple town cars outside the building. No matter the time of day, there they'd be, checking their watches if they had them, looking vaguely incensed, following to a T the pecking order about who stood where and who talked to whom. And although I had been in this environment for only a week, I now knew that while these women may have looked decorous, they were sharp operators. And it was true that the locus of power at the company did at least *seem* to be female—but a mercantile version of consumer women's culture, I guessed.

It was interesting to think about how I happened to work in the company's sole man-based domain (*Details* didn't count—it would never count).

The current on-trend look in the Condé Nast building in the summer of 1994 was a long slip dress, typically worn with a contrasting T-shirt underneath. Mostly this meant white dress, black shirt. We found ourselves at the rump end of what was known as grunge, the no-style plaid-flannel-shirt look having been co-opted two years before into some kind of fashion statement. The hair was to be long and sleek, the bag was to be Prada, and the overall impression was one of rigid control. Which was kind of the exact opposite of the grunge ethos, but whatever. What *was* obvious was that the clothes were armor and talismans against . . . what? Against fear—they were a way to assert your superiority over the abyss. I've always known what clothes are for.

As the copier man and I went through the lobby, I idly wondered if he'd ever taken other assistants out to lunch. I supposed he had, or had at least tried to, although I couldn't have imagined that many of these other women would have been too receptive to the invitation. I was beginning to notice that a lot of people in this building seemed like little spinning tops, whirling around in a perpetual speedwobble, as my father would say (that's one of his words). And I had no idea if their bosses had made them nuts or if they had started out that way.

The copier doctor and I rode the elevator up to my floor. Before there was the narcotizing screen of the smartphone, what did we used to gaze at in elevators so that we didn't have to look at other people? The wall? The buttons, some illuminated, some not? An elevator's inspection card, or otherwise an official document stating that the inspection card could be viewed in the lobby upon request? (Which would always get you thinking about what it was the elevator inspectors were trying to hide.)

"We should do this again," the copier doctor said as the door dinged open and I exited onto six.

Visitors to *GQ* editorial were to wait in the chairs by the receptionist's desk. A great number of these visitors were models—models of the male variety, that is to say. The receptionist, Ruth, had a notably dark and low voice, and her face was always set in a sly half smile. I suppose Ruth had to have been somewhat amused by the spectacle of those young portfolio-clutching men as they accumulated before her throughout the day like so much human flotsam and jetsam. There was always something vaguely prey-like about these guys— handsome and symmetrical though they were, it always seemed as if their eyes were set just a bit too far apart, like lost rabbits.

This has always interested me, the whole idea of display—what's real and what's fake, what's shown and what isn't.

As soon as I got settled back at my desk, the most senior editorial assistant came up to me. She was our leader, to the extent that we had one, and I would have done anything she told me to do. I could have seen her in law school, absolutely. She would have been a killer there.

She placed both hands firmly on the white ledge above my desk and looked at me hard. "About *lunch*," she said.

"Yeah?" I asked as lightly as could be.

"You're going to have to tamp down that thing *now*."

I had various thoughts about this. First of all: *Way to be classist about the copier man.* And also: *What "thing"?* There was not and there never would be a *thing* with the copier man. (Oh, but *now* who was the classist one?)

Another thought: *Someone is actually watching me?* I had come from a place where no one ever noticed or cared what anyone else was doing, and I'd always taken that freedom for granted. (This is not to say, however, that I was being *thought about*. Being *observed* and being *thought about*: different things.) Now, strangely, I was an actual part of the world. But there was a problem with being a part of the world: it imposed its ideas on you, coordinated your thinking, and told you who you were.

Also, I now had a corporate identity, and that was another way that other people got to tell you who you were.

I HAD THE RIDICULOUS GOOD FORTUNE TO START AT GQ AT WHAT SURELY must have been one of the greatest periods ever of any American magazine. The issue on newsstands when I started contained the piece "My Mother's Killer," by the superb American crime novelist James Ellroy. One of my bosses, the assistant managing editor, had edited the piece, Ellroy's blistering account, now rightly considered a classic of magazine journalism, of reading the 1958 police file for his mother's murder. Ellroy later expanded the piece into his excellent book *My Dark Places*. There was lots of Ellroy activity on my desk that first week, and it was fantastic.

As I was told during my job interview, "There are two things to know about James. Number one: he is the nicest man in the world. Number two: he will bark at you."

Both of these things were true, and it was Ellroy, aka "The Demon Dog," who provided me one of my first lessons about how, with writers, you just kind of had to roll with it.

That summer, there was a reception at the Museum of Modern Art for *GQ*'s retiring fashion director, Nonnie Moore. Art Cooper asked me (by that I mean he told me) to help another assistant check in the guests at the door. I figured I was being tested, or auditioned, because being asked to work at a party was understood to be kind of an honor for an assistant. Maybe "honor" is too strong a word. But at any rate, in this regard, Art reigned over an absolutist system; he got to choose the cast of characters for every *GQ* dinner, party, gala: guest list, seating chart (if there was one), which of his editors would be invited and which ones excluded, and which assistants would serve as his attendant Byzantines for the evening. It would turn out that I was often one of those Byzantines.

But favor would wax and wane, of course. I would always remind myself of that.

Nonnie Moore was an elegant lady in her seventies who seemed of another, less vulgar era—though also, doubtless, a more difficult era in which to be a professional woman. I had never spoken with the dignified Ms. Moore and never would, but I was certain that she was a great lady: she wore cool black clothes that seemed to me somehow interestingly Asian, she always had on fantastic jewelry, and, crucially, she always appeared to be the picture of serenity and grace amid the institutional frazzle dazzle.

The night of the event, the other assistant and I got ourselves set up in the MoMA lobby at our check-in table. This other assistant, also from the Midwest, was imposingly poised and knew how to tie an Hermès scarf with considerable élan—a word now sadly tainted, because you only ever see it in the worst possible fashion writing. She and I would later chat about how we had both read this ridiculous thing in the same magazine about how the "perfect" female breast size was, evidently, the size of a champagne flute. But what did that even mean? A tall, narrow flute or the broader coupe glass of, for instance, *Casablanca*? We debated this. The answer was inconclusive, although we agreed that if we were talking about the tall, narrow flute, we were both in good shape.

But we had some immediate professional concerns. The more high profile the assistant duty, the greater the possibility for disaster. Gravely, we pondered what would happen if we somehow didn't recognize one of the prestigious guests whom we were expected to recognize tonight. What if we embarrassed ourselves, and the magazine, by messing up and not knowing who was who?

Because whatever happened that night, we just did *not* want Art Cooper to yell at us the following morning. Because when Art, being the lighthouse he was, shone his beam upon you, you knew there were two possibilities: you were (1) in trouble, or (2) going to be invited into his office for drinks. (No one could decide which of the two scenarios was worse.) We finally reached the comforting conclusion that these VIPs were seasoned professionals in all regards, and they would certainly know how to handle themselves at the door. Noted: Art Cooper did not acknowledge us as he trundled past. This hurt my feelings, although I knew it shouldn't have.

The scene at the party in the MoMA garden was almost unbearably exciting. Nonnie Moore was clearly such a legendary figure that even Art yielded her the floor that night. The fashion celebrities turned out to be completely polite and great with us, the attendant Byzantines—another mark of the high regard in which Ms. Moore was held. Calvin Klein was delivered to the front door of MoMA in a sleek gray Mercedes. The disconcertingly boyish Tommy Hilfiger looked just like Tommy Hilfiger (or maybe he looked like an actor playing the part of Tommy Hilfiger). Donna Karan was the one who held my particular interest, although I could never possibly speak to her, of course. (I'd been a Donna Karan watcher since her Anne Klein days. What a brilliant career!) I now functioned within such a rigid and complex caste system, it was understood that the other assistant and I were certainly not permitted to hobnob with any of these fashion-world celebrities. But I think we were both relieved about that—attempting to mingle with the powerful and well-known felt to me like summoning a demon somehow. I was already suspicious of those who had power and of those who wanted it.

The following morning, as I sat at my desk, alternating taking big bad-mannered bites of my enormous salt bagel with cream cheese and clipping the newspaper gossip columns, an editor stopped at my desk to chat.

"Well, *that* was *fun*."

"Yes," I said. "Last night was great."

Conspiratorially, he stage-whispered, "I wonder whom the *next* retirement party is going to be for."

He was the most overtly erudite person on staff, had an impressively formal way of speaking, and could be really, *really* flinty.

"You *know*, Art is going to be *sixty* in three years," he said.

Art was only fifty-seven? (Actually, it turned out he had a couple of months to go until he turned fifty-seven.) Man, he seemed a lot older than that—already into his *King Lear* years, if you asked me.

"And you know *that* isn't a birthday he's going to want to celebrate," the editor said.

I was getting this sense that growing older was a crime for which every high-echelon media figure—women and men both—would eventually be punished.

In these couple of months at Condé Nast, memos had been circulated announcing that someone with a very senior position was no longer with the company and welcoming a gleaming new replacement person to that same very senior position. These magazine jobs were high status, yet high risk, which had to mean that the sense of power they provided was, in part, an illusion. Didn't it? This was a theory I was working on. Everyone seemed to be clinging on to what they had by a thread. It was not impossible that that also included Art Cooper.

Remember (*remember, remember*): we are always a part of things, never the whole.

6

In college, I spent a lot of time driving around the ghost towns of Butler County, Ohio, listening to Mozart and Cole Porter and thinking about how the people who lived in these places really were up against a lot. I used to have this haughty idea that human unhappiness could be corrected if people were given the right tools—and the tools to self-liberation, I was pretty sure then, were to be found in art. I used to think that if I ever got into bad shape, if I ever had to have a different kind of life, the way to save myself was to remember the great artists (such as Mozart and Cole Porter and Nabokov and whomever else I was into at the time). Everything we needed was there.

It's fair to say that I was always sending messages in a bottle to my future self. But why did I believe I was heading for future trouble?

During that first summer in New York, I flew back home for some weekend visits. On the drives home from the airport in Cleveland, I noted how happy I was to see the great flame leaping volatilely from the smokestack of the LTV steel mill along the interstate—that very iconic feature of the Cleveland skyline. In high school, I'd believed that I was so clever for having all sorts of darkly poetic associations with the famous LTV flame stack, entirely unaware of its ugly reality—that it dispersed lead, carbon monoxide, benzene, and asbestos—but now that fire for the first time seemed interesting and hard-won and maybe even beautiful.

During these trips back home, my parents and I would ride bikes on a path along the Ohio and Erie Canal. This was one of my favorite things in the world to do. A hundred, a hundred and fifty years before, mares and donkeys used to tow canal barges along the path, before the railroad came and changed everything. Imagine that—a whole world, now vanished, right along the canal. My mental soundtrack for these bike rides was always that wonderful old song "Low Bridge," recalled from third-grade music class.

> I've got me a mule, her name is Sal.
> Fifteen miles on the Erie Canal.
> She's a good old worker
> and a good old pal.
> Fifteen miles on the Erie Canal.

Everything about animals has always just killed me—the Chagall painting *I and the Village* (a boy and a cow, or maybe it's a lamb, stare at each other, a faint dotted line connecting their eyes) so beautifully captures the profundity of the human-animal bond, and I'm always a puddle of tears whenever I see it at the museum—and as my parents and I biked along the canal, now overgrown with soft green grass, we saw blue herons, and beavers, and frogs. I thought about the animals, all so beautiful and peculiar, and the boats, and the people, the people whose lives *were* the canal—the voices lost to us, voices never heard, buried in history. My parents and I rode our bikes in a straight tense line, trying to take up, as always, as little space as possible—my dad in front, my mom in the middle, and me in back—and I watched their legs pedal, and I thought about how I'd never live at home with them again (although I hadn't lived with them since I was eighteen), and I thought about how everything was shifting and changing and changing again. These were always very emotional homecomings for me, those first couple of years.

But why was it always this way with me—when I was in Ohio, I couldn't wait to get out of it (this *is* not *the place to be, my friends*), and now that I was out of it, I wanted to go back? Why was it that whenever you achieved exactly what you wanted, the allure of that thing dissolved in the grasping?

Every morning before work, I had to buy all four of the daily NYC newspapers. The day's first job task was to clip the gossip pages from each of them. I'd paste each cutting onto a piece of paper, copy the page, and make twenty gossip packets to distribute to all the senior people at *GQ*. I minded this chore less than you'd think.

I bought all four of my daily papers from my man Jerry, purveyor of a famous newsstand on Astor Place. His stand was located in front of the new Starbucks, which had until recently been the Astor Riviera Café. I liked the sound of that: the Astor Riviera. When I first became his customer, Jerry was a black-haired character actor; throughout the years, I saw him age right before my eyes, dark hair going gray, then white, while I, of course, stayed exactly the same.

On my first day at *GQ*, Peter Richmond, one of the best writers at the magazine, and who once brought in extravagant masses of lilac branches, cut from a bountiful home bush, had this suggestion for me: "Whatever else you do, make sure you read every New York paper every day." Good advice. And so, on my big four-stop, fifteen-minute commute to work, I would peruse the papers—all still black and white—although I really can't say I found much to enjoy in them. This was the summer—the first summer—of O.J. and surely had to be the grim pivot point when we entered our current media age and everything became tabloid journalism. The news got canceled that summer, and it stayed canceled.

So far in my life I'd been aware of some pretty weird non-news news cycles—Gary Hart, Donna Rice, and the inauspiciously named yacht *Monkey Business;* Jim Bakker and his whole freakish crew; that time when Ronald Reagan looked into the camera and said, re: Iran-Contra, "My heart and my best intentions tell me that's true, but the facts and evidence tell me it is not" (the very moment when I knew that politicians would lie, just lie right to your face); that baby who fell into a well in Texas; that time when Dan Quayle put an "e" on "potato"; Tonya Harding and Gennifer Flowers and the now omnipresent bimbo eruptions—but suddenly everything felt different and extremely weird. The media had finally found the formula: take one story, usually involving the abuse—or, preferably, the ghastly death—of a female person, and hammer away at it forever. There were now media distortions in every direction, and people were seemingly oblivious to obvious facts—and that seemed to be just fine. No one really seemed to care all that much that our culture was suddenly—was it suddenly?—and irrevocably broken.

Also troubling to me was the fact that the media had become the enemy. I was but an ultra-low-ranking member of the media, but did it mean that *I* was also the enemy?

This was another thing to start worrying about.

In the early days at *GQ,* a couple of wizened (not really—they were about twenty-seven) old-time assistants took me under their wings. Sometimes we'd get margaritas after work; sometimes we'd pick up huge focaccia sandwiches for lunch and take them to Bryant Park. These women explained that the park had recently been redesigned, and the consensus was that the new green chairs were attractive but not very comfortable, and then someone said that if you squinted at the London plane trees at the perimeter of the park at just the right angle, you could almost believe you were in Paris. But why were we pretending we were in Paris? Were we not exactly where we wanted to be, in an echoing green in the middle of everything?

Mostly, these get-togethers with the slightly older assistants (who, like me, did not have advanced degrees and who, also like me, did not have particularly sparkling CVs) functioned as complaint sessions and as warnings, as they would recount tales of the tyrannies, injustices, and humiliations, petty and not, they'd endured in their brief careers. They seemed to feel expendable, disposable, replaceable . . . although maybe one of the big secrets was that everyone else felt that way, too. This was another one of the theories I was working on. Nearly every assistant wanted to get her stuff in the magazine, but this was many years before publication was seen as a self-evident right and also before magazines had online components onto which to dump an assistant's, or a freelancer's, stuff—gratis, of course, or close to it.

During lunch, one assistant asked me how frequently I had seen *any* assistant's byline in the magazine. I didn't have a great answer for that. "Think about it," she said, "*zero* times." Publication in *GQ*, or anywhere, was tough, nearly impossible, and there were all sorts of gatekeepers blocking our points of entry, they warned me, this somewhat square and shy but always hard-feeling midwestern kid who didn't understand why these people, all allegedly on the same team, weren't being more helpful toward one another.

The assistants would pitch story ideas to their bosses, and they'd get no response. They'd pitch more ideas to their bosses and still would get nowhere. One of the assistants related that she had written up a pitch and had unwisely circumvented her boss by giving it directly to Art Cooper—a bad idea that backfired in a very bad way. The easiest (only?) way into the magazine as a female writer seemed to be the celebrity profile, fitness-based pieces, or else personal essays about your romantic life.

On one very hot afternoon in Bryant Park, when three of us were sitting in the beautiful green chairs, tackling our very large sandwiches, a pregnant woman passed by us.

"Remind me never to be pregnant in the summer," said the first assistant. The pregnant woman did look quite uncomfortable. She was wearing a black dress.

"You have to make sure you plan it right," said the second assistant. "The best time to have a baby is in the late fall."

I was interested to learn that other young women had given this much thought to the then (to me) seemingly abstract ideas of pregnancy and birth. I mean, I suppose I did picture myself as a parent to some unimaginable infant in some ethereal future realm, but five, ten, fifteen years stretched out in front of me like some other kind of eternity.

"I wonder if I'll ever have a baby," said the first assistant. "Sometimes I don't think it will ever happen for me."

"All I want," said the second assistant distantly, "is for someone to save me."

Not that I was in any way noble, but dreams of rescue had never actually occurred to me. I was from the blank soybean fields of central Ohio or the rusted factories up north—take your pick; we didn't think that way. We couldn't afford to. I'd just always felt that everything was up to you alone. You assumed responsibility for yourself. You were in charge of your own happiness. These women were smart and independent people, but they were giving me a glimpse into a somewhat unhappy future that I was determined would not become mine.

I PROBABLY SHOULD HAVE BEEN A MORE INACTIVE DATER THAN I WAS. In general, I found dates tedious and boring, and I was never as astonished by the guys as they seemed to think I should have been. Date situations, once I was out of college, often seemed to occur in restaurants (remember when they used to let you smoke in restaurants?), and in my view, there wasn't much to like about the whole date-in-a-restaurant contrivance: the hard chairs, the little stage set of the restaurant, the asymmetrical-power aspect of the guy's paying for the meal (not that *I* was going to pay; I never had any money), the forced camaraderie, the fake heart-to-heart. *Let's talk.* The fiction of *getting to know each other.* The lie of *Who are you?* How could you possibly answer that, when you were only in your twenties (or any age, really), and *you* didn't even know who "you" were?

What was closer to the truth: *Let's see if you can accept my self-inventions.* And thinking about these guys' self-inventions was never a great use of my time.

In college, I had briefly gone out with a slightly older guy who lived in Cleveland with his parents; sometimes he would make the stupendously dull five-hour drive to see me at school, although I'm not even sure why he bothered—mostly he'd just sit in my dorm room and listen to the CDs he'd brought. He'd slip on his headphones, close his eyes, and he was off, pantomiming drums; sometimes you'd get the odd strike on a phantom cymbal along to—wait for it, wait for it—Mother Love Bone, Mudhoney, or Nirvana. *Old* Nirvana, that is. This guy would get himself all worked up into a lather of self-righteous indignation about how there were people— "posers," to use his striking lingo—out there in this world of ours who preferred *Nevermind* to *Bleach.*

"Sometimes I just gotta crack on them, you know?" he'd say.

Ours was not in any way a glorious or even remotely interesting pairing. Rarely have I ever been as thrilled as I was when he'd finally leave at the end of these weekend visits, and I could light my scented candle purchased from the only decent gift store in town, put on some Mozart, and get back to my reading, possibly the Anthony Burgess translation of *Cyrano de Bergerac,* whose rhyming couplets still, by the way, give an electric thrill:

> Take down this truism in your commonplace books:
> Molière has genius; Christian had good looks.

At least the futile thing with this dude did help me understand that in any kind of relationship, you have to be in the same theater together.

Where did I even meet the young men I dated during those early years in New York? I do know that they would actually have to *call* me to arrange a date, an act that now seems as quaint as the code of social etiquette in a Jane Austen novel. That first fall, a guy from Seattle took me to Strauss's *Arabella* at the Metropolitan Opera. I'd never been to the Met before (that other great NYC Met), and I was dazzled by everything—by the scale and enormity of the proscenium and stage; by the famous golden Sputnik chandeliers as they, at curtain, ascended into the scalloped golden ceiling; by Kiri Te Kanawa, our evening's superb star; by the costumes, the sets; by the opulent spectacle of it. I will admit that I had a hard time following along with the opera—this was the very last year before the Met installed subtitle players on the seat backs (and also, I didn't know as much about music as I wanted to, or pretended to)—but who cared? It was just so exciting to think about all the meticulous and gifted people involved in putting on the performance that night, and I just happened to be there to get to see it.

During the intermission, my date, who was wearing a tuxedo, and I met a friend of his for a drink in the mezzanine lounge. The raffish friend, also in a tuxedo and wearing, in addition to his bow tie, a patterned silk scarf (a nice touch), ordered me a glass of champagne at the bar without asking what I wanted (helpfully, champagne).

I was keenly aware of an unwelcome new experience: feeling underdressed. I had never been to the Met before, and I'd been surprised by my date's attire. Why had he not told me that I could use this occasion as an opportunity to ditch my wide-legged gray cashmere pants and go superformal? (I was, after all, now the owner of a floor-length John Galliano fishtail skirt, acquired at a sample sale—a new and wondrous reality.)

The friend in his tux and patterned scarf handed me my champagne. "So you are the Vassarian," he said.

I had to think about this for a moment. I considered the walls, which were covered in velvet of the deepest, most luscious scarlet.

The Vassarian.

Vassar. Right. Some other girl.

My date, twenty-three years of age but dadlike in the extreme, seemed mildly embarrassed. He told his friend where I worked. He had a sip of his champagne.

The raffish friend with the scarf had a question for me, a blunt one: "How'd you get that job?"

"A friend of a friend," I said. (Why not keep it vague?)

"No," he continued. "I mean, what authority do you have? You look very young."

I suppose this guy didn't know that authority was not a requirement to get yourself hired as an editorial assistant, but it *was* becoming ever clearer that people just loved putting other people into vicious little class boxes. And it was of course true that I'd had no background in editorial or in assisting. But experience was also unnecessary—reading comprehension skills were important; taste was a plus but not mandatory. I found myself explaining that in school the previous year, I had been a teaching assistant, though I didn't want to get into too many details about it with these young men there in the Met mezzanine lounge.

Neither did I get into my experience of reading student papers, where I'd bear witness to the authors' struggles with the Gordian knot that is, evidently, the English language. When I read these papers, I'd picture their student-authors toiling away in lab coats, trying to work out the formula—to the voice in *The Return of the Native,* maybe? (No, no, it was worse than that. The voice was . . . *Theodore Dreiser.*) And I was never remotely clear who the students believed their audience was. Whom were they addressing? When I had conferences with students, my pep talks always seemed to boil down to the following advice: "Just try to sound like a normal person! It *is* the twentieth century, after all."

Essentially, I could never figure out what to do with the papers other than rewrite them, in longhand. Years later, it was pointed out to me that maybe I shouldn't have been using a fountain pen on the papers, and not actually rewriting them, either.

So that was what my experience had amounted to.

"It's incredible that that was good enough to get you the job," my date's friend said.

We never really see our own limitations, even when everyone else does. Our subjective self always exceeds our objective self, meaning *you* always know your own possibilities, even when no one else does.

Or, to put it another way: if you are a woman, you will always be underestimated.

Later that year, I went out with an oddball who wore eyeglasses in the then sleazy (fashions change) aviator style and who—seriously—drove a Rolls-Royce. I had a couple of very short rides in this improbable vehicle, and I can report that the interior was a universe of burled-wood and beige-leather ridiculousness and that there were about three million dials on the dashboard. The car also seemed pretty old to me, like maybe from the seventies, although who was I to judge? This guy drove his gigantic boatlike Rolls, very slowly, everywhere; the couple of times I went out with him, he bizarrely insisted on picking me up at my building, although our dates took place in restaurants only a few blocks away. He worked in some soul-withering yet highly remunerative finance job, and an elevator opened directly into his loft in SoHo.

I'd been in New York for several months by this point, and I was becoming aware that there was a whole new world of pure money that I knew nothing about, a place that had been previously hidden from view. Maybe there was some sort of closet Bolshevik lurking deep within me, because I did know that being around that kind of high net worth made me extremely uncomfortable. And it wasn't only that—I didn't actually believe that this man had any more innate merit than anyone I'd gone to high school with. I didn't believe he was entitled to live like a king on earth.

But . . .

I seemed to like money, unfortunately, possibly quite a lot. (My tastes were, and remain, ruinously Palladian.) Yet at the same time, I didn't want to get too close to anyone for whom the central emblem of his (or her) character was a desire to be around money; I've always been snarlingly disdainful of men who demand "luxury"— those flyers of first class, those who talk ceaselessly about restaurants and about the quality of service in hotels, five-star ones. Although having money seemed like a very pleasant thing, I couldn't imagine doing anything you actually had to *do* to make money. It was like that with a lot of things you wanted in life—you wanted them, but you didn't want to be the kind of person who wanted them.

Not too long after that one, I went to a post-holiday party hosted by a hedge fund, or whatever the things before hedge funds were called, with some other finance guy. I have no idea how drunk this young man was that night, but I must not have been drunk at all, unfortunately, because I can still vividly recall the sight of him, in his parka and with his red chapped cheeks, gazing down at a pile of discarded Christmas trees on the icy sidewalk a block away from my new apartment on Waverly Place.

Maybe it is true that we're all telepathically sharing the same thoughts, à la Jung's collective unconscious, because for just one moment (and only that), our minds met.

"Please don't," I said.

"Oh, come *on*," he replied unscrupulously. "It'll be hilarious."

"Please don't do it," I said. "I mean it."

He offered me a small evil smile. Lumberjack style, he hoisted one of the pine trees from the pile over a shoulder. He was a big preppy guy, and I watched him as he advanced a few unsteady steps with the tree, weaving down the sidewalk on Waverly Place.

He stopped. He set the tree down on the ground, holding it upright.

"Please just leave it," I said.

"Um, *OK*," he said, as he bent over and grabbed hold of the trunk.

He dragged the tree down the sidewalk, through gray puddles, over gray ice, into the lobby of my building. We went past the doorman (who was no help at all), into the elevator, up to the eleventh floor, and down my hallway, leaving a dissolute trail of brown pine needles behind.

When we got into my apartment, he leaned the tree up against a window. This sad old Christmas tree, which had been urinated on, and worse, by mammals of all kinds, still had some abandoned ornament hooks on it, errant tinsel, and it was now somehow my problem.

"I can't *believe* I have to deal with this," I said.

And deal with it I did: for years afterward I was still stepping on old brittle needles, those bad boys pricking my bare pink feet.

"Just put it in the stairwell. Who cares? Let someone else get rid of it."

Oh man. These guys. What a total waste of time. No, I wasn't interested in any of them in the least—these men without self-criticism or conscience. Identity just really didn't seem to be much of a problem for these dudes to solve.

My only important relationship in those years was with a much older married man. As a result of this situation, I learned that each unreal relationship is its own Prospero's island and that dreaming and unreality keep you on your island. I learned, too, that the false dream is better enacted than actually lived.

But there were many real-world consequences for me, too: I became a rather weird, fatalistic individual about relationships and had, for a time, the idea that they needed to be conducted under a cloak of secrecy. I became used to thinking of myself as a vaguely illegitimate presence in the life of someone important to me, and I became accustomed to providing protection to brilliant, narcissistic, charismatic, fiercely ambitious men—men who never quite thought about extending the same protection to me, no, not quite.

7

My desk has always been the place where I feel the most comfortable. This is the main thing in the world I like doing: hunching down at my desk, wherever that desk may be, and getting back to work. I was promoted at *GQ* after a year, from editorial assistant to assistant editor (I was still very much an assistant, though), but I tried not to get too excited about the title change. Status—any status—was subject to flux and change, I kept reminding myself. I barely told anyone I'd been promoted. Such was not my character. How could it have been? I was a nobody from nowhere; I was from the plains and the Rust Belt both. Let's not get too excited about where we are. Let's keep on moving forward. Let's dream up a different drama.

Granger would take me out for lunch sometimes at a sushi place close to the office. We'd be seated, he'd rub his face with one of the refreshing hot towels they give you at Japanese restaurants, and he would inevitably ask, "So what's next for you, A?" For my birthday that year, he took me to a French restaurant called Adrienne and said, "You're going places, A, I can tell." He was, or could be, excessively generous to me, and I had absorbed many lessons from him. One of those lessons was to always be on the move. He was not going to remain a number three editor at a magazine forever, and I never had any doubt that he would be an editor in chief somewhere, and soon.

I'd always liked being around ambitious people. I supposed I was ambitious, too, but I already had worries about myself: in order to succeed in this particular world, your ambition needed to be highly specific and also fairly conventional.

It's very hard to move from assistant to non-assistant.

But was being a non-assistant even a grand enough aspiration? To be honest, wasn't it, as far as aspirations went, just sort of boring and ordinary?

Granger's mentorship style was indirect, to say the least, but from observing how he worked, I osmosed the following lessons: to be a good editor you have to have a curious mind and a questioning spirit; you help the writer develop a voice and a tone; you give the writer room to breathe, and explore, and live. You trust your writer enough to let him follow his obsessions, but you're the moderating influence, too, and the voice of reason. You also have to try to save the writer from his worst impulses.

This is the most important job of all, actually, for an editor: to save the writer from himself. In this manner, being an editor certainly has to be the most psychologically intimate job in the world. Frequently, I would wonder if some of Granger's writers would even be able to function at all if they didn't have him as their ideal reader.

There was always a very palpable buzz in the office when a story from one of his guys came sputtering out of the fax machine.

I'd get a call from the writer, announcing that he was about to fax a draft of his piece, and I'd scurry back to the machine and carry the papers through the office as if holding a fragment of the True Cross. All these men were outstanding practitioners of the art of literary journalism, and it was fascinating to get to peer behind the curtain and read these pieces in their original states. (A journalist friend, by the way, has always objected to the word "piece"—"sounds like an amputation," he says, correctly.)

Some writers tended to send in polished, spick-and-span pieces, and some of them usually needed a few more drafts to solve the puzzle. I also got to see how great journalists can, and do, fail, until they get it right. Failure, I learned early on, is a crucial part of the game, and anyone who does anything worth doing in the world is going to fail, and fail quite a lot. When a writer gets in a jam, it's usually because he can't find the life in the story; one of the tricks Granger would suggest to free a stuck writer was to have the writer pretend to compose a letter to him in which he'd try to explain what he wanted the story to do. I loved that.

I also intuitively understood that these writers' jobs seemed both ideal and also thankless—living from deadline to deadline, pulling all-nighters, perpetually cramming like grad students. And the stakes were just so awfully high: one error in reporting and that would be *it* for them.

But the thing you had to say about them was that they were their own men (and yes, they were men, all of them). They were creating something that was theirs alone in the world. This already seemed to be the most important thing.

From these guys, and others, I would also learn that writers are sensitive instruments.

I was responsible for writing the table of contents page, an un-enviable task because *everyone* hates writing the TOC. I ended up doing it for years. This meant I had to read the galleys for every piece in the magazine, often wondering as I did if I was the only person there who actually read the issue cover to cover. *GQ* was, like every general-interest magazine, a high-low amalgam, which in this case meant, approximately, literary journalism/political reporting/essays/criticism/occasional literary fiction + men's fashion + service and celebrity pieces + boobs (– nipples).

As has been pointed out at length, there was some tremendous writing in the magazine, but there was also plenty of not-great stuff. The most egregiously written pieces in the magazine were always the celebrity profiles; the worst of these profiles inevitably had actresses and models as their subjects—or, God forbid, *aspiring* actresses and models. My time at *GQ* coincided with the advent of the so-called lad magazine; when *Maxim* was birthed in the United Kingdom in 1995, you could see *GQ*'s treatment of women get lewder and stupider right before your eyes. The then raunchy Sharon Stone cover (cover line: "Sharon Stone Undressed"; seems tame now, I know) was a turning point of some sort.

MAN: high culture.

WOMAN: low culture.

(MAN: high power; WOMAN: low power.)

"Mass media," writes bell hooks, "do the work of continually indoctrinating boys and men, teaching them the rules of patriarchal thinking and practice." I would note all the policing of masculinity in the magazine—a "man" does this, but a "man" does not do that; a "man" is this, but he is not that. Why *was* "being a man" so important? It was about power, that was why.

Regardless, I saw writing the TOC as my opportunity to slither my way into the magazine. My predecessor was a true virtuosa of the TOC, and on a shelf above my desk I kept a black binder filled with photocopies of her old pages. In *Telling Stories,* Joan Didion says that writing editorial captions for *Vogue* in the fifties, which she likened to training for the Rockettes, taught her that "less was more, smooth was better, and absolute precision essential to the monthly grand illusion." I would study these old TOC pages from *GQ* issues past and try to absorb the style and voice. Their concision, when really analyzed, was quite artful. Here was a new concept, following the lead of Didion (following, indeed, Tacitus): don't use three words when one word will serve.

But do I continue, lo these many years later, to follow that particular lesson? Not exactly. My heart has always been with those wild old Ciceronians—the spiraling subordinate-clause-upon-subordinate-clause approach—rather than with any no-fun, tightfisted Tacitus. Which is to say that my TOC entries could run the length of a paragraph and were always appallingly pun-heavy.

After a couple of months at *GQ*, the literary editor asked me if I wanted to choose a book and attempt a short capsule review of it. Yes, I certainly did want to. My selection was *The Quantity Theory of Insanity*, by Will Self. Soon thereafter, I was concocting little reviews every month. This was a very big deal for me.

There isn't a lot of room in a capsule book review to do much else other than summarize the book, which, if the book is any good, can't be done anyway. (Was it Edward Albee who said that if a play could be described in three lines, that play should be exactly three lines long?) The sad thing: I never really improved at the format. I certainly wish I'd known then what I know now: the reviewer's job is to evaluate the book on its own terms and to determine how well the book succeeds—or doesn't, as the case may be—within those terms. I suppose that I had believed that my job was to imperially confer, based on little else than my sensibility and idiosyncratic preferences, based more on emotion than on rationality, a Caesar's thumbs-up or thumbs-down.

Conveying subtleties and fine distinctions is not easily done (or encouraged) in such a structure, and it didn't take too long to figure out that the stronger and louder your voice in these reviews, the more positive reinforcement you'd receive. Let me just say that that was one happy day, when an editor at the magazine appreciatively remarked, noting my breezy savagings of various recent novels, that I was getting to be quite the trash artist. He actually said that: "trash artist." I didn't understand that I was hiding behind a pose, a mask; that I was disguising myself and feigning a lot more confidence and knowledge than I had, pretending as if I had emerged into being fully formed like the mythical Spartoi, who, from dragon teeth sown into the ground, spring up whole—and victorious. All I was doing was judging and declaring victory.

Being a reviewer (Gore Vidal enjoyed reminding everyone of the distinction between a *reviewer* and a *critic*) is easy work, especially for a young person—you are always standing safely at a remove; nothing is risked, nothing is bloodied. Writing reviews can become your first little frisson of power, and if you're not rigorous with yourself (you won't be), your aesthetic judgments about a book can become moral judgments: *this bad person*—"bad" because he has such a minute understanding of the human experience—*wrote this bad book*. I also didn't understand that while I had been given a modest platform, I had no innate authority.

And whatever I believed I was doing with these book reviews, it had nothing to do with cultivating appreciation.

Back in those pre-email days, when you'd see the author's own crazy handwriting on the heartrending self-addressed stamped envelopes, you were always so acutely aware that a real human being was attached to each submission. For better or worse, I've given a lot of thought throughout the years to what Sid Luft said about Judy Garland's response to having her TV show in the sixties canceled: it was like canceling a person. *Well, nice work,* I'd think with every rejection letter I'd send, *I've just ruined this guy's day.* Sometimes, depending on the kind of mood I was in, or how much time I had that day, I might draw a goofy picture on the rejection letters or else write a boosterish "FANTASTIC!" It was just that these slush-pile authors seemed so vulnerable and trembling in a way that the actual published authors did not. (Why was it that typeset books rendered the persons who created them unreal?) Little did I know, every writer—high, low—is always vulnerable and trembling, all the time. I'd learn that soon enough.

But I will say that, at first, I did approach the short-story sub-mission stack with more purity of purpose than I did the book-review stack. I had this idea that the slush pile was the place where my taste and my judgment really could come out and shine. At *GQ,* I dreamed of bringing a brilliant short story by some undiscovered writer—some unblinking genius who knew her own worth even if no one else did, someone whose sense of self, even after the thou-sandth rejection, had still not been eroded—to the literary editor, and he would love it, and he would pass the story along to Art, and Art would love it, and it would be published, and the world would change forever. I'd always believed I had something of an eye for spotting literary talent.

Since I'd been at *GQ,* I'd become a keen reader of *Esquire*'s fiction, past and present. Arguably, *Esquire* had been the chief platform for American short fiction from the forties through the seventies. The magazine had published major works by Norman Mailer, Vladimir Nabokov, Raymond Carver, Saul Bellow, Wil-liam Faulkner, Flannery O'Connor, and Barry Hannah; Tim O'Brien's classic "The Things They Carried"; my beloved F. Scott Fitzgerald's tragic and unreadable Pat Hobby stories; Dylan Thomas's "A Child's Christmas in Wales"; and, most famously, Ernest Hemingway's "The Snows of Kilimanjaro." And *GQ* had published . . . what memorable fiction exactly? But in my view, the current literary section of *Esquire* had become moribund, geriatric, small, boring—and, mostly, *expected*. And work by women was, to say the very least, grossly underrepresented in the magazine.

I'd always loved what Kafka wrote in a letter: "I think we ought to read only the kind of books that wound and stab us. If the book we're reading doesn't wake us up with a blow on the head, what are we reading for?" If there were one job in the world I wanted, the ur-job, it would be literary editor of *Esquire.* Of course, this was insane. But I could really shake things up there, I thought. I'd publish fiction that wounded, that stabbed.

THE MID-NINETIES WAS THE GOLDEN AGE—OR, MORE CORRECTLY, THE last gasp—of the print magazine. There was no competition from the Internet, and print was still king. I don't even want to begin to calculate the amount of time I spent at newsstands those days. Like many other people I knew, I was a connoisseur of *The Baffler* and *The Face* and the magazines that wanted to be *The Face*—the ones that always had Jarvis Cocker or Liam/Noel Gallagher (and is there a distinction between the two?) on the covers. I likewise developed an interest in a satirical magazine from San Francisco called *Might* and nerdily saved every issue. I brought the stack in for Granger to examine.

"You should get this guy David Eggers to write for us," I suggested. (Dave was then, professionally, a David.)

It was also the era of the low-fi, low-res fiction reading. I'd been going to my fair share of readings, though I didn't *quite* go out of love (but does anyone?) so much as out of professional obligation. Most of these writers were men, and most of the man-writers' readings would go a little like this: the writer would walk up to the podium, carrying a great bundle of papers, which he would drop onto the lectern like a granite tombstone; with a solemn look, he would gaze upon the audience and declare into the microphone, "This is pretty long, actually." There would be a throat clearing. There would be a leafing through of the papers. Upon the room a great silence would descend, and it was at this very moment that you, as captive audience member, knew that all you could do was settle into your chair (if you had one) and kiss your evening goodbye.

In 1995, *GQ* organized a reading at a bar downtown for a young writer, Donna Tartt, who had published a short story in the magazine. She was a real hotshot—her first novel, *The Secret History*, had come out to great fanfare three years before—and it was clear that *GQ* considered it a coup to have her story "A Garter Snake." I didn't yet remotely understand the pecking order of the whole short-story submission game (a game watched by perhaps dozens of people, even if we were still in the golden age of print), which was to say that if *GQ* was publishing it, the story must have been rejected by at least four or possibly five other magazines. (This is not a disparagement; it is a clear-eyed statement of fact. And if *GQ* ran a short story, it had certainly been rejected by *Esquire*.)

Mostly, I just thought it was cool that (1) *GQ* was publishing an ambitious short story by an ambitious woman, and (2) Art Cooper hadn't required some sort of corset-themed photo shoot for her.

The reading was at the scruffy East Village bar KGB. I was the assistant/drudge whose job it was to deal with the invitations, RSVPs, venue setup, and whatnot. I was just happy to be involved, and the whole event was so obviously excellent for *GQ*, and for writers, and for books, and for the so-called literary world.

But there was also something mephitic about the thing.

The bar was packed, and I wondered if the bourgeois sensibilities—shared, sadly, to a degree by yours truly—of, for example, Art Cooper were somewhat offended by the place's grubby downtown aura. There were red walls and kitschy framed Soviet-era posters. Art stood back by the bar, enjoying a martini, but not doing too much in the way of circulating. Not entirely his milieu, I suspected. The guests, upon further inspection, were all rather nicely scrubbed up—a colleague later said derisively, "I think all of them owned *art galleries*"; there was lots of tight, shiny clothing; there were barrettes, worn high on the forehead, in the style of the day; I actually saw one cigarette holder (certainly used parodically, although it was no mere prop: there was an actual lit cigarette in it). Before the reading began, a number of Tartt's friends and acquaintances installed themselves at a big table in the front.

I overheard Art Cooper's wife say to a female assistant, "Do you work in the fashion department?"

The young woman did.

"I *knew* it," Art's wife, Amy, said. She had been the editor in chief of *Mademoiselle,* so she was an expert in these things. "I can always tell when a girl works in the fashion department. You all have that extra little something. A real spark. An extra *pizzazz.*"

But as excited as I was to be there, it was impossible not to pick up on a kind of weird energy in the room, like some kind of miasma hanging over the city of Thebes.

I had a couple of mildly sour mini-chats with young men who were, or who claimed to be, fiction writers, and I also found myself talking to some peculiar young fellows on the book publishing side of things. I couldn't figure out why the literary encounters I had had in my brief career so far, particularly with dudes, seemed to have this borderline surly and defensive tone. Was it me? It definitely could have been me, but did anyone else also feel that these happenings were essentially Kierkegaard's idea of ressentiment personified? And the larger question: Was this really all there was of the republic of letters? Did anyone actually have any interesting conversations about books—or about *anything*? It just seemed to me that the collective thought circulating around this room and all rooms like it boiled down to: *Who here is writer numero uno, and why am I not he?* (Most authors eventually grow out of this adolescent need to be the top dog, by the way, but I have also known some who, well, never quite did.)

While fiction writers may have had the imaginative high ground with respect to journalists, I will suggest that journalists were pretty much always more straightforward to deal with than fiction writers. I was working on a hypothesis about this: fiction writers were all maybe just a little bit crazy because their lives were so insecure and so defined by reputation—and reputation was abstract, subject to ebb and flow, flux and change, and was something one had very limited control over.

But if there was one thing a fiction writer *could* control, it was his persona. I now considered the scene before me at KGB. It struck me that a lot of these guys often seemed to be playacting the part of the archetypal Writer—and that archetypal Writer often seemed based, in some way perhaps no one was really even conscious of, on Hemingway. (In much the same way that the archetypal Composer is always Beethoven.) But the conscientious actor must fully understand his part, and thus it seemed important to remember that the persona of the demotically possessed male artist, the rugged loner, was actually a creation, a copy of a copy with its origin in the Romantic movement of the nineteenth century, and it had to do with, yes, Beethoven, with Nietzsche, with the rise of the middle class, and with the deification of secular idols. In other words: always remember that every idea has a whole human history behind it, so make sure you think twice about what narrative it is you're enacting before you go around believing you're any kind of renegade.

There's a line from the Richard Corliss *Time* review of *Amadeus* (when I was thirteen, I collected reviews of *Amadeus* from newspapers and magazines and put them in a scrapbook; I was an odd child): "Mozart ... comes raucously alive as a punk rebel, grossing out the Establishment." I've often thought of that line with respect to many writers I've known and their timidly chippy rebellion: *Ah, there he goes again, grossing out the Establishment.*

A small dinner, hosted by *GQ,* took place after the reading. Tartt was welcomed to bring a couple of her friends to it. I was not invited, as indeed I should not have been and did not want to be, and I fled out into the night.

The next morning, the literary editor handed me the bill from the dinner, an expense to put through for speedy reimbursement. I looked at the receipt. Had I ever seen a meal whose tab reached comfortably into the four digits? I had not. Had perhaps more than a "couple" of Tartt's friends been included in the dinner? This was not for me to say. When I got home that night, I called my parents and told them about the dinner bill.

"It will be interesting," said my father, "to see what happens when the company goes public." This was always his take when I told him about any of the alarming (to me) profligacy I had witnessed at work. He added, "I just don't see how any of it is sustainable."

And it wasn't sustainable. How could it have been? "I believe in waste," said the famous former Condé Nast creative director Alexander Liberman. "Waste is very important in creativity." Not that I was in any sort of position of power (obviously), but never once did I hear the word "budget." These magazines spent enormous amounts of money on writers, photographers, and illustrators, on shoots and events; the expense accounts were big (although the editors' salaries were not so big, but no one needed to know *that*—sort of ruined the fantasy), everyone took black town cars everywhere (this included, yes, frequently, assistants), there were not one but two Christmas parties for even the lowliest members of the editorial staff at *GQ*, and assistants got overtime if they stayed past 7:00 P.M. and, if they played it right, were even reimbursed for their lunches. (All I had to do, it turned out, was submit a receipt and a petty-cash voucher for a "working lunch." And "working lunch," for me, usually meant sitting at my desk, flipping through someone else's copy of *Esquire* as I very slowly speared into my container of salad with an uncouth plastic fork. [Like everyone else in the office, I would pore over each new issue of *Esquire* with varying degrees of interest and bewilderment. One extraordinary cover line from *Esquire* during those years: "Heather Locklear Plumbs the Hermeneutics of Desire."])

And so if Condé Nast was a wondrous gravy train, it was also an effective reality denier. Where would we be without it? *What* would we be without it? What would happen if—when—we were fired like everyone else? Because people were fired from our magazine and, it seemed, every other one *all the time*.

Word had it that assistants in our building were fired in this manner: there would be a call from our lady in HR, and she would say, "Um, can you come and see me?" That was it. That was when you knew it was all over for you and that you'd have mere minutes to pack up your things and get out. Additionally, someone must have told me very early on that when assistants were given the ejector seat, they weren't allowed to take their Rolodexes with them; Rolodexes, evidently, were company property and had to remain at the desk. Of course I was sufficiently *cattiva* (and enough of a doomsday planner) to make copies of each card as I went along.

But when people at more middling levels got the heave-ho, there frequently seemed to be more of an attempt at group civility. Sometimes goodbye cards, hidden inside manila folders, would be circulated around the office (but what to write on them? "Good luck!" "So long!" "SORRY!"?). There might even be an awkward office party—OK, a *nonparty,* let's call it. These nonparties would take place in the hallway in front of my desk, and the fired person would usually be forced to make a little "All Hail Our Dear Leader" speech and may or may not have received an attractive pen (ballpoint—no fountain pens for you, friend), presented in a keepsake box. There would probably be a few bottles of Veuve Clicquot. That merrymaker, the Widow Clicquot. Would there be cheese and crackers? There *could* be cheese and crackers at these nonparties; this was not a given.

I'd watch these sad and magnanimous little speeches, pondering what the firees were going to do with their days now. A job was helpful for a number of reasons, one of which: your days were automatically filled for you. Because what would you do with yourself otherwise, when condemned to freedom? Eventually you always get thrown back into who you are, and when that happens, you'd better have something there. I'd already figured that out, at least. You build up an image of yourself as an actor, but you'd better not get too invested in that image, because then that's all you were.

After these speeches were over, we'd all stand in the hallway, clutching our prop cups and our prop plates, ponderously chitchatting. It always felt (to get back to Jung's theory of the collective unconsciousness) that we were all joined in the same thoughts then—each thinking more about ourselves than we were about the person who'd just been cast out, each of us considering how it would soon be our turn. Ask not for whom the bell, etc. . . . And when it *did* toll for thee, how much grace would thou display?

A question: How much can you give up and still be "you"?

8

One winter afternoon, Whitney, another assistant at the magazine, and I went to lunch with a *GQ* journalist and a notorious restaurant maître d' at a German biergarten in midtown. Why did these two men invite us to lunch? Who knows, but lunches were big in our business, and whenever a professional contact asked me to dine with him in those days, I'd usually comply. I'm not sure why the biergarten was selected—for the anachronistically down-market nature of the place, I guess. To say that the restaurant was on the casual side was redundant in the extreme: there were long picnic tables; there were squeeze bottles of mustard and ketchup on the tables. The journalist and the restaurant maître d' were both older than my father.

The journalist was a known bon vivant, not to mention a real wisenheimer, and he always seemed to be snickering about something whenever he went down the hall in the office. Once at a work Christmas party, as the Sinatra recording of "Jingle Bells" ("I love those J-I-N-G-L-E bells / Oh!") played on the restaurant sound system, he announced to several assembled people, "Adrienne doesn't even consider me male!" That comment embarrassed the hell out of me, although it was also from him I first heard the magical words "the Crillon," so it all evened out, I guess.

The maître d', whom I had met once at his restaurant, was high-spirited, "colorful," as they say, and struck me as a confabulator of the sort I could appreciate—in small doses. I knew he was completely full of it, but I was along for the ride. The maître d's restaurant was a temple of power, a shrine to the worship of power and to the display of it. Art Cooper took me to lunch there once, but I didn't understand why: my interactions with Art were distant and transactional and would remain so even after the lunch. (The king does not want to make himself too familiar.) I was comatose with nerves and nearly catatonic during the entire meal. I'm sure Art considered our lunch a spectacular dud, if he even considered it at all, which I can guarantee you he did not, but on the upside, he insisted that I join him in a martini—my first ever. (And then another. These were vodka martinis, as opposed to my parents' gin ones.) From my end, I will say that I came away from the lunch with somewhat of a better understanding of Art as a man who had started in the periphery. Through a combination of luck, industry, and will, he had gotten himself from the middle of Pennsylvania to the center of it all. To the red-hot center, you might even say.

But back to my skepticism about people with power. I always had this idea that you can never trust anyone with it—that that's the only way you can remain free and maintain the independence of your thinking.

At the biergarten, the journalist and the restaurant maître d' put themselves in charge and ordered a pitcher of beer for the table. They ordered our meals for us, too: bratwurst, sausage, spaetzle.

Beer was distributed into plastic cups (ladies first). The journalist and the maître d' set about entertaining Whitney and me (as she and I exchanged quick little surreptitious eye rolls across the table) with some high-level gossip about the NYC restaurant biz. The talk was simultaneously expansive and narrow, and the stories were mean, funny, and absurd, and nowhere in them did any women appear. As the men spoke, it occurred to me that I wasn't sure how much I cared about food (I've always had a simpleminded food-is-food attitude; I'll save whatever money I have for more durable satisfactions) or about restaurants: restaurants as entertainment, restaurants as theater, restaurants as stagecraft, restaurants as conferrers of power, restaurants as analyses of power, restaurants as the main (the only?) event of the day.

It was curious: the whole of the maître d's world seemed to exist within the confines of this one particular restaurant, as if there weren't a life outside of it at all. Which, come to think of it, was a lot like the stance toward the world you saw when you worked somewhere like *GQ* in this, the still-golden era of magazines: if "we" didn't cover it, it didn't happen.

Somehow, I now found myself lurking about in the periphery, in the shadows, of a world of pure power, ruled by men. But what was interesting to learn was that power, once someone had it, was a force rarely scrutinized. I had begun to observe that powerful people (or those who think of themselves that way) didn't really have much of an incentive to examine themselves or their own subjectivity.

In other words: themselves = subject; everyone else = object.

"What about your *boyfriends*?" the journalist asked. "Would your *boyfriends* be jealous if they knew that you were having lunch with two handsome, witty, and charming men?"

Although I was pretty friendly with Whitney and admired her mordant sense of humor—and we had even gone on a weekend trip together—I had no idea whether there was a boyfriend or a boyfriend-type individual in the picture. The subject just never came up. There is something hidden in people, something kept private, and they will tell you exactly what they want you to know. You've got to respect that. (Also—and I realize this may be impossible for the males of the world to comprehend—women don't actually *always* discuss men. It is a fact that two young women can spend a few days together and find other things to talk about.)

An order was placed for another round of beer. Bratwurst, sausage, and spaetzle arrived on the table, on platters.

Before the maître d' cleared us to dig in, he indicated that he had an announcement: a *gift* for us. He reached into his bag and produced something round and roughly the size of a golf ball. There it was: one splendid black truffle.

The maître d' passed the truffle underneath each of our noses. I'd had no previous truffle experience; I was interested to learn that it smelled pleasantly of meat, dirt, and some deep, unidentifiable scent from Middle-earth. Again, the maître d' reached into his bag. This time he pulled out a truffle slicer made of, in memory, polished silver. He paused with it for a moment, allowing it to gleam in the light. *Flash, flash,* it went. *Flash, flash.* He then began shaving wantonly away, strips of truffle falling onto the plates in great decadent heaps—onto bratwurst, sausage, and spaetzle. The three of us—the journalist, Whitney, and I—exploded into a round of applause.

The maître d' talked a little about whence the truffle had come, what type of truffle it was, etc. He was a man accustomed to holding forth, but I had spent the last two years being around men like that; this was a now familiar archetype. What I didn't understand or appreciate was how powerful the maître d' was in his world . . . or should I say how powerful he considered himself to be. I also didn't understand that the amount of power you have (or believe you have) shapes your demands of life and of other people.

Oh, but still, this seemed to be a great kind of world to live in: surprise truffles and spontaneous applause, rich food, rich people (or, better yet, mean stories about them), and no apparent reason to be too worried about returning to work before anyone noticed that you'd been gone for three hours. It was also delightful to think that there were people who considered food more than mere provender—that food can be grand, and entertaining, and enchanting.

"Everyone should always bring truffles with them all the time," I observed.

Somehow, I now seemed to know a lot of guys who put hot sauce on everything, so it was fun to know that there were also people out there who deemed truffles a basic utility, like electricity.

"If you want your daily truffle," the journalist said, "you're going to need to start hanging out with rich guys."

It was a cold day. All four of us were wearing black coats. After lunch, in the taxi on the way back to the office, the journalist rode shotgun. In the back seat, the maître d' sat between Whitney and me. Is it important to know who among us was wearing a skirt?

Without warning, a male hand suddenly appeared on my knee.

I looked at that hand. I looked over to Whitney, whose dark, expressive eyes widened. I looked at that hand again, which had now made its way to my thigh and was creeping upward.

The grotesque maître d' then lurched toward me and forced his tongue into my mouth. He tasted like beer, truffles, salt. I moved away.

He sat back in the seat for a moment. He fixed his hair. Undaunted, he turned to Whitney and started attacking *her*.

She moved away.

The unctuous maître d' came back to me again and again jammed his tongue into my mouth; like some pestilence that can't be gotten rid of, he went back to Whitney again; back to me. This went on for a couple more rounds.

Whether the journalist up in front noticed the assault happening right in back of him, I have no idea. He never turned around.

During each brief pause in the maître d's assault, Whitney and

I exchanged quick glances. We were stunned, we were mortified, we were aghast, and we had no idea how to react or what to do. I'm sure we both wish we had risen up like goddesses, like Athena striking down Hephaestus with a stone, but that was not how it played out. (Often our behavior is unequal to our conception of ourselves.) The tone at the *GQ* office was informal, jocular, frequently unprofessional, often lewd, and it was confusing for us to know how to react and how to behave in our workplace.

Although we were not at our workplace. The maître d' had nothing to do with our work.

"Look at me," the ghastly maître d', who was not a native English speaker, said, sitting back again. He made a sweeping gesture there in the back seat of the taxi, taking in his kingdom whole. "I have a nice lunch, and I kiss two very pretty girls."

Whitney and I hadn't perceived an id so unchecked, an imbalance of power so vast, that the maître d' felt entitled to his own personal editorial assistant harem. She and I had gone into this lunch thinking that it would be a weird, fun little adventure, thinking we were all on the same team, thinking that each actor at the table would play an equal role, and we left it thinking, *Man, your soul is just so bad.*

(Happily, years later, the proverbial chickens would come home to roost when the maître d', after years of accusations of sexual misconduct, was forced to resign from his restaurant following a guilty plea to misdemeanor assault charges. And then the restaurant went out of business.)

What we didn't know was that power was the motivator.

THERE IS SOMETHING TO BE SAID ABOUT SPENDING ONE'S FORMATIVE years in a place where there are not many grand notions of power or profit. When I was young, I had only one big glimpse into the world of incredible wealth, and that was thanks to the first family of Akron, the Seiberlings. Frank Seiberling, Akron's own Henry Ford, was the founder of Goodyear (confusingly, and in a seemingly uncharacteristic act of self-denial, he didn't name the company after himself but rather after Charles Goodyear, the scientist who—quite accidentally—discovered the process of vulcanization and who died a pauper), and the Seiberling family lived like kings in a sixty-five-room Tudor Revival mansion in west Akron. The mansion, now a museum, has a name because why not: Stan Hywet—"stone quarry" in Old English.

I'd always had an obsession with Stan Hywet (so much so that I set a novel there), and the obsession surely must have had something to do with the knowledge that the place offered my first view at an entirely theatrical identity: the Seiberlings playing the parts of English aristocrats in a Tudor drama. The estate was built around the time of World War I, and though you may have expected to see Henry VIII prowling in a corner, the world of the Tudors would have seemed as remote to people then, during that age of Kafka and cubism, Stravinsky and revolution, as it does to us. What the house really was was a modernist dream of self-improvement—a theater in which identity games were played. The ideology, the quest, the goal: to imagine a better self.

The Seiberlings were known as famous hosts, and on house tours the docents still brag about visits by Helen Keller and the 1940s movie star Stewart Granger. But the greatest star was certainly the brilliant actor George Sanders, the man born to play Humbert Humbert. Sanders's most famous role, and maybe my favorite film performance ever: the vainglorious theater critic Addison DeWitt in *All About Eve;* further to recommend him: the title of Sanders's autobiography is *Memoirs of a Professional Cad* and the title of a Sanders biographical treatment, *A Dreadful Man.* So there you go. Sanders's evening at Stan Hywet must have been somewhat more alcoholic than Helen Keller's, though—displayed in a glass case on a lower floor of the house is a copy of a letter old man Seiberling, a proud teetotaler, sent to the actor, scolding him for some dramatically disruptive behavior at a formal dinner.

Interestingly, a daughter of Seiberling's would bring the two founders of AA together at Stan Hywet, and the place is considered the birthplace of Alcoholics Anonymous. Which makes perfect sense when you think about it, because isn't this really the idea at the heart of modernism—that people can change?

No, not only that they *can* change. That they *must*.

To imagine a better self.

No, no: to surpass the self.

9

I was now teaching myself to become a professional reader. I had to adopt an aesthetic attitude and also learn how to balance competing interests. I was no longer reading to please myself, not entirely. I was reading for some idea of what the magazine was but also, practically, reading with an eye toward what I believed my bosses would like. That was the way it had to be; otherwise, left entirely to my idiosyncratic sensibility, I would have been reprinting excerpts from Thomas Bernhard's novel *The Loser* all the time. (So bitter. So Austrian.)

And what about Art Cooper's taste in fiction? Art's taste in fiction was . . . was . . . well, who knew anything about Art's taste in fiction. Did he have any? Was there a "*GQ* Short Story"? And is that even a given anyway, that a magazine editor who began his career as a newspaper journalist even *has* a particular taste in fiction? I knew that Art loved anything Mordecai Richler wrote, and of course Ellroy, and also Peter Mayle (whose charming and amiable columns in *GQ* about his life in France eventually became his book *A Year in Provence;* he also wrote charming and amiable fiction), and Art harangued me about getting him an advance galley of one of Patrick O'Brian's *Master and Commander* naval-based novels (which I just could not force myself to read a page of—yes, I know his books are supposed to be great), but, really, let's be honest: Art remained an old newspaperman at heart.

It does seem fair to say that Art had an old newspaperman's fixations. Like all old newspapermen, Art revered the *Washington Post* and was, by extension, obsessed with the identity of Deep Throat. A favorite *GQ* parlor game involved guessing plausible suspects for the world's most famous secret source.

"So who's Deep Throat going to turn out to be?" Art would ask, that bullhorn-amplified voice of his blasting down the hallway.

Who was Art addressing? It didn't really matter—let's just say it was always some guy, and the guy, whoever he was—editor, writer, visiting dignitary, etc.—was always going to comport himself as if in the running for the slot of number one kiss-up. The oily sycophancy was always a superb thing to witness.

"Pat Buchanan!" the guy might say, whoever the guy was, happy just to be involved in any encounter with the king. Inevitably someone else would invoke that chilling word "Kissinger." But Art would have his own ideas.

"Wrong," he would say, as he'd turn away. Art walked in a sort of midriff-led way, as if his belly were self-propelled. "It's *David Gergen.*"

In the stage play of *Amadeus,* there are two characters called the "Venticelli": the little winds. They're the whisperers, the ill breezes, the purveyors of fact, rumor, and gossip—a kind of caustic Greek chorus, commenting throughout on the action. Eventually, I came to think of myself as the Venticella of the office, sitting quietly at my desk, watching these men watchfully. *Yes:* the Venticelli may seem inscrutable, but they see and hear everything—and store it for use at a later date. They are players of the long game.

I BEGAN RECEIVING SOME SUSPICIOUS MAILINGS, POSTCARDS WITH images of cloud formations, blue and white. INFINITE PLEASURE read one. INFINITE STYLE. INFINITE WRITER said another. These mysterious teasers were clearly the early stages for some massive advertising campaign for a forthcoming book, and they put me rather too uncomfortably in the mind of an Absolut Vodka advertisement. Or maybe they were supposed to be a parody of the Absolut ads? Who knew. My reaction? The old eye roll, followed by the old lip-gloss reapplication. What *was* this novel, *Infinite Jest*? No clue, and the publicity materials, with their ominous cloud formations that put me in a hazy, hereafter frame of mind, only raised more questions than they answered. And *who* was this author? The one with the wacky bandanna and the melancholy face (a later comment about the author photo from the author himself: "Yes, that's the post-lobotomy picture"), this person with so radically name-y a name: David Foster Wallace.

"How in the hell have you never heard of him?" a writer friend asked.

"I don't know, man," I said. "I can't keep up with *everything*."

"Isn't that sort of your *job*?"

The writer explained to me that David Foster Wallace had also published a couple of books and a bunch of other splashy nonfiction essays in magazines, notably in *Harper's*—there was this one about a state fair, and there was this other one about a cruise. The essays, evidently, were really just cripplingly long, and *Harper's* published them as a folio insert—pages of a different paper stock, and uninterrupted by ads. *GQ* did not run folios, though it had plenty of writers who were stars, or who considered themselves to be (a cheap joke—these were exceptional writers, some of them).

"What, is it like stunt journalism?" I asked.

"No," the writer said. "He's *intellectual.*" A pause. "He seems like a dick."

Then I started paying attention. I soon noted that the general tone when anyone spoke of David Foster Wallace was, essentially: *That fucking guy.* John Adams once said that the principal human urge was "the passion for respect and distinction" (I would have phrased it "the *rage* for respect and distinction"), and my time working at *GQ* had certainly helped clarify what he meant by that. Resentment, or ressentiment, it destroys art and ruins souls. But it's also possible that resentment makes the world go round.

The galley of the mega-novel *Infinite Jest* finally arrived. My friend Allison, a fellow *GQ* assistant, and I chortled about how, as the Prada backpacks every woman in the Condé Nast building then carried were getting smaller and smaller, the books (not to mention the CDs—the epical *Mellon Collie and the Infinite Sadness* had just been released) seemed to be getting bigger and bigger. Now here was an idea to launch a thousand magazine think pieces! We would have assigned it if we could have. Some editors and writers in the office started asking me if I could get them their very own copies of *Infinite Jest.* That was something I *could* do, it turned out.

The week before Thanksgiving, I committed myself to review *Infinite Jest* for *GQ.* (By that point, somehow, and probably unwisely, I could review anything I wanted to review.) Even in those pre-9/11 times, I knew the meaning of the word "terror": the review was due the Monday after the holiday. Six days to read 1,079 pages—a project the author believed (I would later learn) should take between two and four months. I was the back seat passenger in my parents' car as we drove from Ohio to my grandmother's house in Martinsburg, West Virginia, for Thanksgiving weekend; my grandfather, who had died six years before, was still dead. I had the flu, and my grandmother (who always referred to herself in the regal third person and with the nickname George) said to me upon our arrival, "George wants to know why Adri isn't dating JFK Jr. yet." I was not in the best frame of mind that weekend, honestly. But even if I had been, I would not have been able to summon the kind of monkish devotion *Infinite Jest* required.

I thought the novel was insane and bizarre and full of grandeur and despair, but I didn't like it. I didn't get it. I was insufficiently enlightened *to* get it, I guess, but "getting it" wasn't even the point. It would take years for me to understand that that which offers redemption does not come in an instant. (During two subsequent readings, I would have the author himself to help guide me along my journeys . . . when, that is, the author felt like it.)

But maybe I wasn't exactly the ideal reader for *Infinite Jest* then. Maybe I never was. I became peculiarly fixated on my loathing for the loathsome character Orin Incandenza, the anti–Sydney Carton and a serial seducer of young mothers whom I wanted to drag out onto the balustrade and slap across the face with an evening glove; the females in the novel seemed archetypes rather than successfully credible characters; I was confounded by the narrative's chronology; I was unnerved by its lack of warmth; I had no interest in drugs; I hated tennis. At the same time, I loved the stagecraft and the theatricality, and the language was so audaciously charged with life—even as the world it depicted was dead: a thing. A book at total cross-purposes with itself: a maximalist work with nothing to celebrate.

Yet at the same time, there was something godlike about it.

I had a hard time squaring the whole together. Did the beautiful and elating parts outweigh the exasperating ones? If you happened to have a conversation in those weeks with someone who was also scrambling to read a review copy of *Infinite Jest,* this was the over-arching question. Come to think of it, this was also much like the experience of knowing David Wallace himself—joy and delight, countered by exceptional frustration and disillusionment.

A *GQ* writer had scheduled an interview with David, which was to take place at his hotel in midtown the day of the *Infinite Jest* party. At the eleventh hour, a publicist called to cancel the interview. Believe me, this did *not* go down well in the *GQ* offices ("fuck him!"), and the excuse—"David's tired"—smelled of unbearable prima donna–ish behavior, and there was plenty of resentment at the magazine for that and for everything else. But it was possible that I was more on this guy's side than not—I was becoming less clear about why it was always so easy to get celebrities to talk to journalists anyway. The entertainment press is never benign. You didn't have to explain to me why Terence Trent D'Arby (I know this is a random one) changed his name (to Sananda Maitreya, amazingly). The real question: Why don't more subjects seize their own stories? When you give up your narrative, your life becomes just another story, one for other people to tell; you will be trapped within the stale pages of someone else's interpretation, made less subtle than you are (at best), made a fool of (at worst), reduced to an object (always), and caricatured into abstraction.

THE PARTY FOR *INFINITE JEST* WAS ON A COLD EVENING IN FEBRUARY. February in New York: that special time of year when you want to pitch your winter coat, gloves, hat, and scarf into the garbage can forevermore (but you still have two more months of wintery torment to go). It was held at a bar in the East Village, and I had a bad attitude about the whole thing. Man, I *so* did not want to go. I'll also admit that in my constructed scenario of the evening, the remarkable guest of honor was but an afterthought. But my incentive to attend came when Granger invited me to ride downtown to the party with him and a writer from *GQ*, Tom Junod, in a town car. No subway for me that night! Things were looking up, slightly. The cherry on top came in the form of my getting to glom on to their plans to have dinner afterward at a restaurant I otherwise had no business in.

The bar was mobbed. There were cinder block walls and red ikat-upholstered furniture. It was stuffy and did not smell all that great. As soon as we checked in at the door (hello, ladies—I'd been one of you before, and I'd be one of you again), I just *knew* that my hair would smell like cigarette smoke when I woke up the following morning. (Remember when you had to air your clothes out from tertiary smoke as soon as you got home from a night out?) The bad news for me was that I knew, or at least recognized, many of the people there—the more junior ones, that is. I scowled at them. They scowled at me. *Hey, how did you get in here?*

About half the crowd seemed to be made up of *Esquire* editors. Granger, Tom, and I made sure to sneer at them good (Sharks versus Jets, etc.). The two men each went their separate ways, circulating around the room, and I hung back in the periphery, taking in the scene with grim fascination (I'm terrible at mingling and have never gotten any better at it). This party was more surreal than most, with people orbiting David Foster Wallace like electrons around a nucleus. Something was happening, and whatever that thing was, everyone wanted to be part of it.

I watched with wonder as people watched David but tried not to watch David, who did not seem chatty—or even, frankly, civil—in the least. "Prima donna" was not exactly the label that came to mind. My main sense was that he was a man apart. His hair was long, auburnish, and he had on round granny glasses and a blue-gray polo shirt about four sizes too small. I, however, was gorgeously attired, wearing a long brown Paul Smith skirt and my most sumptuary garment—a Paul Smith blouse of the palest red-and-white silk brocade. (It wasn't a matchy-matchy thing; the skirt and blouse were from different seasons—one current, one not.) The shirt looked as if it had been spun by monks, and probably it had.

I'd found it somewhat interesting, but mostly just deeply irksome, to watch the culture industry gear up around David Foster Wallace and announce: *We now present you with the* BOOK *and*

the AUTHOR *of the moment, and you are powerless in the matter.*
ENJOY. It was also a paradox not lost on me that I was, nominally,
a cog within that machinery. Also, I now understood that celebrity
worship is a deep human evil, and I'm sure that this diagnosis had
its basis in my idea, nurtured in my more crabbed and pessimistic
moods, that most humans are incapable of self-government and
have no common sense.

My anti-celebrity-culture stance certainly also had to be at least
somewhat connected to my forced reading of so many magazine
celebrity profiles. I needed someone to tell me why it was that the
profile writers (who were thoughtful people, usually) always produced these old, stagnant, lazy things. And about David: it made
no sense—why did people take such a personal interest in the lives
of writers, when the writer's real life is never visible? People wanted
gossip and biography; people wanted things prepackaged for them,
placed into categories—they wanted everything but the thing itself, which is the work.

So anyway, I didn't read any of the profiles about David Foster
Wallace. Didn't have to. I already knew what was in them: David
would be presented as an already mythic, mystery-shrouded figure;
there would be genuflection before the male genius; there would
be resentment. I already knew that the pieces would have more
to do with the profile writer's ressentiment than they would with
anything else.

I had an exchange with a woman I knew, an assistant at a literary agency. She didn't like me, and I didn't like her, although
we did both agree that David could have spruced himself up a bit
more for his own party. But we endured each other because we
had no one else to talk to. (I now have a theory, developed after
many years in New York, that parties exist only so that we may be
thrust into conversations we do not wish to have, thereby sharpen-
ing those artificial-good-humor skills so necessary to face the real
world.) This was one of those conversations during which one finds

oneself planted like a redwood, and with no exit strategy (I've since learned: *always have an exit strategy*) . . . but thankfully Tom materialized. I'd already reached my allotment of literary encounters for the evening (one), and I was content to drift silently (I, silent; he, not) to and fro with him.

OVERHEARD: "It's great to be able to put a face to a byline!"
OVERHEARD: "They say it's going to win all of the prizes next year."
OVERHEARD: "So what does everyone *really* think of it?"

David's editor stood up on a table and gave a quite impassioned speech about the novel and its author, those accumulators of much recent stupefied praise. The editor was young and fair-haired and did not seem to be by nature a table-stander. The act was significant. After the speech, I watched as some of the more brazen types approached David, like, for instance, one woman who crept up to him in slow motion and had the following to say when her moment in the sun came:

"I'm half dog!"

Tom and I were standing in the bathroom hallway, evaluating the party and analyzing its dramatis personae, when David slunk by, en route to the john—to sneak some chewing tobacco, as would later be explained. Tom introduced himself to David. Tom introduced me to David. Really wished he hadn't done that. Had a bad feeling about what was coming next.

"Adrienne here is the person who wrote the *Infinite Jest* review in *GQ*," said Tom.

Sea, I thought, *swallow me. Go ahead and swallow me whole.* I knew as well as I'd ever known anything that my review of the book was crude and short, and I didn't even begin to get at anything I wanted to get at in it. Those three hundred words contained nothing real. I had not read the book or written the review with anything like full obligation. Not even like 20 percent obligation, and I knew it.

David said nothing. He studied the floor.

Tom asked, "So. Do you feel as if your head has been emptied out since you finished writing *Infinite Jest*?"

David gave a shrug. "Yeah," he murmured. "My brain really *is* empty now, I suppose."

With that, David scuttled off into the bathroom like a raccoon.

Plainly, Tom and I were immobilized by this failed encounter—all we could manage to do was continue to stand there in that little hallway and blink at each other. Why were we not suaver conversationalists? Why were we so wretchedly unappealing? What was *wrong* with us?

When David finally emerged from the bathroom, Tom and I were still stationed there, not having budged an inch. In the manner of an antisocial second grader, David ducked between us, not bothering with any token courtesy like, say, eye contact or an "ex*cu-use* me," and darted away.

How about that? Rejected by the man of the hour not once, but *twice*.

I watched as David joined the crowd and thought, *There he goes again, grossing out the Establishment.* But we were clearly in the presence of someone who was extraordinarily unusual in every way. And those were the first words I heard David Foster Wallace say, directed, more or less, toward me, or not: "Yeah, my brain really *is* empty now, I suppose."

10

I wasn't really too successful at being twenty-three, twenty-four. In general terms, my physical existence alternated between the following locations: *GQ,* apartment, gym. (My route to and from my gym took me by the old Tower Records at Broadway and Fourth Street, where a poster for the album *Fashion Nugget,* by Cake, remained in a window for what seemed like a decade.) At the gym, I'd occasionally chat with a handsome blond-haired guy who always worked out in purple sweatpants; he explained that he was a painter, and when I once rather inanely asked him if he ever did any art for magazines (my mind-set was still: if it's not in *GQ,* it doesn't exist) he replied, "Oh, I'm not an illustrator. I'm an *artist*." And an artist he was. That man was John Currin.

Dates still remained not the best uses of my time. For better or worse, most of the men I tended to meet now were writers. Were they my tribe? Sure. I guess, maybe. Mainly, I enjoyed talking to writers about books, although talking to writers about books would also inevitably serve as a reminder to me of the huge number of things I should already have read but had not. It was not that I felt I couldn't keep up with anyone I talked to, however, and only a ferret-eyed doofus will ever casually quiz you about the Great Books; it was merely that I understood I was smarter than I was educated. But I didn't want a mentor or anything like that, and a Trilby-Svengali dynamic was so not going to work for me. The mind, remember, must be sovereign. I didn't want instruction—what I needed was *information*.

And so what is it that writers *really* want to talk about, even and especially on dates? Their own work, of course. I became accustomed to this arrangement: if I were to go out on a date with a writer of fiction, I might receive, at the rendezvous's end, a batch of six to ten short stories (or, God help me, a part of an in-progress novel) to read and comment on—*ASAP,* if you please. I understood that every writer is always desperate for readers, so I tried to be helpful in this regard. But, depending where the guy was in his career journey, I might also be asked to evaluate lines in rejection letters ("I'd welcome the opportunity to consider more of your work in the future") as if interpreting smoke signals from the pythoness at Delphi. From writers in somewhat later phases of their career journeys, I would learn that there are agents who forward to their clients editors' rejection letters and that there are ones who do not. (Is this interesting to know? You decide.)

Often I'd find myself wondering why it was that these dudes never really asked me about any of my own extracurricular writing, by the way, but these situations were never as reciprocal as one might have wished. But maybe that was my own fault. I hadn't written much. I wanted to write—always believed I would—but I hadn't yet. And as talent-free as I may have privately believed most of these guys were, I did admire their initiative and their persistence. I worried that I had neither.

What else was I doing with my life? Not enough. There were more readings; there were movie screenings (the best: Sergei Eisenstein's restored *Alexander Nevsky,* with a new recording of the Prokofiev score; the prescreening party, with its mounds of caviar and fountains of vodka, has now in memory expanded to the status of legend). Occasionally, fashion department people would give me their tickets to the shows. I had no professional reason whatsoever for attending a fashion show, but I did enjoy them (though I was too high-toned to have admitted that to anyone). Fashion shows always started late, so I'd bring along *Pale Fire* as my go-to reading material. (Yeah, I was just *that way:* the young lady who brings a Nabokov novel—and *that* Nabokov novel—to a fashion show.)

There were press luncheons. There were drinks dates, there were dinners, there were parties. And then there was the subset of the party, the dread book party. My tales of the peculiar torment of the book party are many, and in my growing view they now had to be avoided at all costs: invite me on a walk, to dinner, to a play—I'll see anything (I'm just a Broadway baby)—or to plant some flowers, but do not ever, ever, ever invite me to a book party (unless you are my actual friend, in which case you must). I can't bear them. The using of people as props. The instrumental nature of most literary relationships: *What can you do for me?* The fact that Charlie Rose was often to be found skeeving around at the more prestigious of them. Weren't these things supposed to have been fun, way back when? And none of them ever had the energy of the *Infinite Jest* party, I'll tell you that much.

THAT FALL, THE FIRST GQ MEN OF THE YEAR AWARDS CEREMONY WAS held. The purpose of the awards: to celebrate the most remarkable celebrities of the previous year. I started asking people in the office to explain the whole thing to me. Why did we need these awards? What, exactly, were we celebrating? What did the awards really *mean* to the persons who received them? Was the whole premise not somewhat toothless and manufactured? A friend put it *Field of Dreams*–ishly: "There is one rule about celebrities: If you throw an awards show, they will come." And another question: Weren't *all* men *always* Men of the Year, anyway?

The ceremony, a black-tie affair for an audience of five thousand, was held at Radio City Music Hall. I worked in an undefined capacity in the pressroom that night. In the days leading up to the event, some friends at the magazine warned me about the ego blow I'd soon endure when I, a resolute non-celebrity, had my first red carpet experience. Apparently, when you'd begin your Bataan-esque march down the red carpet, there would be a moment when everything would be held in suspension: the photographers would try to figure out who you were, their cameras at attention; but when it was determined that you were a big nobody in their books, you'd see the cameras collapse as if heliotropes in a dying sun. The worst part: the cameras would instantly spring back to life upon the arrival of the next—and, with any luck, more radiantly exciting—person in line.

But why did we even believe that we *should* be celebrities (or at least mistaken for them)? If global fame were the goal, were we possibly in the wrong line of work? And, secondarily, was it also possible that we all had a greatly inflated view of our own importance? This was also a thought I was beginning to have a lot at work, particularly when an issue of the magazine was closing and my colleagues were running around like marauding pirates. Back to the John Adams line about the passion for distinction being the principal human urge.

I found a side entrance at Radio City that night. No red carpet for me—then or ever, and I wanted to keep it that way.

This year's big winners—not that there was any suspense: they were that month's cover subjects—were Mel Gibson, Michael Jordan, and Jerry Seinfeld. The run of show: celebrities presented other celebrities with awards, Phil Collins performed a concert (of course there had been crotchety commentary around the office about how Art Cooper's awareness of music had clearly stopped, suspended like a martini olive in aspic, in 1985—actually it was 1965), and other celebrities presented other celebrities with some more awards. Because if there was one group of people who needed more presents, more prizes, more, more, more, that group was *celebrities*.

But down in the pressroom was where all the real action was. As everyone else from work scurried around with clipboards, looking as if they were about to spontaneously combust, pretty much all I did was bask in the red-and-gold art deco fabulousness of Radio City and gape at the dazzling stars. I'm sure I should have appreciated far more than I did then what it actually took to organize and execute an event of this scale.

Items: Mel Gibson was a pygmy, Liam Neeson was a monolith, and the singer for Hootie & the Blowfish (the nineties! it was actually a pretty slimy decade) seemed endearingly bashful. But who cared about any of those guys, because James Brown was there. Seriously. *James Brown*. How did they ever get *him*? I watched James Brown up on the little pressroom stage, as he posed for the cameras with a prop microphone, his black shirt unbuttoned to the navel. He had on a black jacket with rhinestone-studded lapels, tight black satin pants, and pointy boots. A fine layer of glitter covered his chest, face, and hands. Silent, antagonistic, Brown went through his photo-call routine in the beam of the flashbulbs—pivoting, posing, and glimmering; pivoting, posing, and glimmering. My main thought about him: *Here is a* pro. When he dropped down to the floor of the small stage and did a side split, I was as sure as I've ever been about anything that he was the single most impressive human I'd ever seen.

Forget what I said about how celebrity worship was a deep human evil. James Brown was a star for a *reason,* and at that moment I would have followed him anywhere.

But there was a big oversight: somehow, no one from *GQ* had gotten around to arranging any food for the press. How could this have happened? How was this even possible? Emergency pizzas were ordered, but I didn't understand that those pizzas were not meant *for me* (some other assistants were also similarly mistaken), and as I boorishly helped myself to the press's food, I pondered what else I ought to do to at least make myself *appear* busy. At one point, I crept up to the publicity director and, trying to at least seem somewhat conscientious, asked whether I could be of any help. I got shooed away. OK, fine. But why *was* I in attendance, exactly?

This was a question I was starting to ask of myself at work sometimes, too. Now, at twenty-four, when taking a lunar view of my career situation, I was beginning to question just exactly how useful I actually was in the world. But then I'd think back to where I was from, and I'd settle on this conclusion: feeling useful is an indulgence that most people cannot afford.

After two years on the job, I did know that I really needed to start taking some rigorous self-inventories. Starting with: How, exactly, did I spend my days? Well, let's see. There was rarely anything *that* unpleasant about my days, but neither was there anything *necessary* about them. I mean, I wasn't exactly working in an ER or anything, and I was bad at math, or bad at whatever it was you needed to be good at to work in an ER. Recently, a question had started to form: Were there not many, many other people in the world who could also do what I did?

Was I *necessary*? I was not. Was I *indispensable*? Nope.

I would now find myself wondering whether a degree of self-delusion was necessary to work as a magazine assistant, or maybe to work anywhere. The French have a word for it: *méconnaissance,* which can mean, approximately, "misrecognition" plus "self-delusion." "Self-misunderstanding," really. Was it possible that all magazine assistants—or, to expand outward, workers of all sorts—suffered from a kind of institutional *méconnaissance*?

But my *méconnaissance* had another layer to it. Could I actually have any self-respect as a female person if I worked for a men's magazine? Yes, yes, there was outstanding journalism in *GQ;* yes, there was great criticism. But weren't men's magazines at least half embarrassing, and maybe even more than that? But yet the representation was not the real—I kept telling myself that—and we should not confuse our actual lives with things we see in magazines.

The questions:

Could right and wrong coexist?

Was I, by mentally jettisoning the bad parts but keeping the good, operating in bad faith?

THE SELF-EVIDENT FACT OF THE MAGAZINE'S SEXISM COULD BE SPOKEN of only with the other assistants. We'd sit at Mexican restaurants with our machine-dispensed margaritas and fulminate about the representation of women in the pages: they were never actual people but were instead personlike ideas, concepts of people. Why, one of us might ask, did the women in the magazine appear unclothed, yet the men did not? Why, for example, did we *always* need some pervy description of each female profile subject's lips? Why, in a larger way, did men feel so freaking *entitled* to women's bodies? And if male readers wanted porn, why didn't they just go buy some porn? (Pornography was then a product that actually had to be bought.) The adolescent in-betweenness of the men's magazine was just embarrassing for everyone. It was easy to see what the obsession with women's ages was about, though: the "*GQ* Woman" must always be in the bloom of her youth, which was another way of saying that she isn't here to stay.

There was never a moment when I wasn't hyper-attuned to the colossal gray area that also came with the job. Until I came to work at men's magazines, I understood feminism only in the abstract; I didn't understand why women actually *need* feminism. Sometimes in my darker moments, I would now find myself thinking of my life as one gigantic discord of masculine voices, each voice talking over the other. What follows are actual lines spoken to me by men, and all in professional, or at least semiprofessional, contexts:

"God, pregnant women are so fucking sexy."

"You can tell how intelligent a woman is by the way she moves her hips."

"Feminists are always saying that rape is about power. No, rape is about *sex*."

"I wanted to say to her, 'Honey, *no one* wants to see your enormous freaking bloomers.'"

"That is one gigantic *can* she's got. I was walking behind it and I thought, *I want to give it its own name*."

"She looks quite a bit more like Brent Musburger than I'm comfortable with." (Actually, David Foster Wallace was the speaker of this one, but I'm skipping ahead chronologically.)

"Whenever I see a fat woman, I think, *Soo-eeey!* I know, I know. I can't help it."

Here is a colleague speaking of a photograph of a female celebrity from a recent shoot for the magazine: "Did you see the size of that *flank*?"

A coworker speaking of another photograph of another female celebrity: "That's the best set of tits I've seen all year."

And another one: "Does it move the sticks?"

I was called into a colleague's office ("Hey, Adrienne, get in here") and asked *this* question: "So what's your favorite part of sex?"

A man asked me, "Do you have a pair of underwear that says DADDY'S GIRL on the bottom?"

Another man asked me, when I was wearing a skirt, to stand

and twirl for him. When, in a mortified fury, I sat back down at my desk, this man came up behind me and said in a low voice, as if he were staging some sort of sinister coup, *"You should wear skirts all the time."*

I'd been raised to never, never, *never* talk about anyone's body. Ever. Mine or anyone else's. When I was growing up, my parents mentioned my appearance only when they'd see me wearing an unfamiliar item of clothing: "Is that new?" they'd ask with disapproval (still do). And I had never particularly thought of the single defining characteristic of myself—my self—as my gender: I was everyone, I was no one, I was facticity *and* transcendence, I was all mind, all essence, I was Adri, I was Matt Miller from the plains and the Rust Belt both. Before I had this job, I had never known, like really *known,* that there were actually environments in which women's bodies were evaluated as if they were tires, or trucks . . . or something finer—automobiles: luxury ones.

And then there was the experience of having to listen to men weigh in on the topic of the Tragic Aging Woman, no longer useful as a sex object, thus a figure of pity:

"Some women, when they get older, they really do start looking like men."

"It's a very sad thing, to see her trying to cling to her youth."

A man said to me of a sublime—*the* most sublime—European celebrity, the ultimate grande dame, by way of justifying her increasing professional indifference to him: "She wants me to remember her the way she *was.*" (OK, the fabulous lady was Catherine Deneuve, and the man was a modestly successful photographer.)

But possibly the most harrowing remark of all was just some careless off-the-cuff thing, a miserly comment I can guarantee you the dude who said it never thought of again, spoken about a female media veteran (who, incidentally, could have made a *meal* out of this guy—and I hope she did):

"She's just your standard-issue suburban mom."

I would hear these things and think: *There is no hope for any of us.* I would wonder how it was that I would survive in the world, in *this* world, as a woman.

I would think: *There is always a* drip, drip, drip. *There is always a stripping away.*

Yet I would be remiss if I didn't offer a reminder that, when presenting the speech of others, individual utterances should not necessarily be interpreted as answers or as the final word. People often don't quite mean what they say (and often don't quite say what they mean), so speech sometimes is nothing more, or less, than partial evidence. (And I'm the queen of blurting out dumb things, too, God knows.) Uttered speech is skywriting, essentially. That's one way to look at it.

The other, more durable way is the Maya Angelou (or Oprah) approach: "When someone shows you who they are, believe them."

I often wondered if these guys, who I, on my good days, believed were otherwise quite smart, had any idea how much their comments affected the young women who heard them. Could they have understood how much their words changed our perception of the way the world really was? And if they understood, did they care?

11

In the winter of 1997, Ed Kosner, the editor in chief of *Esquire*, killed a short story scheduled for an upcoming issue, "The Term Paper Artist," by the writer David Leavitt, purportedly fearing that the homosexual content of the piece would offend a particularly conservative American automobile advertiser. (Kosner would deny this as the rationale for killing the story, by the way.) The well-respected long-term *Esquire* literary editor Will Blythe resigned in protest, and the whole thing blew up and became quite the brouhaha in what is politely called the literary world. (Magazine short stories making headlines!) Not long after that, Kosner was gone from *Esquire*, too.

Granger was hired as the magazine's new editor in chief in the spring of 1997. This felt impending, inevitable. The morning he gave me the news, he glanced around the *GQ* office, as if on the lookout for an army of clever spies, and said, "After I tell Art, you're never going to see me here again." I watched as he squared his shoulders, inhaled deeply, and deployed himself into Art's office.

I let the knowledge of my new reality marinate in my brain. You make yourself, but you unmake yourself, too. If I didn't play this right, I could very well end up back in Ohio.

After a minute, two (maybe not even), Granger emerged from Art's office.

"He was very gracious," Granger said.

Here is where we might expect the story to leave me, for at least the moment, and to follow one of the men—maybe we could go out the door with one, into the office with another. But this is my story, not theirs.

In a few days, I was scheduled to leave for Chicago, for the gargantuan annual book trade event BookExpo (now BEA). Why Art suggested the trip I have no idea, though I supposed it was meant as a gesture of goodwill toward me. I had no business to do in Chicago, no reason to go there, and I had not planned for the expedition in the slightest. This was a year of high drama at the book trade event, though, as far as these things went: many of the big publishers and chain bookstores had boycotted the event, protesting its expense and overall antiquatedness.

A few minutes after Granger had departed, Art emerged from his office. He walked down the hall and stopped in front of my desk.

"Are you looking forward to your trip?" he asked. Did I detect a flash of tension in his voice, a telltale strain? And why my imminent voyage to Chicago was at the forefront of the Cooper brain right after Granger's announcement, if even for just that one second when I happened to be right in front of him, don't ask me.

"Sure," I said. "It's going to be so great."

Art turned to go down the hall, hesitated. "Go to Charlie Trotter's," he said. "Have the *tasting menu*. Tell them *Art Cooper* sent you."

My days in the office were numbered, of course. Art would consider Granger's departure to *Esquire, GQ*'s chief rival, a defection and a betrayal. I could likely function as collateral damage, being an unpleasant visual reminder to Art, as he viewed me toiling away at my very public desk, that his power was not absolute. And I was, of course, expendable and disposable, and so very easily erased from the picture: a *girl*.

That afternoon, I furtively started packing up my books and papers, those obstinate things.

In Chicago, I was transported via shuttle bus from hotel to convention center, from convention center to hotel, and back again. For three days, I wandered around McCormick Place ("the largest convention center in North America," crowed some press materials) in a daze. Truism: nothing kills the magic of literary creation quite like a book convention. Books, you were reminded, were a product like any other product: cans of sardines, kazoos, toilet-bowl brushes. Despite the flashy publishers' boycott, the event seemed formidably well attended—the main floor was the size of an airship hangar, an overlit hell world jammed with exhibitors' stands and booths, thousands of them. A thought I'd been having a lot lately: *Everyone is a writer.* I'd never even met one writer before I came to New York—college teachers didn't count, naturally—but now was there any person upon the fruited plain who *wasn't* a writer?

Well, *I* wasn't.

Every night in Chicago for dinner, I'd pick up a falafel sandwich from the same place and bring it back to my hotel room. (Now, with hindsight, I think, *Why* didn't *I go to Charlie Trotter's?*) I sat at the desk in my room, fomenting my plan.

I understood that I would not be anyone's first choice to be the literary editor of *Esquire*. I understood that I would not be anyone's 100,000th choice to be the literary editor of *Esquire*. Yes, I got that I wasn't "qualified" to do the job, but my thought was *Who is?* It's not as if one can earn a Ph.D. in "literary editor." Instinct, taste, and judgment can't be taught. And I knew I had instinct, taste, and judgment. I was my own first choice, and that's all that mattered.

At the hotel, I worked on a letter to Granger, developing, as I composed it, a range of techniques I believed to be epistolarily persuasive. I promised that I would deliver him vibrant, *necessary* fiction. When I returned to NYC, I lobbied hard for the job. Granger had me come in for a few interviews with him. I probably should have prepared a PowerPoint presentation (though it was 1997, and I'd never seen a PowerPoint presentation), but I loved Granger and was confident in my ability to talk to him, and I was also confident in my ability to talk about short stories and books. The interviews went well, I thought. But I was also aware that on my visits to the office, I'd been observed by the Venticelli of *Esquire* editorial: some sour male assistants from the old regime who were hanging on by a thread. They were spies—the Venticelli always are—but they weren't terribly clever ones, I'd soon discover.

One morning after one of those *Esquire* interviews, I came to work at *GQ*. Yes, there it was, the old workspace, shrinking by the second. It was not where I wanted to be, yet I was ready for business, as always: I had my bagel, my coffee; I had my four newspapers.

I flipped through my morning gossip pages and discovered something of interest: an item in one of those gossip columns—the granddaddy of them all—was, ludicrously, about *me*. I was named in it, and identified as a twenty-five-year-old *GQ* assistant who was interviewing for the revered, indeed *famous,* job of literary editor of *Esquire*. The tone of the item was an aghast, pearl-clutching *How could this be?*

How, one might wonder, did this item make its way onto a gossip page in a New York paper? My hypothesis: persons of insidious intent had planted the gossip item after they viewed me in the *Esquire* office for an interview.

As calmly as you please, I continued gnawing away at my gigantic bagel.

The big black phone on my desk rang. Two rings: the call was external; one: internal. This was a one-ringer. The fun calls were always from the outside.

"Would you come and see me, kiddo?" said the female voice on the other end.

Our woman in HR always called me "kiddo." I would see her on our floor every now and then, when she was en route to or from Art Cooper's office—her presence on the floor typically signaling some sort of personnel issue—and in passing I could count on a hasty "Hi, kiddo!" from her.

I had been in this woman's office only once before—three years ago, when I had my interview with her. In college, I had been an assistant at my university's poetry press, and my claim to fame there had been that they'd used a detail from a painting by Pieter Bruegel the Elder, *The Hay Harvest,* I'd suggested for a book's cover. On *GQ* interview day, I'd brought a copy of the published book with me to show off. As I handed it across the desk, the HR woman had something interesting to say about Bruegel.

"He's so great at painting regular people," she had said.

Now, three years later, I stood again at her open door.

"Come in," she said, indicating the chair across from her desk. *"Sit."*

I came in. I sat.

She placed both hands upon her desk, locked her fingers together. (The careful reader might perhaps notice that the author doesn't dwell too much on women's appearances. Men are fair game, but because I've spent so much of my reading life tussling with physical descriptions of females [fictional females and nonfictional ones], I find that I've now become protective of the women. Even the one who would attempt to demote me to professional Siberia.)

"We would like to offer you a *job,*" she said.

She wasn't evil, though, this lady, not even in an Eichmann-banal way. I understood my place in the system, more, probably, than I ought to have. She was just doing what she had to do. My beloved grandfather, a great and good man, had worked for years in HR at Western Electric, and I'm sure he'd had to fire his fair share. Not that we, his family, would have known—like so many men of that greatest World War II generation (with the gregarious exception of that era's crop of white male novelists), he had a mum's-the-word approach to life.

The new job, as she explained it, was at a women's fashion magazine. In the fashion closet. As an exceedingly junior-level assistant. A sub-junior-level assistant, really.

"You will be apprenticed to Rachel Archambault," she said. (Note: Rachel Archambault was not this person's name, but it definitely could have been.)

"You're *kidding* me," I said.

So much for my pose of equanimity.

"This is the job you have been offered," the HR woman replied.

In her famous attack on Diane Arbus, Susan Sontag condemns Arbus for, among other atrocities, photographing her subjects—those "assorted monsters and border-line cases—most of them ugly"—smiling. Essentially, Sontag's argument is: How self-aware *are* the Arbus deviants? Are they in on the joke? Can the Grand Guignol ghouls even see how ridiculous they are?

Arbus (a famed *Esquire* contributor of the legendary Harold Hayes era) always had a great defense: her people smile because they'd already experienced the trauma the rest of us spend our lives dreading. The freaks laugh because they know it can't get any worse.

Back at my desk, I gathered up my crafty duplicate copies of my Rolodex cards and stuffed them into my bag. This was the moment for which I'd been sending myself all those messages in a bottle for all those years: when you get thrown back into who you are, you'd better have something there.

I could have counted on two hands the number of times I'd been in Art's office: that first day, a time or two when I was summoned in to have drinks with him and some other assistants, a couple of occasions when the collective had something to toast, and once (because he was the one among us with a TV) to watch the greatest American trauma of the era: the O.J. verdict, back when the only Kardashian we had to worry about was Robert. I had never been to his office unbeckoned.

I walked in, smiling. He was at his desk, smoking. There was a sharp look in his oystery eyes when he saw me.

I advanced to his desk and stood before him. "I was not aware that interviewing for a job was a fireable offense," I said.

Art's face went ashen. He leaned back in his chair, the cigarette smoldering between his fingers. I could see the gears in his head moving. I tended to be either debilitatingly shy or really brashly forthright—these were two modes between which I tremulously vacillated. One never knew what to expect with me—even *I* never quite knew what to expect of my reactions to things.

"You'll be a star," Art said.

I watched the cigarette, which remained immobile.

"I have always said that," he continued.

He had? News to me. Of course I knew that I was but a pawn in the chess game between him and Granger. But I could play, too. I'd been thinking a lot about this line from *A Room of One's Own* recently: "I refuse to allow you, Beadle though you are, to turn me off the grass." I was always fortified by it.

"You," I said, jabbing my finger at him (I was no longer smiling), "are a *bully.*"

He leaned back in his chair, paused a few beats. The cigarette had still not proceeded to his mouth.

"You're a star," he said again, wearily now.

Was it a craven reiteration? A magnanimous one? He looked at me straight on. In three years he had never really looked at me. Art talked at you, not to you. This isn't even a criticism.

"You don't need me," he said.

The very first piece of mail I received when I started my job at *Esquire* was a card written in opulent purple ink with an immoderate hand, the likes of which will never be seen again: "I told you you'd be a star."

12

What I knew was this: I was twenty-five years old and I had my dream job. I was the literary editor of *Esquire*. I was responsible for finding, acquiring, and editing all the short stories published in *Esquire*. There was no editorial board, no circle of readers; there was only me and my judgment, and Granger. I also controlled the book coverage—choosing what books to review and to whom to assign the reviews—and I could also edit feature stories, front-of-the-book pieces, and anything else I happened to bring in. I had a job that others would, as I was continually told, kill for. (Male editors and writers of a certain type are fond of their martial metaphors.) Imagine that. What a mad thing it was.

Why had Granger hired me? No idea. We got along well, and I

must assume that he believed I was smart (or at least smart enough to read short stories) and also that he believed I had the potential to be a good editor . . . but, honestly, was that enough? You didn't have to tell me: I'd been an assistant for three years. That was all I had done in the world. I was just some dumb kid from Ohio. I knew that I had been given a far bigger opportunity than I deserved. I understood that I had little of the grounding I would need to do this job. I would have to prove myself. And in order to prove myself, I would need to get smarter, fast.

Previously, only men had had the *Esquire* literary editor position, including the legendary Gordon Lish and Rust Hills, both pivotal figures in the landscape of mid- to late twentieth-century American literature. Lish, so associated with a swashbuckling persona cultivated at the magazine that he had an actual nickname, "Captain Fiction," was, famously, Raymond Carver's closest editor. Unlike most other editors, who understand that their work is best when it is invisible, Lish had what might have been called an exhibitionistic approach to editing. Through his aggressive cutting of Carver's stories, Lish helped to engineer the dry, reticent, menacing (minimalists scare me) tone that would come to be so influential on a generation of American writers. (The famed title of the Carver story "What We Talk About When We Talk About Love" was itself a Lish creation.) Lish also championed authors as varied as Jane Smiley, Amy Hempel, Stanley Elkin, Cynthia Ozick, Hilma Wolitzer, Barry Hannah, Mary Robison, and Ben Marcus and acted as a mentor to many others. (There were also the notorious private writing seminars that further burnished the Lishian myth.) If you happen to have some picture of a wildly charismatic and conceited male literary editor from the golden age of magazines (the flowing white hair, the wacky ex cathedra pronouncements, the Zorro-like slashings with the red editorial pen), it probably has a lot to do with the role created and performed by Gordon Lish.

Rust was still at *Esquire* in a somewhat emeritus role when I started, and he would stay on at the magazine for two more years. He'd been intermittently associated with *Esquire* since 1957 and had been integral to the careers of Norman Mailer, Don DeLillo, Richard Ford, John Cheever, Ann Beattie, William Gaddis, Cormac McCarthy, and Rust's own spouse, the amazing Joy Williams. He was in his seventies when I knew him.

The first thing Granger said after he told me I had the job: "You're going to have to find a way to work with Rust."

I didn't meet Rust that first week, though; he didn't have an office at the magazine and mostly worked from home.

The first person I *did* meet was Dave Eggers. Yes, *Dave Eggers,* of the bundle of *Might* magazines I'd delivered to Granger at *GQ* a couple of years before. Dave was a new editor/writer at *Esquire* and had the office next to mine. We started our jobs the same day.

We met when we were both taking a "tour" of the *Esquire* mail area. The mail area was not a fancy setup: on a long table back by the service elevators were chrome trays for each editor's mail (although, what with the quantities of fiction submissions the magazine received, I had a rather different situation: two of those big white UNITED STATES POSTAL SERVICE bins).

"Whoa," Dave said of the mail zone, unimpressed. "Low *budge.*"

I have no memory of my response, although I can guarantee that I replied with something sarcastic—too sarcastic, I'm sure.

"We're going to have a problem someday, you and me," Dave said, and regarded me skeptically.

The *Esquire* office was in a Hearst satellite building along with some corporate back offices and a couple of magazines I'd never heard of before. It was on a dingy block in midtown west; downstairs was an Irish pub, and across the street was a food stand, the real-life inspiration for *Seinfeld*'s Soup Nazi. (I went there only once, though—you'd have to wait in line for hours and hours unless you wanted to pick up your lunch at some irrational time like 4:15.) No longer were there town cars awaiting magazine staffers as if winged chariots. It's fair to say that Hearst was more of a no-frills/no-drama place than Condé Nast, and it was honestly kind of a culture shock, as well as a bit of an all-dressed-up-and-no-place-to-go situation, after the society-of-the-spectacle situation that was the Condé building, to ride these empty Hearst elevators that, spookily, never even seemed to stop at any other floors.

Esquire editorial was on the seventh floor, and the art, copy, and research departments were on eight. Everyone kept saying that the office had been designed by a famous architect, but no one could recall which one: there were translucent glass walls, a shiny black floor that was buffed nearly nightly, and a waiting area with black leather Corbusier-esque furniture. A metal staircase connected floors seven and eight.

On the wall by the stairs were rows of framed past *Esquire* covers, with an emphasis on those weird and brilliant George Lois ones from the sixties: the boxer Sonny Liston scowling furiously in a Santa hat, Muhammad Ali in the pose of arrow-pierced martyr Saint Sebastian, and Andy Warhol drowning in a can of Campbell's tomato soup. But my personal favorite was from the eighties and designed by the artist Barbara Kruger: a black-and-white close-up of Howard Stern overlaid with the caption "I hate myself."

I had an office now, an interior one with a glass front wall: clear glass up top and glazed glass down below. The walls of my office were lined with empty black bookcases that would soon find themselves bloated with review copies of books. My desktop computer came with the flying toasters screensaver installed on it. My metal tanker desk had a distinctly retro vibe, and I usually tried to keep some fresh flowers on it. My salary was $45,000. A princely sum, that, it seemed to me—at first. My starting salary at *GQ* had been $18,000.

When I started the job, of course, I needed to introduce, or reintroduce, myself to my professional "contacts," those names and numbers I'd compiled from the verboten duplicate Rolodex cards back at *GQ*. The first calls were to some writers and literary agents whom I gauged to be friendly—or at least neutral—parties. Manuscripts were submitted to me in various ways: directly by authors, by referrals, and by literary agents. It was important to get the agents on my side ASAP.

There had been two shocking and gruesome celebrity deaths that summer: Princess Diana and Gianni Versace. During these agent calls, the first minute or two of perfunctory chitchat would inevitably focus on how crazy it was to lose two big stars back-to-back like that; some speculation might follow about who'd be the next celebrity to go down (the smart money mean-spiritedly said Elton John). Some of these folks might express their ire that the media—albeit the scuzzy paparazzi division that had nothing to do with us (*did* it?)—were being blamed for Diana's death; there might be a comment that all these celebrities who moaned about their fame were self-pitying egomaniacs, because in the whole history of Western civilization, no person had ever become famous who did not want to become famous (which is true).

Now the call with the agent could finally get down to business. As I'd half observe the flapping wings on those pixilated toasters and toast on my computer screen, I'd go into my little spiel about my professional mandate: to make it new (apologies to Ezra Pound) but also to reintroduce a refurbished *Esquire* to some of the more notable literary grayheads of yore.

During one of these calls—I had believed it was actually going pretty well—a male literary agent said, "You don't have any authority to do this job, you know."

At that moment, I happened to be gazing at the word "zwieback" floating by on my computer screen (this particular flying toasters screensaver had captions running across the bottom). Vaguely, I thought: *Zwieback, zwieback, zwieback.* I also thought: *This jackass is actually right.* Authority is never automatically granted. I knew that.

Also, I intuitively understood that few people go around rooting for the career success of a very young woman. A man's early professional success may be attributed to . . . well, if not to merit at such a young age, let's just say to his self-evident brilliance. Watch and enjoy as the world coalesces around the myth of his greatness. *He was the most astounding student I ever had,* etc. The woman, conversely, gets the job perhaps thanks to . . . what? Well, surely not as the result of her brilliance, because no one is ever going to accuse her of *that.* Luck? Appearance? Favoritism? Her ability to play the game? Something somewhat darker?

Early on, I was haunted by the fear that my presence at the magazine was largely ornamental. I never could quite shake the fear that I'd been hired because I was young, female, and (seemingly) controllable. And while I understood how self-defeating this line of thinking was, was it further possible that I was there because the magazine maybe didn't actually even care all that much about its literary program? An *Esquire* dinner my first week, attended by my new colleagues, did nothing to assuage my worries.

We went to an Italian restaurant. I ordered, I regret to report, the veal. (What was I *thinking?* I always just get the vegetarian pasta.) After my order was placed, a coworker declared to the table, "Veal? You *are* veal." This fellow was a friend of mine, and I must assume that he was trying to be funny, and if I'd been in a different mood, I might have laughed right along. But I wasn't in an indulgent frame of mind that night. I wasn't concerned about protecting men and had no interest in sublimating my ego; I was thinking about how on earth I was going to do this job. I rose from my chair, bolted into the ladies' room, and exploded into tears.

This should have been one of the happiest weeks of my life. It was and it wasn't. Most of my friends were underemployed, unemployed, or in grad school, and few could relate. If you'd have asked me (no one did), I might have said that I was really scared. But I was so excited, too.

THAT FIRST WEEK, I DISCOVERED, IN THE BOTTOM LEFT DRAWER OF MY metal desk, paper contracts for recently published *Esquire* fiction. (Initially, it was of some passing interest to see how much more *Esquire* paid for fiction than *GQ* did—as in two to three times the amount.) Also in that contracts drawer was one other document, an internal memo about a short story that had been submitted to *Esquire* and rejected. The story was "The Depressed Person," by David Foster Wallace.

The memo was a tortured thing, having clearly been left behind as an artifact of historical import, a sign of life: the letter the outgoing president leaves to the incoming, the Voyager Golden Record sent off into the universe. As explained in the memo, "The Depressed Person" had been read by nearly every single editor on staff—not only by those in the fiction department—and their responses had been divided into two agonized factions: those who were repelled by the story and loathed it, and those who were repelled by the story and admired it (in a cold, arm's-length sort of way). As I recall, the phrase "tough going" was used to describe the overall reading experience. The memo had also certainly been left behind as a self-protective gesture: the editor who wrote it had been in the pro–"Depressed Person" camp and had been prescient enough to know on what side of history this opinion would eventually prove to be. (When I finally read "The Depressed Person" a year later, by the way, I will admit that I had a completely contradictory interpretation of the story. Wasn't its parody of a therapy voice meant to be comic? Wasn't the story just kind of a hoot?)

But my main takeaway from the memo then: *How many people had it taken to make a goddamned decision around here?* An editor in chief should give his editors a degree of freedom and autonomy, yes? Fiction by committee? Lord, already I couldn't imagine that *that* scenario would have worked for me at all. I liked the way things were rigged up for me at *Esquire*. In these early days, I'd tell Granger I wanted to do something, he'd say "fine" and tell me how much I could spend, and that was that, pretty much. (It was possible that I was, and would never be, a great "collaborator"; in school, I'd always shuddered whenever the teacher told us to "break into groups.") Only one of the editors implicated in the "Depressed Person" memo was still working at the magazine—Rust Hills. Everyone else had quit, or had been fired, though their fates were entirely unrelated to the outcome of "The Depressed Person."

Rust had thick white hair and sort of a shambling, craggy quality. "Hello, it's your wandering Uncle Rust!" our weekly calls would begin; he'd come into the office every few weeks or so, and then less than that, to root through fiction submissions. I was never clear when he last had an actual physical office. He was one of those mystical time-dividers with multiple homes and lived what seemed to me a graciously old-school peripatetic existence.

It was also not evident to me then what his expectations for his role still were or how much his association with *Esquire* actually still mattered to him; throughout the years, he had quit working at the magazine and returned three times. Had I been more perceptive, I would have understood that his involvement most certainly did matter to him, possibly quite a lot.

And what did Rust make of yours truly, if in fact he made anything of me at all? A tin-pot Torquemada? A mini Al Haig? An inoffensive nincompoop? An overly enthusiastic yet information-challenged youth? Looking back on it, he was always remarkably courteous toward me and treated me as an equal. It now makes me queasy to admit that I had quite a lot more power, if you wanted to call it that, at the magazine than Rust did. But my situation didn't make me queasy at all then, at least not at first—power, to review, is a force rarely scrutinized. Power is also invisible when you have it. But you can't see anything straight if you're too close—you keep losing your perspective.

Throughout the years, several writers, including Richard Ford and Cormac McCarthy, would tell me that Rust was a genius at novel excerpts (it's true—I actually talked to McCarthy on the phone once): give the man a finished manuscript of a novel—the longer, spikier, more tentacled the better—and a day or two later, he would emerge with a stand-alone story from it, gorgeous, lapidaried, immaculate: *complete*. I also loved the drollery with which Rust would speak about short-story submissions: "It's not a *gripper*"; "Oh, it's amusing in *spots*, I suppose."

I must say that Rust's approach to the writers he wanted us to consider was weirdly in resonance with his Literary Universe project: he'd come into the office with a piece of legal-pad paper filled top to bottom with the names of writers. Names, names, and more names. Most of these writers had been in the Literary Universe ten years before; frequently appearing at the top of the list were two elegant writers graced with, I would come to appreciate, ideal prose styles: Christopher Buckley and James Salter. How correct you were, Rust, to put them right there at the top.

I'd heard from various writers that Rust maintained an elaborate index-card system of writer info, these cards described in Carol Polsgrove's captivating history of the Harold Hayes *Esquire* years, *It Wasn't Pretty, Folks, but Didn't We Have Fun?*: "On the cards was listed every fiction writer anywhere, it seemed, and their agents, and publishers, and past publications." Some writers who'd claimed to have seen the cards would tell me that they were so lavishly detailed that they may as well have cataloged the writer's blood type.

Rust had brought in *Breakfast at Tiffany's* for the magazine, excerpts of Styron's *Sophie's Choice*, Arthur Miller's "The Misfits," and he'd had the unenviable task of handling Mailer's *An American Dream* (story line: the hero murders his wife and, in so doing, finds himself), which Mailer composed as a serialized novel *in real time* over the course of eight issues in 1964. Rust had worked with Dorothy Parker, who'd been the magazine's book reviewer, but I was unable to pry any tales out of him about that experience, or any others, really. (*Dorothy Parker.* I mean, *seriously.*) I wanted to hear about Nabokov, O'Connor, Salinger, Cheever, Vidal, Italo Calvino, Philip Roth, and about Rust's famous (and famously intoxicated) *Esquire* literary symposia. Terry Southern had, mind-explodingly, subbed for Rust in the office one summer. I needed details about that. I also needed to hear everything about Harold Hayes. And what about the magazine's publication of "Le Côte Basque, 1965," an excerpt from Truman Capote's in-progress (and never finished) novel *Answered Prayers,* a painfully mediocre satire of the ladies-who-lunch set and the novel that killed Capote—artistically, socially, and probably even literally? Gordon Lish? What exactly *was* Rust's relationship with Gordon Lish? He *had* placed Lish in the red-hot center of his 1987 literary power chart, after all. Was it sort of a Wozniak-Jobs situation with the two of them? But I got nothing.

There was never much in the way of institutional memory at *Esquire,* and later, when Rust was gone, there really *was* nothing. Former editors were rarely spoken of, as if the instant they left the magazine, they were flushed down the giant toilet bowl of publishing history. Although I was only twenty-five years old, I had enough sense to know that this would happen to me, too, eventually. Not for a long time, hopefully, but it would happen. The feeling was always that we were to look forward, not backward. This was also a warning: do good work, but don't get too attached to the title or to the place.

When you get thrown back into who you are, you'd better have something there.

My own position: Would a little ancestor worship have been such a bad thing? Being the amateur student of history I was, it's always been my belief that looking backward can do a lot to help you find your direction forward. When speaking once of this topic to David Foster Wallace, he remarked that if *The New Yorker,* not *Esquire,* had published "The Snows of Kilimanjaro," *The New Yorker* would have kept a statue to the story in its offices, and you'd have to bow to it as you walked by.

Rust could also be rather cranky. During a lunch with him at a Japanese restaurant near the office, he complained, over colossal iced teas, that a misbehaving author had recently sent him what he amusingly described as a "nightmarishly circumstantial *rant* of self-justification." He then drank in one swallow the shot glass of simple syrup for his iced tea and promptly asked a server for another.

I proceeded to ask Rust a question about the Nabokov story "The Visit to the Museum." I mentioned the year it had been published—1963.

"Years?" Rust replied, perturbed, hunting around for the server again. "I don't remember *years.*"

Maybe Rust thought I was looking for gossip, but I really wasn't. I wanted information. I wanted a rip-roaring ride through the literary past, but he was not about to give it to me. It wasn't Rust's *job* to provide me that, of course. With him, I always felt like a miner outfitted with the world's dimmest headlamp.

13

Not long after I started the job at *Esquire*, I went with a friend to a talk by Norman Mailer. The idea was for the friend, who worked at the Wylie Agency, which represented Mailer, to introduce me to the grand old man after the speech. Mailer was, possibly after Hemingway, the fiction writer most closely associated with *Esquire*. He'd been regularly publishing in the magazine since the fifties: he had a regular column (title: The Big Bite), there was *An American Dream* and excerpts from *Harlot's Ghost*, and there were features, most famously "Superman Comes to the Supermart," about JFK and the 1960 Democratic National Convention, and "Norman Mailer versus Nine Writers," in which he was given seven (count 'em, *seven*) feature-well pages to assess recent books from nine rivals. (Let us sample this beauty about Bellow from the essay: "Yet I still wonder if he is not too timid to become a great writer." And about Styron's "bad maggoty novel" *Set This House on Fire:* "four or five half-great short stories were buried like pullulating organs in a corpse of fecal matter.")

In more recent years, Mailer had done an interview with Pat Buchanan (thus bringing the number of Buchanan references in my narrative so far to an improbable two . . . although maybe not *too* improbable: Buchanan was Trump before Trump) and an astounding—not in a good way—interview with Madonna, the introduction to which Mailer wrote in third person and which contained the sentence "Madonna, on the face of it, had to have an ego even larger than his own." You don't even want to know how much he was paid for the piece (I saw the contract). Mailer had also appeared on the cover of the magazine a couple of times; his eerie resemblance on one of the covers to Golda Meir was not infrequently noted around the *Esquire* offices.

Repeatedly directed toward me at work, like the plangent bleats of a foghorn, were the questions "Who is our new Mailer? Who are our titans? *Who are our titans?*" They wanted Big (Male) Writers of the Mailer school. Implicit in this line of thinking was that a writer with enough talent and charisma should be able to force the culture to care about novelists and novels again. The fault was with the writers, not with the world, in other words. I supposed it was true that no one (except for David Foster Wallace) was trying as hard, and on such a heroic scale, as Mailer, as Roth. That was part of it. No one seemed to *want it* as much as they had. But how could a Mailer, or a Roth, or any communal national literature, ever exist again? Those big, grandiose books about America and Americanism couldn't be written today: as the country went more and more off the rails, we all did the sensible thing and retreated inside our heads (and into university writing programs), and, broadly, our novels were now internal monologues—the dream world of the self.

I loathed Mailer. Yes, I would have reluctantly conceded that *The Executioner's Song* was a near masterpiece; yes, I understood and appreciated that *The Armies of the Night* was a very good novel. Yes, yes, I got that Mailerian work ethic was in fact heroic. But I wouldn't be the first one to point out that the prose was ludicrously overwritten and that the whole Mailer novel-writing stance—*man asserts his manhood by writing manly novels*—was preposterous. I would further argue that his novels had barely made any sort of dent at all on American fiction; his early nonfiction is another story, however (but novelists want the novel to be king, not the non-novel), and pieces like "Superman" actually probably did change literary journalism forever—now reported stories could be flamboyant and oracular and ridiculous and sound like novels.

In my view, the best Mailer *Esquire* piece was not something Mailer had written but was rather *about* him—Germaine Greer's glorious takedown of their infamous 1971 Town Hall debate (and exploration of Mailer's mother issues), "My Mailer Problem." (In more recent years, Greer's positions have become tragically retrograde and wackadoo, alas.) It was a piece that spoke more truth to power than anything Mailer ever wrote (and was fabulously illustrated with a photograph of a female performance artist as Mailer in a werewolf costume): "the tragedy of machismo," Greer wrote, "is that a man is never quite man enough."

What I couldn't accept about Mailer: How could a writer whose work was so pugnaciously sexist be widely considered "great"? How could this even be allowed? But this probably wasn't an argument I'd even need to have, once I ventured away from the *Esquire* editorial offices. There *were* no young Mailer fans, and I'd never heard anyone my age mention his work, ever . . . so that was progress of a sort, I guessed.

Mailer's talk, a stop in the publicity campaign for his latest novel, *The Gospel According to the Son,* was at a school on the Upper East Side. The typical Mailer loyalist out in the audience looked as if he'd died about ten years before. The novel: the "autobiography" of Jesus. Mailer as God. The jokes just wrote themselves, folks. Onstage,

Mailer, who had a weirdly affected Brahmin (was it?) accent, held forth about God, Jesus, Christians, and Christianity as if he alone had the special wisdom monopoly on these topics—and all others. It seemed to me even then dangerous for a writer to come to regard himself as grandee; the writer's concern should always be getting to the truth—and how can you get to the truth of the story if you *are* the story, not the one standing outside of it? (In his irritatingly excellent book *The Spooky Art*, Mailer in fact acknowledges his early fame as the central tragedy of his career.) Never get too comfortable in the temple: this was another message in a bottle I'd send my future self.

During the book-signing portion of the evening, as my literary-agent friend and I advanced toward this terrifying white cannonball (who, to be fair, was not without a large degree of personal charm, and his captivating final wife, Norris, whom I would later briefly meet, seemed to be just about the loveliest person ever—Norman, you were a lucky man), it occurred to me that there was nowhere I less wanted to be. I had in my brain the demented bravado of *Advertisements for Myself* ("the sniffs I get from the ink of the women are always fey, old-hat, Quaintsy Goysy, tiny, too dykily psychotic, crippled, creepish, fashionable, frigid, outer-Baroque, *maquillé* in mannequin's whimsy, or else bright and stillborn"), a book *Esquire* had excerpted. As Greer had written of *The Prisoner of Sex* in "My Mailer Problem," "Every page bespoke the terrors of the dying king."

The question: Could I really levitate above it all with a special sort of Apollonian detachment? *Should* I?

When my turn in line with Mailer came, I'm sure I burbled something to him as nuance-free as "Hey, you should write for *Esquire* again." As a matter of fact, that is exactly what I said.

Mailer's blue eyes considered me with distaste. After a rich pause, he intoned, "I feel about *Esquire* the way I feel about an ex-wife: *I don't care.*"

Sometimes in life things can be the best and the worst at the very same time. This particular encounter was an example of this phenomenon.

(The silky, urbane Mailer voice sounded a lot younger than it was, by the way, and that accent *was* a total put-on.)

The following day, I shared the sad tale of Mailer's swiftly terminal response with Dave Eggers. I stood in Dave's office, navigating the many empty Snapple bottles on his floor. He would usually, but not always, arrive at the office sometime before noon. In memory, he is always in shorts.

Based upon my past close readings of *Might*—whose sensibility lay somewhere between the *Onion, National Lampoon,* and *Letterman* from the Chris Elliott era when I was making videotapes of it every night (I'm sure Dave would correct my appraisal, though)—I probably would have pegged Dave as a manic prankster with a hand buzzer built into his palm. A real madcap, in other words. I would have been wrong about that. Dave was jangly, restless, supernaturally confident, cantankerous when necessary, well meaning, and fixated on the idea of integrity—his own and everyone else's. He would spend one somewhat embattled year at *Esquire*. I never really understood what his job was. I'm not sure he did, either.

I always enjoyed getting his take on things and typically felt that his overall worldview was in alignment with mine. In the case of the Mailer flop, however, he did not supply the response I'd wanted.

He shook his head slowly, very slowly. "You, sister," Dave finally declared, "are a dork."

In my view, Mailer had brushed me off because he had regarded me as a mere girl, nothing else to see here, please move along, but I supposed there was more to it than that. Mailer may indeed have had (and should have had) some vestigial loyalty toward Rust, who always had a soft spot for the old cannonball. But mortifyingly, when I approached Mailer, I hadn't quite known how terribly checkered his history with *Esquire* actually was—a pattern that might be summarized as: Mailer leaves; Mailer comes back; Mailer leaves; Mailer comes back; Mailer leaves; Mailer threatens to sue (and does); Mailer comes back; lather, rinse, repeat.

The first grievance in many grievance-rich decades occurred in 1960, when the headline "Superman Comes to the Supermart" was changed from the more pragmatic "Superman Comes to the Supermarket." Mailer did not appreciate the odd, anachronistic "supermart" and felt that the headline had been snuck past him. (Another of the tenets of old-time magazine editing: try not to share display copy with authors if you can possibly help it.) Rust Hills had valiantly patched that one up, but a lifetime of exciting squabbles was to follow.

It was now clear to me that there were many ancient *Esquire* feuds being perpetually enacted all over the place—mostly by writers, but also by agents and by other literary-world figures. Almost everyone I encountered these days seemed to have some sort of beef with *Esquire*. A writer had been jerked around in various ways by the magazine; a story had been acquired, then killed by the magazine; a submission had received a discourteous rejection letter; a submission, God forbid, had not been responded to at all. Not infrequently did I feel I had to apologize for something someone I'd never met before (and possibly had never even heard of) may or may not have done years before.

One well-known fiction writer sent me an email nobly headlined "WHY I DO NOT WRITE FOR *ESQUIRE* ANYMORE," presenting a bravura inventory of *Esquire*-generated offenses. At a party, I was introduced to a veteran female literary agent (and truly one of the worst people ever), and I offered my hand for a shake but received only a vehement glare in return.

Said another old-time literary agent at another party, "I would *never* recommend to a client of mine that he appear in a *men's fashion magazine*." With a smile, I told the agent that he and his authors were free to ignore the fashion pages in the magazine—*I* always did.

"But *Esquire* used to publish Camus!" Camus had been an actual client of his, so I suppose he felt he had the right to rub it in. *"Camus!"* he declared again as he wagged a finger in the air and walked away.

Another affronted writer said to me of his own uneasy situation with the magazine, "But don't you know what *happened*?"

Hell no, I didn't know what happened. I was flying completely in the dark. How was I supposed to know one damn thing about some writer's decades-steeped rancor toward Gordon Lish?

Hearing about these various traumas was helpful in a very important way, though. They introduced me to one of the most important aspects of the editor's job: defusing writer rage. That was a very big element, it would turn out. Some editors had that talent, and some of us would really need to work on that one—and on everything else.

AS SOMEONE CONSPICUOUSLY LACKING THE GIFT OF "SPONTANEOUS eloquence" (Nabokov's phrase, applied to himself), I've always been dreadfully susceptible to the charms of the swift tongued. I've always wished I could be more like them, those suspiciously showy elocutionists, rather than being the way I am: slow and deliberative about what it is I want to say before I say it, and even that doesn't get me too far. In the editorial meetings at *Esquire,* I would watch transfixed as many of the men would just gab away—just gab and gab—without seeming to give much thought at all to what it was they were saying.

At some meetings, editors and staff writers might have to pitch a few story ideas. Most of the ideas were about famous people (the subtopics: persona, if the celebrity was a man, and appearance, if the celebrity was a woman). I could just never get over the feeling that there was something so dreadful about seeing people as "stories," although I must also add that I was no longer quite as sanctimonious about celebrity profiles as I had been. I had now written some of my own, and, good God, they were *terrible*. Very crudely, the *Esquire* house style (the tone and usage conventions each magazine follows to give the sense of one consistent voice) those early days seemed to be something like bombast plus sentimentalism (plus a weakness for the second person), and it proved chillingly easy for me to absorb. But I'm passing the buck. Something happens to you when you just want to see your own byline.

One of the best comments to come out of these story idea meetings: a man suggested, invoking Devo (Akron's fourth-finest export after Rita Dove, LeBron James, and Jim Jarmusch), that we change the motto of the magazine from its bland "Man at His Best" to the mordant "Are We Not Men?" One of the worst comments: a man—someone situated squarely in the middle of the talent pool of life—made a remark that if a reporter from the *New York Times* called and asked you some sneaky background questions about yourself, you knew that an advance obit was being prepared about you. You were *that* powerful in the world.

If I could repeat that John Adams quote—the one about the passion for distinction being the principal human urge—on every page without ruining my narrative flow, I would.

Outside my office, they gave me two, or possibly three, depending on how you did your calculations, dedicated fiction department cubicles. I now had a staff (a grandiose noun) of three freelance readers. Were these women officially interns? That depends on what your definition of "intern" is. Some were students, some were adults; some were paid twelve dollars an hour, some nothing at all.

Throughout the years, a few of the brilliant and judicious women who came and went as *Esquire* fiction readers/interns would become my closest friends. I needed smart women around me, and in eight years at *Esquire*, I would hire more than a dozen women, but only one guy. I was never much of a mentor to anyone, though; I had little wisdom to supply, and I was uncomfortable being an authority figure. To clarify: I wanted authority, but what I wanted was literary authority, aesthetic authority; I didn't want the authority that came with being someone's boss. I was better (though rarely great) at being a buddy.

One of my first readers/interns/assistants/Venticelli was a woman named Amanda Davis. She had springy auburn curls and a minuscule nose ring, drove a truck, and lived in an area of Brooklyn that then seemed terra incognita but is now jammed with art galleries, tech start-ups, and luxury lofts.

Mere days after Amanda started at *Esquire,* she asked me if she could write short book reviews. After she'd been there for a few weeks, she started receiving postcards from celebrated authors, communiqués to be tacked up on the wall of her cubicle like the trophies they were. After she'd been at the magazine for a couple of months, she asked for a raise; after a few more months, a promotion; after six months, she wanted health insurance. (She was a freelancer and got nothing, alas. Recall: *it's very hard to move from assistant to non-assistant.*) For an afternoon snack, she'd go out and get two York Peppermint Patties, and even though I'm not sure she really liked me all that much, she'd give one to me. Six years later, at the age of thirty-two, when she was on a tour for her second book, Amanda was killed, along with her parents, in a plane crash in Asheville, North Carolina. It still seems incomprehensible that this ebullient young woman who loved writers and writing and teaching, who loved the Bread Loaf Writers' Conference more even than seemed reasonable, and who was so perturbingly well read in contemporary fiction, is gone forever.

THERE WERE, AND ALWAYS WOULD BE, EDITORS AT *ESQUIRE* WHO BElieved that fiction should be assigned. They wanted fiction to be approached like journalism, to be reported like journalism. This topic would inevitably come up in meetings: short stories ought to be "relevant" and should incorporate current events. *Esquire* wanted the social realism of Sinclair Lewis or Theodore Dreiser or, more appropriately, Tom Wolfe: their idea of what *Esquire* fiction should be squared perfectly with Wolfe's infamous manifesto about how to save the American novel, "Stalking the Billion-Footed Beast," which insists on "a highly detailed realism based on reporting, a realism more thorough than any currently being attempted, a realism that would portray the individual in intimate and inextricable relation to the society around him."

The idea was that I would approach writers with story ideas from the news and commission them to write short fiction on such-and-such topic. I wasn't so sure that fiction worked that way—didn't it have to come from the inside out, not from the outside in? (Hail, muse, etc.?) Any acutely topical fiction would certainly be of dubious artistic substance and would serve only the moment but not much else. Whenever someone again suggested that I commission a short story (Timothy McVeigh was one such concept), I will admit that I saw myself as "the Lord High Executioner of middlebrow culture," in Louis Menand's nice phrase about Dwight Macdonald (*Esquire* writer, by the way, and the magazine's film critic for a period in the sixties). The approach was anti-literary, most certainly middlebrow, though I don't believe any other editors there saw it that way.

But yet it wasn't as if anyone was ever looming over my desk or anything, like black-cloaked Death in *The Seventh Seal,* grimly pressing the phone into my hand: *Hello, Mr. Roth. Any chance you'd be interested in writing a short story for* Esquire *narrated by Posh Spice?*

But in the early days, it was still easy for me to acquire any short story I wanted to acquire. My principal struggle then was to woo the writers I wanted to publish and try to convince them that they didn't *always* need to automatically think first of submitting to *The New Yorker* (although it made a lot of sense that they did, I had to admit).

I suggested to Granger that *Esquire* run a short short story on the back page. The back page of any magazine is prime real estate and is usually a listicle, product placement, or an attempt at humor. Remarkably, he went for it, and the back page became a 650-word flash fiction. My slug for it, Snap Fiction, was possibly not for the ages and brought to mind (for me) crisp English peas and the brightest springtide green. But I just loved that this page existed. In truth I did always approach it with a sense of leave-taking and end times, knowing that it couldn't last, surely. It actually hung on for a couple of improbable years. We published some wonderful stories on that page, though David Foster Wallace did say to me about one of the least successful of them, "What, did he write that on a fucking *cocktail napkin?*"

Rust Hills was also not a fan of Snap Fiction.

"Six hundred and fifty words for a *complete story?*" he asked. "I can barely get a *drawer* open in *six hundred and fifty words!*"

THE DUBIOUS ACHIEVEMENT AWARDS, *ESQUIRE*'S ANNUAL ROUNDUP OF all things preposterous, was created in 1962 by art director Robert Benton and editor David Newman (both of whom would go on to write the screenplay for *Bonnie and Clyde*) and is, or was, the signature issue of the year, I guess you could say. The format: an all-caps header as punch line, followed by a summary of a news item. Traditionally, there was always a photo of an alarmingly youthful Richard Nixon, grinning broadly, with the caption "WHY IS THIS MAN LAUGHING?" (In later years replaced with "WHY IS THIS DEAD MAN STILL LAUGHING?") The whole enterprise aspired to sound very *Harvard Lampoon*—mischievous, smug, caustic, and often pretty funny.

To locate the Dubious pop-cultural era when I was new at *Esquire,* there were jokes in the January 1998 issue about: the Heaven's Gate cult (those Hale-Bopp comet cultists who were talked into committing mass suicide with their Nikes on—because people can be talked into anything), Boris Yeltsin, Dudley Moore, Marv

Albert (he of the sex scandal, and wearer of ladies' underwear and a very convincing toupee), Michael Jackson, and JFK Jr. and his superlatively clueless magazine, *George*. There were *five* jokes about the Trumps and a sidebar devoted to the nutty things Norman Mailer had said during interviews about *The Gospel According to the Son* . . . which just went to show that there was never any lingering institutional loyalty toward you, or even any hint of vestigial affection (impossible to imagine *The New Yorker* mocking its most recognizable writer, John Updike, similarly—but *The New Yorker* house style was impersonal, never knavish), even if you'd once been the magazine's star writer. You will always become a self-parody and made a fool of in the end.

During past editorships and regimes, Dubious was, as I understood it, an all-hands-on-deck situation—every editor and writer could contribute to it. But I don't recall being included in one meeting that year about Dubious, although it's possible there *were* no meetings that year about Dubious, as freelancers and Dave Eggers did most of the work.

These, in my view, were the best jokes in the Dubious Achievement Awards of 1998:

I'M SORRY, COULD YOU SAY THAT AGAIN, ONLY MORE SLOWLY AND WITH YOUR BUTT?
Responding to critics, Jim Carrey said, "I don't care if people think I'm an overactor. People who think that would call van Gogh an overpainter."

In reference to the death of Princess Diana:

AT LEAST SOME GOOD HAS COME OF THIS TRAGEDY
Andrew Lloyd Webber's publicist said, "Andrew was a friend of Diana's, and I think he was too near the subject to think of it as a musical."

And the freakishly prescient:

AS THE REIGNING ASSHOLE, I HAVE TO KEEP UP APPEARANCES
Donald Trump hired a personal trainer to help Alicia Machado take off the twenty-two pounds she had put on since being crowned Miss Universe and invited the press to watch her train.

DAVE EGGERS WAS SOMETHING OF THE SPOKESPERSON FOR DUBIOUS that year and did some media for it. One cold night, I tagged along with him to a studio at a media conglomerate on Sixth Avenue for a TV interview. As we rode the elevator, I asked Dave the one thing you shouldn't ask someone who's about to go on a TV interview:

"Nervous?"

He regarded me for a moment. There was a small experimental tuft of facial hair below his bottom lip.

"Um, *no*," he said. He added, somewhat reproachfully, "Nice *pants*."

I was wearing leather pants—and a black Katharine Hamnett jacket—and they *were* nice (so was the jacket). When I was back at *GQ*, I had tried to get some custom leather pants made for me, but my guy (recommended to me at work as *the* leather guy) did a fitting in the office, cashed my deposit check, and stopped returning my phone calls. These particular leather pants—I'd saved up for them for months—were from Charivari, the best store in the history of the world (it would go out of business the following year). I was vain about these pants.

"Why are you hanging out with me?" Dave asked, referring more to the pants than to me. Leather pants: not as ubiquitous then as they are now, and more statement making back in the day. (Divergent aside: I once interviewed Simon Le Bon—that's right,

Simon Le Bon—and I noted that he referred to his leather pants as his "leathers." I'll always remember that. *My leathers.*) "You look as if you should be some rock star's girlfriend."

"But I don't want to be the *girlfriend*," I said. "*I* want to be the rock star."

This was not true. I did not want to be the rock star. Well, I did and I didn't. In the abstract, being the center of attention seemed like a nice thing, but being the center of attention also meant that you had to deal with people, and my preference was to not have to deal with people if I could help it. And there were few things I could imagine wanting to do less than a TV interview, especially one in which you weren't speaking for yourself but were instead representing an institution—*two* institutions, *Esquire* and Dubious—and the potential for a high-profile screwup seemed limitless. But Dave was cut from a different cloth from I or anyone else.

Dave was my office buddy that first year, and I'm fairly sure I would have lost my mind without him. He was great to talk to and usually had controlled and impressively sane responses to things. Example: we'd seen *Titanic* together, and I'd squirmed in my seat the whole time, overcome with thoughts of self-immolation. "Well," I said as we left the theater, "*that* was ridiculous." But levelheaded Dave conceded that he actually believed that *Titanic* was very good at what it was and likewise very good at doing what a commercial movie should do—not demand too much of its audience.

Dave could be disarmingly puckish: "Do you like *seafood*?" he might ask, take a big bite of something, and open his mouth. He once pilfered a notebook of mine from my office desk and returned it with the following note on the inside cover: "This belongs to Adrienne, who no one really likes." (Question: Shouldn't that have been "whom"?) And there was that one time when he and his younger brother mercilessly ridiculed me, in those early-Internet days, for using the word "flame" as a verb (I deserved that one). He gave me his copy of the Madonna book *Sex* because he didn't want it lying around his apartment. I soon discovered I didn't want it lying around my apartment, either.

The elevator arrived on the TV studio's floor. Dave was shuttled off to the makeup chair or wherever they took him, and I loitered in the greenroom.

The other guest on the show that night was—wait for it—Ed Koch, the one and only. In my youth, the main thing I'd known about Koch during his seventies and eighties mayoralty of New York City was his catchphrase "How am I doin'?" I suppose I had imagined that Koch, sitting there in that late nineties greenroom, would be this loud, feisty, wisecracking, glad-handing fellow: a stand-up comic as ex-mayor. This was the total inverse to the aura Koch projected that evening. He sat at the cliff edge of his seat, long legs extended straight in front of him (Koch was a tall man—did not know that), arms rigidly crossed against his chest. He seemed grumpy as hell; he spoke to no one, made eye contact with no one. He had no reading material. His only activity: scowling silently into the middle distance.

I helped myself to a cookie—that greenrooms vacillate wildly in terms of snack quality was a lesson still to be learned—and watched Dave's interview on the monitor. He was swift of tongue, systematic of mind, as poised as a statesman, and terrifyingly telegenic. It occurred to me that I had to revise my take on Dave somewhat. This was another Dave to contend with—not a punk or a smart aleck, no, but a head of state, an orator, a leader—*the* leader of . . . something.

A skittish young guy—thin as a dime and wearing a beanie—who worked on the show kept darting in and out of the greenroom. He'd stand with his chin cupped in hand as he watched the monitor, mesmerized by Dave, and then he'd scurry out of the room. He'd come right back, though, would watch Dave for a few more seconds, and dash off again. This sequence was repeated several times.

"*Whoa,*" the guy said appreciatively, considering the TV on one of his stops. "Check out the soul patch on that dude."

Ed Koch, in his chair, scowled briefly at Dave on the TV. Unimpressed, he went back to staring abstractly into space.

"Funking them out!" the bro exclaimed to the monitor. "Funking them *out*! Yeah, man: that dude is *funking them out.*"

It was of interest to me to see how people could sense where the power, or charisma, or star quality, or whatever it was, was. People wanted in on it, wanted to grab a little of it for themselves. Guys—and, indeed, they were always inevitably guys—did tend to accumulate around Dave. I'd been observing this phenomenon as it happened right in front of me. After work, sometimes I'd get something to eat with him at one of the diners close to the *Esquire* office (Howard Johnson's was one), and it often seemed that young dudes would just start showing up at the table. These chaps were always of a rather specific and narrow demographic, but yet: Who *were* they? Whence did they come? How did they know Dave? Who told them to meet up at the HoJo? We shall never know the answer. Dave was then a fairly new NYC arrival. He was known, in a nerdy, cultish way, as the impresario of *Might,* yet this was all before *McSweeney's* or Dave's memoir, *A Heartbreaking Work of Staggering Genius,* was a gleam in anyone's eye. Anyone except for the Eggersian eye, of course.

Dave once made the remark to me, by the way, that in restaurants he never wanted to sit with his back to the door; he surmised that this probably had to do with his need to always be on guard in case of invaders or assailants. And still to this day, when I'm happily facing a restaurant wall, I find myself thinking again about how I have absolutely no inner Viking.

14

I had been spending my professional life, at *Esquire* and *GQ* both, reading fiction by men about men. The sub-subjects: The Land of Marriage. A middle-aged man coming to terms with something. Extramarital affairs. Hotel rooms. Adult life as unwinnable game. A man trying, and failing, to be a man—whatever that thing was. A wife. A waif. Oh, God, the *mothers*. How many trailer parks *were there* upon the greensward? There sure were a lot of trains. Why were there so many prostitutes? And why were so many of the women dead? Rarely did any children appear in the stuff I read, and when they did, they tended to serve as devices for the teaching of moral lessons—touching ones, usually. And the women—voluble, irrational, rarely all that smart, but, with any luck, sexy, sexy, sexy—functioned as instruments to male enlightenment. Oh, if I had a dime for each time I read the sentence "She made me feel *alive* . . ." (to which my private stock response was always "And you made her feel *dead*").

Occasionally, I'd find myself reading some crazy stream-of-consciousness story (although usually without the consciousness), and I would come to note some regional peculiarities such as the appearance of John Denver in a great number of the stories submitted by writers in the Aspen, Colorado, area (in later years John Denver, RIP, was replaced by the ghost of John Denver), but mostly we were still in a post-Carver moment then: the stories were hammer-and-nail stories and their authors were trying to build solid realist houses.

I had been at *Esquire* for six months, and I knew that I wasn't too interested in anything I regarded as workshoppy, meat-and-potatoes fiction. I'd read a story submission that I fervently wanted to publish: "Adult World," by David Foster Wallace. *Infinite Jest* had come out two years before, and David was largely regarded as the young novelist to top, but he was not yet the most influential American writer since Carver . . . and then, eventually, since Hemingway. I had done no wooing of David—his agent came to the office for meetings and hand-delivered a copy of the story (that's some good agenting: never happens)—but it was exactly the kind of fiction I had promised I would deliver. "Adult World" had beauty and strangeness; it wounded, it stabbed, and, like all true works of art, there was something ineffable about it. I argued for the story—in a memo and in person—and we took it. "Adult World" would be the centerpiece of the July 1998 fiction issue.

"MS. MILLER?" DAVID FOSTER WALLACE BEGAN ON THE PHONE, NOT entirely as politesse but as a provocation. This was my interpretation, at least.

It was late winter 1998, and Monica Lewinsky was the only "news" of that season—and of that year. Two years before, *Esquire* published David's essay about the tennis player Michael Joyce. David had written the Joyce story for *Details*, but *Details* had killed it. David would tell me that *Details* didn't believe his piece conformed to house style. So, *Esquire* to the rescue! Though David would remark to me that *Esquire*, a magazine he then deemed low prestige and high cynicism, was the absolute last place he'd wanted it to run. (He did end up having a good experience with the editor who worked on the piece, however.)

In my time at the magazine, I had learned another important lesson: no editor ever went broke by underestimating the number of grudges collected by your average writer (not that David Foster Wallace was your average writer). Writers work their grudges over and over like cows with their cud, and maybe that's the right thing to do.

The only purpose of David's call then was to relate that he had sent in a disk, a "homemade DOS disk" (I supposed that meant a floppy disk) with "Adult World" on it. I told him that there was no way in the world my office could read one of those things. Floppy disks were, like Linear B and Evel Knievel–branded bikes, things of the past.

David mentioned something to the effect that the codes on the disk had to be "displayed" rather than "functionalized."

I told him that I had no idea what he was talking about (still don't).

"Ask a techie or a techette to help you."

We set up a time to talk again, a week later, after the disk had arrived. My big fear, not that I mentioned it to the author, was that I would have to actually retype "Adult World." We're in pre-scanning days here, and if a writer couldn't email a copy of his or her story or get me a technologically relevant disk of it, the piece would have to be typed. And that typist would be I. And I had indeed keyed in pieces by some technophobic old-timers (Updike was one), duct-taped to my chair, anesthetizing myself by listening to *Ladies and Gentlemen*

We Are Floating in Space. I could imagine no bigger nightmare than trying to format the labyrinthine structure of "Adult World."

The story is narrated from the close third-person perspective of a naive young wife who is concerned about her sex life with her husband. It has two parts: the first is, or seems to be, a fairly straightforward story of marital sexual dysfunction, but the second part abstracts out into a densely structured, formally outrageous outline (meta-outline?) plotting the young wife's epiphany (she realizes that her husband, a shifty Wallace grotesque, is a secret compulsive masturbator [thereafter known in the story as "S.C.M."]) and her subsequent process of self-analysis. (He would tell me that he'd used an ex-girlfriend's voice, presented through indirect discourse, for the young wife. This did not seem a promising disclosure on a number of levels.)

It did occur to me that I might have asked my readers/interns/assistants to type the story if it came to that, but asking people to do stuff for me was just not my style, never would be. (Also, I was a bit of a control freak.)

I relented and made a call to the IT guys—"you are not going to believe this, but some author sent in a *floppy disk*"—and a goateed techie came to my office. Somehow he got the thing to work. On the appointed day, at the appointed hour, I called David with the info, being mindful that his time zone was one hour earlier than the East Coast one. David lived in Bloomington, Illinois, then, teaching at Illinois State, and enjoyed reminding people of the central time zone issue—his folksy chomping-on-a-toothpick shtick was always a useful personal and professional strategy, and also a bulwark against whatever spell he was casting. (He was, he knew, much harder to observe when he was wearing a mask.)

I told him that they were able to read the disk.

"Yes, I told you they would. I'm absolutely *shocked* that you bought this story. I just about fell off my chair when my agent told me," David said.

Yeah, we'd already gone over that.

"You could have knocked me over with a feather," he continued.

These were subtle insults to *Esquire*, to be sure. My interpretation: he didn't believe that *Esquire* was smart enough to appreciate his work. But I wasn't intimidated. A printout of a piece of writing is a great equalizer: one writer's manuscript looks like any other writer's manuscript. So if I'd been asked then if I found editing a piece like "Adult World" intimidating, I would have said that it was a piece of writing like any other piece of writing. It was a puzzle to solve, and I was going to solve it.

I needed to know a bit more about the kind of imagination that could produce a story like this. Question for him: I wanted to know how he'd come to the decision to fragment the second part of the story out into that crazy outline.

"Here's the thing," David said, "I don't want to be manipulative. I don't want to write thrillers. I generally hate epiphanies in fiction, and I really hate epiphanies when they're dramatized in scene, so what I tried to do with this one was write something urgent but formally strange." He added that he wanted to do something weird and fractured but also something redemptive and moving. I didn't know it yet, but these were all Wallace buzzwords.

He remarked that the young wife's maturation was meant to be an emotional gut punch for the reader. Yet it seemed to me that the female character's coming of age was being treated comically—mockingly, in fact. I'd soon learn that there wasn't too much that annoyed David more than being told that his fiction was funny (which it was). That was a real DFW bugbear.

I didn't know this guy at all, but I could tell he was a tricky one. It seemed to me that keeping things pleasant and unobjectionable was probably going to be a good defense with him.

"It's interesting that you would want to rock the boat on something as marginalized as magazine short fiction," David continued, rocking the boat himself. David, I would also learn, was a gold-medal boat-rocker, an absolute virtuoso of the art. "Tell me why you wanted to publish it."

Jesus. He was testing me. He was actually *testing* me. Again, I loved the story—even if it did assert that marriage was at best an accommodation, more likely a sham, and that true intimacy within it was impossible.

"Well, I'm going to be pretty surprised if I open the magazine and it's actually in there," he declared.

"Adult World," he said, came out of the reporting he had recently done for his *Premiere* article about the porn industry, "Neither Adult nor Entertainment" (later republished as "Big Red Son"). He reiterated that he never expected this treacherous, twitchy (a favorite Wallace word), experimental, and, frankly, X-rated short story to be published in a magazine that, as he put it, needling me already, *smelled good.*

"But you have to be cruelly savvy within the pragmatics of what you're doing, I suppose," he added.

David was incorrect to suggest that there was anything at all cruelly savvy about *anything* I did. Whatever the opposite of "cruelly savvy" was—that was me. He'd figure that out eventually. The few times I have tried to be professionally strategic, the outcome could only have been compared to Gore Vidal's assessment of Dawn Powell and that great comic novelist's "many unsuccessful attempts to sell out to commercialism."

But *Esquire* wasn't cruelly savvy in those days, either. Maybe it never was, not in that era. What it was was weird, and idiosyncratic, and, it must be said, somewhat uneven. But the fallibility, in my opinion then, gave it heart.

Granger was publishing stuff that no other magazine would have had the nerve to touch—"Adult World": great example. At the same time, I should add that the magazine's editorial decisions those days did, frankly, seem so odd, so unsafe, that everyone working at *Esquire* was half expecting we'd go belly-up any second.

What was unknown was whether we'd go down with the ship or if we'd each get deep-sixed individually. A highly contentious, yet ultimately prescient (though still invasive), recent article by one of the magazine's best writers suggesting that Kevin Spacey was gay did nothing to fill us with any confidence about our *Esquire*-related futures.

David explained that he wanted "Adult World" to be treated as two unattached pieces—not run back-to-back, but instead separated by other stories in the magazine. His argument was that the division would be "less hard on the reader's central nervous system"; otherwise, he said, if the two sections of "Adult World" were to run adjacent to each other, the format change between (I) and (II) would look, for reasons best left to his own understanding, "gratuitous"—"a heavy slapping of the reader in the face with the change of format."

He also wanted to use two separate titles: "Adult World (I)" and "Adult World (II)."

I said that I'd see what I could do.

(Maybe. This sounded like a horrible idea.)

"Thank you," said David, and made a rude comment about the glossy magazine "syndrome of subscription blanks." Could I talk to someone "upstairs" about that? (Was he joking?) And would I like to know the first thing he did whenever he got a magazine in the mail? (No, not particularly.) He ripped out the subscription cards.

"Do you always display this much of an attitude with your editors?" I asked.

I was amused—somewhat, but only somewhat. He was giving me a hard time, and he seemed to be enjoying the little performance. But I needed him to understand that he would treat me with equality.

"You want to know the first thing *most* writers say to me?" I asked.

"No," David said. "What?"

"*Thank you.*"

"I'm making a mental note that any attempt to intimidate you backfires."

"You know, John Updike said thank you."

That was true. But Updike had also complained to Rust in a letter about how his author photo had been handled by the magazine (it had been completely my fault). I neglected to mention this to David.

"Um, *O-K: thank you,*" David said. "How old are you?"

"Come on," I said. "Twenty-six." I shouldn't have told him, though.

"I'm thirty-six, a whole decade older than you," David said. "How tall are you?"

I told him: six feet. (I'm five-eleven, but I say six feet when I sense that power needs to be asserted.)

He said he was six-two. He said he weighed 210 pounds.

The weight seemed about right. The height, however, did not.

"You're not that tall," I said.

He assured me he actually was.

"I met you. You're not that tall," I reiterated.

(He was not that tall.)

"No," he said. "I am."

I told him that our meeting of sorts had occurred at his *Infinite Jest* party two years before.

"Yes, I remember," he said. "What you saw that night was just my being a spaz. I probably looked a lot shorter than I really am. I can at least guarantee that that night was more of a Boschian nightmare for me than it was for you."

I just *had* to mention that shirt he wore the night of the party.

That shirt was a relic from high school, so the story to me went, and seemed, in his view, to grow tighter throughout the evening.

David said, "I just kept thinking, *I've gotten so fat. I am not going to get laid at my own book publication party.*"

Why was he telling me this? Mildly odd, that. All my interactions with the grander of the writers with whom I'd worked so far at *Esquire* had been cordial (best case) or so distant as to be nonexistent. Examples: I did speak with Updike about his story "Oliver's Evolution" (the last piece he would publish in *Esquire*), but let us just say that he did not seem to want to have a deep editorial exchange. I'd had one very brief (and very awkward) call with Garrison Keillor, and I never had any direct contact at all with my man Martin Amis—his extremely short commissioned piece was faxed by an intermediary and that was that. None of the old guys wanted to engage me.

David continued, going into far more detail than anyone could ever have possibly needed about his pitiful attempt to "get laid" (he said that *again*) the night of the *Infinite Jest* party. He said he asked about six different women up to his hotel room, and when he finally found one who assented ("the seventh," said he), the situation ended up being thwarted by, weirdly, a young man I knew.

"*Wait,*" I said. "I just went out on a couple of dates with him."

In truth, they were more like non-dates, and while this guy's account and David's never *quite* matched up (you can bet I asked the guy about it), it did seem certain that he, a tall blond scenester, had shown up at David's hotel room and prevented whatever was going to happen from happening. The subterfuge of a pizza delivery may or may not have been involved, but that depended on whom you believed.

"Please tell him I wish him a violent death," said David, and added that he'd even worn his "good" pair of underwear that night—"the ones with red rocket ships on them."

I thought: *Very bizarre.*

Did he actually think that it was a "positive" for me, a new female professional contact, to know that he had spent the evening of his greatest literary triumph—the greatest literary triumph any writer could imagine or hope for—debasing himself?

But you know what? Maybe *I* was the problem here. Maybe I wasn't conveying any sense of gravitas. And maybe *I* was the one with boundary issues. Perhaps David, to the extent that he was giving "me" any thought at all, believed that I, a young female men's magazine editor, was raunchy and unembarrassable, a gal who knew how to knock back a few cold ones with the fellas.

Well, I supposed that I *was* just another one of the fellas to the extent that I could quote pretty much all of Gunnery Sergeant Hartman's lines in *Full Metal Jacket:* "You are nothing but unorganized grabasstic pieces of amphibian shit." (And: "If there is one thing in this world that I hate, it is an unlocked footlocker. You know that, don't you?" Oh man, I could go on.) But unless the guys in question were Stanley Kubrick (chef's kiss to you, Stanley, in perpetuity, for all of it), Stephen Sondheim, Wolfgang Amadeus Mozart, or Thomas Jefferson, being one of the guys was of no interest. At various professional men's magazine–based events, when I'd witnessed the spectacle of women mimicking men—drinking whiskey, smoking cigars, cursing like boatswains, etc.—I'd always sent myself the following message in a bottle: *No matter what happens, never do that.* But, to quote Robyn Hitchcock, "everything you say you won't is what you will eventually" ("honesty is money in the cemetery"), so was it possible that I'd *already* become one of the guys?

Or was it that these men felt comfortable enough with me to be the brutes they actually were?

No, not that, either. The more likely scenario: these men just forgot whom they were speaking to.

David went on about his *Infinite Jest* party: "And I ended up spending pretty much the whole party in the restaurant kitchen, smoking cigarettes and crying."

"The kitchen?"

"Yep."

"Crying?"

"Yep."

This sounded marginally insane.

David and I began speaking of another gentleman we had both spied at the party and whom we both knew slightly. David, who had total recall for slights real and imagined ("it is burned into my frontal lobe," he would declare of various affronts), told an interesting little story about how this guy had once insulted him. David observed, "He has eyes like a fish. If you poked his tummy, your finger would get stuck in foam."

I explained that I'd been invited to the party because I'd reviewed *Infinite Jest*. When I later admitted to David how quickly and crudely I read the novel that first time, he said, "You have just confirmed all of my worst suspicions about book reviewers." But as a measure of the kind of person David was or could be, he didn't hold the existence of that appalling little review against me.

The next time David called, he volunteered the tentative title of the book he was working on, a short-story collection in which he would include "Adult World."

"But please don't tell anyone," he said.

This was the first of many disclosures throughout the years I would be expected to treat as classified information. Although how top secret actually *were* many of these confidences? It's a question.

The title: *Brief Interviews with Hideous Men*. Nice one. Was it going to be—ahem—funny?

"Yeah, talk about a laugh riot. Parts of it are funny, I *guess*, but there are parts where you'll need a damp cloth on the solar plexus."

"Sounds great," I said.

Looking back on it, there was, right away, a tone that felt correct when talking to David: one had to be extremely direct and also gently ribbing. Soon enough, I would understand that he would also frequently need to be rebuked, sternly, as a child is rebuked.

"Everyone's going to hate this book," he said. "Just wait."

David remained consistent to me in his prediction that *Brief Interviews with Hideous Men* would be critically panned. He said he felt vindicated when it was. (It wasn't, but I'm here to tell you that he believed it had been.)

He called again a couple of days later.

"Can you please say hi to the Icky Brothers?" He introduced me telephonically to his dog Jeeves. "And *this* is Cancer Boy."

His other dog, Drone, had recently been diagnosed with lymphoma, and David was a mess about it and would become a bigger mess still. He said he knew Drone was sick when he noticed that he (Drone) was drinking abnormally large amounts of water. (With every animal I've had since then, I'm always on the morbid lookout for this portent of doom.)

"So," David said. "This is it. Welcome to the Love Grotto."

A call a couple of hours later:

"I was hoping you'd help me out with something," David said. *Yes?*

"Well, I don't like everything I do, and I have no confidence that anyone else will, either. I mean, I do 'like' the story, but I'm nervous that people just won't *get it* if it's in *Esquire*. This whole issue is not unrelated to the weird, hard reading you're asking your audience to do with this, yet at the same time, you can't ignore the business of the magazine, which is to sell ads. We're both trying to have our cake and eat it, too, I suppose."

He quizzed me again—again!—about why I liked "Adult World." Would he have grilled Maxwell Perkins in such a way? Gordon Lish? Rust Hills? Yes, there were plenty of sexist overtones in this, and, yes, I was alive to them all. I had intuited that he'd also wanted to see if I had any independent taste of my own, or if I liked "Adult World" merely because the author was David Foster Wallace. Either that or he was the most cripplingly insecure person I'd ever encountered. (Probably both, actually.)

I told him that what I found most moving about "Adult World" was its view that sex cannot help two lonely people transcend the fortress of self that separates them. Despite the comic elements of the second half, it's a damn sad story.

"OK. You understand. I'm just real grateful for your degree of certainty that an apelike *Esquire* reader will feel the same way about it that you do."

An apelike Esquire *reader.* This, I would come to recognize, was a classic Wallace move—flattery barbed with an insult, a surprise thumbtack in your flan.

"Adult World" had been rejected everywhere else, he said.

"Perfect," I said.

"You still want it?"

"Even more." I added, ever so lightly, that his work probably wasn't to every editor's taste anyway.

And by the way, I *was* rather annoyed to learn that so many other magazines had already seen the story. This was not pleasant information to receive, that *Esquire* was at the bottom of the DFW submission totem pole.

David: "The challenge of fiction at *Esquire* is that it doesn't want anything too arty or too boring, and it has to appeal to both yuppies and homosexuals. It's an interesting paradox of the glossy magazine. You're in the luxurious position to have your pick of American short fiction, yet your demographic restricts you quite a lot. You have many unique challenges in your job. I can appreciate that. And like every other magazine, you can't, or won't, do anything that's not in the house style."

Although most of us, other than the ever-clairvoyant David, were not prescient enough to see what was coming, we were then at the tail end of the magazine industry as we knew it. Back then, in these last-hurrah days before all hell broke loose and the business became the Wild West of our era, each publication was, to a certain extent, its own closed system; each magazine had its own writerly (or anti-writerly) sensibility.

But "David Foster Wallace" and "house style" were two things that did not go together. (Let us recall, for example, that David, during the editing of his Roger Federer essay, convinced the *New York Times* to swerve from its obstinate style rules for him and cede to his use of the Oxford comma—the first, and I should think last, author to claim such a distinction.) David was too much his own man, for better or worse: too allergic to received wisdom, too much of a rhetorical provocateur, and too much of a monomaniac to have written in any voice but his own.

"The particular fiction in a glossy mainstream magazine is there to amuse and entertain, not to provoke and push," he said. "All of these sections sort of drift along ghostlike, and ninety-nine percent of the stuff in them doesn't seem alive."

I did not entirely disagree with that (an "it's not a *gripper*" aura hung heavy over much magazine fiction), but of course I had to defend myself. I reminded him: at least a few glossies actually *were* still engaged in the noble and important enterprise of publishing fiction. But if David's response to magazine fiction was tepid at best, who actually *were* the enthusiastic readers? Were there any? Maybe there *weren't* any. Whenever a reader sent a letter to the editor about a story in *Esquire,* a photocopy of that letter was given to the story's assigning editor. And since I'd been at the magazine, I had to admit that there hadn't been one letter about a story I'd edited. These sorts of things contributed to the way an editor's work was perceived internally.

"But do you know what's even worse than that?" David said. "The fiction in them is there only to signify literary respectability and to win awards. Come on. I don't have to tell *you* this, of all people."

The fact was that *Esquire,* in its incarnation at the time, was not *too* concerned with literary respectability. (If it had been, I would not have been hired.) It had a *very* short list of "approved" literary writers: Mailer, Roth, Updike, and the man in the white suit,

Tom Wolfe. (They always wanted a short story by Stephen King, and that was a good day for me when I finally did haul one in.) But after those big men, *Esquire* was not quite as much a literary "club" as you'd think. A submission from a young cultural phenomenon, like, say, David, was not *quite* viewed as a gift from the literary gods; come to think of it, many of the authors' names on the manuscripts I presented may as well have been obliterated with a Sharpie. This was a freeing and democratic, if frankly eccentric, editorial approach.

But it was also, possibly, I worried, anti-intellectual and *ill-*literary: If we had no real reverence for or even any interest in (or awareness of?) an author's body of work or accomplishments, was it possible that we were neglecting our most essential artists? Did we even know what we were looking at? These were questions.

"So here's what you do," said David. "You do your bullshit service crap, but you also do hard-core lit. You hear that? *Hard-core lit.* You have the harness of power, but I can also sense that your mouth is clamped. I'm probably bitching to the wrong person, actually. But why does *everything* need to be run through the same grinder? Not everything *is* for the same reader—the halfwit knuckle-dragging ape. People feel so lied to in this world; they want something nourishing, something that doesn't seem so blatantly false."

Perhaps he expected me to defend the role of the big soft glossy—the "BSG," as he, rather excrementally, would call it in his short story (Russian novella?) of magazines and excrement, "The Suffering Channel." Maybe David wanted an argument. At that point, I had never spoken with any other magazine editor who'd worked with him, and I had no way of knowing if this was just the way he was. Or at least the way he started off. Maybe he put all new editors through a sort of grisly hazing process. Maybe he wanted to see whether I could be trusted.

"I'm sorry I'm being so outspoken and bad-tempered," he said. "I seem to have no filter when I talk to you. It's weird."

"Not a problem," I said.

Or *was* it?

"It's just that sometimes I think, *You know what? That's it. I'm not gonna play anymore.* But then the other side of me is like, *Gotta be in the magazine, gotta be in the magazine.* So that's that. So here I am."

David was fired *up* today. But whom, or what, was he mad at? *I* wasn't the one making him play. And what *was* he complaining about exactly? (Later, he would apologize, sort of, to the extent he was ever actually able to apologize, for being such a difficult person in this era ["dick" was the word]: "I was not a healthy man then.")

I reminded him that the magazine *was* paying him $10,000 for "Adult World." (Those were the days.)

"I *know*. I've been telling everyone how much you pay for fiction."

He later admitted that *Esquire* could have gotten "Adult World" for free.

"Look, I'm very grateful to you . . . God. *Sorry.* I'm sure you're used to foul tempers, talking to fiction writers all day."

That was true. My job had already taught me a lot: first and foremost, all art is compensatory, and well-adjusted people do not become artists. Quoth the brilliant Wallace story "Octet": "You are, unfortunately, a fiction writer."

"You have to be kind of a shrink, too, in your job, I guess," he said. "But this whole magazine question really does drive me nuts. All of this stuff is so diluted all the time; it's as if all of these glossies are edited subject-matter-wide. *Esquire* does not *have* to compete with *Entertainment* fucking *Weekly,* you know. Tell them that. You go in there and you fucking tell them that . . . Damn. Sorry. I'm not your problem. I'm my own problem. I'll leave you alone now."

Now came calls from David with story ideas.

"You should have six well-known but ridiculous people review the same book," he said.

Courtney Love was one such potential author. *Wall Street Week*'s Louis Rukeyser—he was another.

"What about doing some trailblazing Internet thing?" he asked. "What about a story in hyperlink?"

Wait, what was hyperlink? Patiently, it was explained. He would later tell me that the footnotes in *Infinite Jest* functioned like hypertext. Later still he would say that he considered *Infinite Jest* "basically an Internet novel." And: "When people finally figure that out, they'll see that I didn't invent a new *form* or anything."

Then another call—this time about writers whom he thought I should approach for the magazine.

But hey, David, why should I even listen to you? What credibility, exactly, do you have in this department?

He had been a fiction editor of the *Sonora Review* when he was in grad school at the University of Arizona, he said. That was why I should listen to him. This, hilariously, was the only credential I was given.

One afternoon—we're in late March here, and we'd been talking for a month or so (he now called randomly to chat)—he and I were grumbling on the phone about book critics. We were joined in the opinion that most book reviewers were simply reacting to other reviews and that the so-called literary world was hivelike, its tastes and opinions imposed from the top down. (As Michael Herr excellently wrote in *Kubrick*, his mesmerizingly great biographical treatment of the master, "There aren't many spectacles more dispiriting than this one: the culture-critical smart set, united in aversion, dreadfully putting on their thinking caps.") David consistently maintained to me that he had only one intelligent interview during the entire course of the *Infinite Jest* publicity campaign, with the critic Laura Miller, who then wrote for *Salon*. That was his story and he stuck to it.

He would tell me, and I believed him, that the acclaim he had received for *Infinite Jest* did not make him feel, in his words, like a big man, but actually had the opposite effect: the superlatives served only to reinforce what a fraud he believed he, at bottom, was. In later years, he told me that no one seemed to have noticed how he had pulled one over on them.

I remarked to him that I wanted to find someone to review books for *Esquire;* I would suggest that writer to the boss and hope for the best. It was damn hard to get too excited about most book reviewers, or reviews—so many were cribbed from press releases or plagiarized from other reviews. I had a dream: I wanted drollery, I wanted elegance and (occasional) vehemence, I wanted someone immune from that dreadful phenomenon of critical consensus. I wanted someone godlike, someone who understood the whole intellectual history of literature and culture, someone who could do high and low but never middle: I wanted the young Robert Hughes of books. As a matter of fact, what I wanted was the actual Robert Hughes—irascible art critic and author of the following sentence: "Truly bad art is always sincere, and there is a kind of forcible vulgarity, as American as a meatball hero, that takes itself for genius; Jacqueline Susann died believing she was the peer of Charles Dickens." Hughes, please. Get me Hughes.

And I did try to get the actual Hughes to write something for me once, but by that point, I had become nicely inured to the experience of being yelled at by brilliant, outspoken, bad-tempered old men. And I spent my life alternating between two modes: indulging these men or else (occasionally) fighting back. Usually, I tried to be polite. Thomas Jefferson believed that politeness is artificial good humor and that artificial good humor is—or was, back before our culture became so poisonous—what makes the world go round.

"Run, do not walk, to get James Wood in the magazine," David said.

David was an enthusiastic early reader of Wood, the now eminent literary critic who would famously give David's work a misread—a reasoned misread, but a misread, a big one. (He changed his tune later, though.) This was a year before Wood's first book was published; Wood was then writing reviews for *The New Republic*.

"*He* should be your book critic . . . *if* you could get him past your boss."

(David just *had* to get that little insult in there.)

More calls:

"I can't stand to be around men. Just watch the structure of a male exchange: 'Whose dick is bigger?' 'How much of the world have I penetrated?' It's *Mutual of Omaha's Wild Kingdom*: '*Now* we observe the *male* of the species . . .' It's mental chess, and it is *always* a pretend friendship. I prefer women to men. *All* of my friends are women."

David, lover of women, all kinds, said that he liked lesbians best of all.

"You don't have any male friends?"

"Not a one."

Later in the conversation, I noted with amusement as he listed the names of many of his friends, in New York and in Bloomington, each and every one of them a man.

And:

"My domestic life is an education in lameness. I have a diet consisting solely of peanut butter and jelly sandwiches, potato chips, and lemons."

"You *eat* lemons?"

"Yes. They're delicious *and* they prevent scurvy."

"Weird," I said.

Dare I ask what his beverage of choice was?

"Milk. It keeps me big and strong."

"Cute," I said. "Real cute."

He said that a woman—actually, what he said, in the man-child way he had, was "an old lady," later explained to be the mother of one of his friends—would come to his house to make him food, which would be divided into storage containers labeled by the days of the week.

"This is the most pitiful thing I've ever heard," I said.

Also: I was clearly being worked over. I was getting this odd feeling that in our conversations he was following some sort of script, running the same record, the same loop, over and over.

"I have something even *more* pitiful for you," he said, and offered that on the last dog walk of the evening he would often relieve himself outside with the Icky Brothers. He would go first, then the dogs would follow, right on the exact spot.

"You're gross," I said.

"You are correct."

"Speaking of *Mutual of Omaha's Wild Kingdom*," I said.

It was a couple of days later that a different David began to emerge.

"My moods swing from OK to fucked up completely," he said.

"You're never in a better mood than OK?"

"Rarely. Are you?"

I thought about that for a moment. "Almost always, I guess," I cheerfully replied.

A pause.

"Should we start thinking about edits to your story?" I asked.

I'd suggested before that we get down to business, but David kept putting me off. Already, he'd taken up quite a lot of my time, and we'd done zero work. I was in fact editing other stories for the fiction issue, too. It was the biggest month I'd had so far at *Esquire*. It was the biggest month I'd had so far in my whole career.

"I would be willing to engage you," David said.

15

When I bought a short story for the magazine, it was understood that the piece was, more or less, complete. Editorial suggestions, I learned quickly, should be conveyed to the author in a positive, cheery way, and the suggestions should be extremely specific. With an author, I might want to discuss the structure of a story, and I'd frequently suggest changes to titles and often wanted some sort of revision to the endings. I liked to work on paper. I'd do a line edit, in which I might query syntax, rhythm, transitions, timing, word choice, pacing, punctuation, character believability; perhaps I'd note that I sensed that something—a line of dialogue, a moment, a scene—was misplaced. I'd send a copy of the edited manuscript to the author. There would be two more rounds of edits, with fewer queries each time. After that, I'd proofread the various sets of galleys and proofs. I spent so much time on each piece that, as I saw it, any error in something I edited was no one's fault but my own.

Acquiring a nonfiction piece on the basis of a proposal was a different beast entirely and always felt more like being a venture capitalist—it's a big risk to take a flyer on a piece with an uncertain outcome, especially if you don't know the writer. It was a gamble that could yield some big payoffs, but you'd also have to be prepared to receive some extremely unruly early drafts requiring lots of editorial work. But unlike the true venture capitalist, there's no shared equity between writer and editor—the editor's work should always be invisible and usually is (unless the editor in question is Gordon Lish).

It is true that there are some writers who do *not* work well with editors; in Nabokov's haughty appraisal: "I have also come across a few pompous avuncular brutes who would attempt to 'make suggestions' which I countered with a thunderous 'stet'!" I'd had a couple of those types so far in my brief career and would certainly have more. I'd work with plenty of high-flying writers who would insist that their agents intercept all editorial communication (the "there will be *no* eye contact with the Emperor Caligula" approach); one of the most famous and successful authors in the world responded to my queries with a note to his agent, which she (the agent) imprudently forwarded to me: "WHY is this person bothering me with this? Tell her the story is FINISHED."

David said he didn't really do email and wanted to go over the edits to "Adult World" on the phone. Although each writer certainly presents his or her own unique editorial situation, most fiction writers tend toward the avoidant personality type—no, correction: what you get more often than not with fiction writers is a self-canceling combination of avoidant and hustler—and most don't want to talk to editors on the phone unless they have to.

David had another request.

"Would it be possible for you to give me your home number?" he asked.

"Why?"

"In case we need to work on edits over some weekend."

"Why would we need to do *that*?" I asked.

Was I along for the ride? Yes, I guess you could say that I was. But I understood that these calls were intrusive, invasive, and inappropriate. And I also believed that he was quite odd, very pushy, and maybe even predatory. I had all of these thoughts. But he also held a certain appeal.

The editing process of "Adult World" consisted mostly of my wanting to talk through the agrammatical stuff in the piece and David's assuring me that this agrammatical stuff—the weird syntax and the crazy abbreviations, etc.—was intentional. Hours were spent on the phone with the galleys in front of us, looking for "boners." Mistakes, typos. *Boners.* That was David to a T—always, if you will excuse me, inserting his personality into everything. As the years went on, I would like to think I had somewhat more editorially to contribute, to his work and to everyone else's, hopefully.

Although I did make a huge editorial mistake: I let David get his way and we ran "Adult World" as two separate unattached pieces, divided by other stories in the feature well (the format was ridiculously confusing). There was also the issue of the accompanying photo illustration to "Adult World": a female model's torso in a black satin teddy. A "merry widow," as David had it. I'd never heard that term before. That merry widow kept David howling for years. I still didn't understand how professionally infelicitous it usually was to share an illustration for a piece with an author before that piece shipped to the printer.

"You're a total angel puff," David said when the story closed. "I hope we can talk again sometime."

The breathtakingly poignant thing about working at a print magazine: you're always on to the next issue. All that effort, and then it ceases to exist. A blighted rose, a will-o'-the-wisp, an angel puff. (Or, to put it another, more Sondheim-y way, "Thanks a lot, and out with the garbage.") I didn't expect to talk to David again—wasn't even thinking about it—unless I were to edit another story of his for the magazine.

But indeed, as Ernest Shackleton was to Antarctica, David Wallace was to phone conversation. (The protracted tête-à-têtes between the brothers Mario and Hal in *Infinite Jest* could only have been concocted by an author who knew a little something about the art of the well-tempered—which is not the same thing as good-tempered—conversation.) He kept calling.

Now, it is just a fact that most people—high, low; old, young—go through life on ego autopilot. Who, after all, really listens to anything anyone has to say? Real conversations ought to be built on a spirit of equality and reciprocity, but are most exchanges truly symbiotic? Who's actually listening to *anything*? It's like this: the other person talks, blah blah, and you sit back, thinking mainly about how to advance your own position when it's your turn to speak again. Most people pretend more certainty than they have, but a guy who asked as many questions as David wasn't someone who thought he had all the answers. Of course, given David's experience résumé relative to mine, he had every right not to care too much about anything I had to say, but the guy really was the best active listener you could possibly imagine.

And it was now also clear that he was *not* someone it would behoove you to try to impress. And little did they know, those who did pretentiously try, that they were fated to become hapless victims of the DFW derision machine: "'*Dayyy*vid. I *assume* you know who I *am*,'" he would drawl, pitilessly mimicking the desperate-to-impress individual. "He's such a vain little twat."

He asked what my salary was. I told him, and he countered with his teaching salary at Illinois State and also the amounts of his book advances and grants. It was weird for him not to be poor anymore, he said.

"But I'm not 'rich,' though! I wish people would stop thinking that I'm suddenly rich."

(Seemed pretty rich to me then.)

He asked how many cups of coffee I drank a day. "I'm trying to figure out whether you fit the profile of an addictive personality."

I had one cup of deli coffee at my desk in the morning.

"OK, you don't."

DAVID, LATER IN THE CONVERSATION: "What are you planning to get your mom for Mother's Day?"

ME: "Flowers, probably, I don't know. Perfume maybe. You?"

HIM: "A Batman mouse pad."

There was one two-hour phone session one night, a couple of longer ones to follow.

"David, are you in the *bathroom*?"

"Goddammit. I was hoping you didn't hear that."

Said David, "I haven't talked to anyone this much on the phone since high school."

Had I ever gotten a B?

"Oh, yes," I said, "and worse. Did *you*?"

Answer: "*What?* No!"

DFW: "If Freddie Mercury had wanted to pop my adolescent cherry, I would have let him."

AM: (Say *what*?) "Are you gay, David?"

DFW (ORNERY): "Maybe slightly."

AM: "OK, so if you're gay, be gay." I added, invoking the great acting teacher Sanford Meisner (though I didn't know it): "Be who you really are."

DFW: "'Being who I really am' would create more problems than it would solve."

The previous night, at an *Esquire* party at a photography studio in the Meatpacking District, I had fainted. I told David this had happened and relayed how mortified I was about it.

"Are you pregnant?" he asked.

"Why would you ask *that*?"

A member of his family, he offered, had experienced some fainting spells during her recent pregnancy.

"I think you're pregnant," he said.

"I am definitely *not*," I replied.

Not that it would have been any of his business if I had been, actually.

Later: "Hey, Adrienne, were you depressed in high school?"

Yes, I guess, mildly, and in college, too, but I knew that high school and college wouldn't last forever. *Sic transit*, my friend. *Sic transit*. This too shall pass.

"Wow," he said, "I wish *I'd* been that mature then."

It was so depressing, he said, how he viewed most of his adult life as an effort to escape the misery of his late adolescence.

David and I learned we were both admirers of the stories "Hot Ice," by Stuart Dybek, and "Bullet in the Brain," by Tobias Wolff; the latter, about a cynical book critic's last moments, was, we both agreed, the greatest critic-revenge story ever. Indeed, it was a piece that gave David some cold comfort during the dark nights of his professional soul, which was to say whenever he made the mistake of reading his reviews. He was great on Hemingway ("there would be no *Esquire* without Hemingway," he said) and, of course, C. S. Lewis. His interest in commercial fiction, now well known, was then baffling to me. Of course, I considered myself far too high minded ever to have read the world's Clancys and Grishams (but I considered myself a populist, too); David would later send me a mass-market paperback copy of *Red Dragon* ("I just think Thomas Harris writes really good prose," said David prosaically), a book from which he could, for better or worse, quote extended passages.

I read it. Skillfully plotted, but constructed of sentences that vanished into airy nothingness the second after they'd been read. I had my literary requirements: I needed to be able to take some sort of pleasure in what I was reading; I wanted my own voluptuous little aesthetic experience.

THE WORLD HAD TURNED, SUDDENLY, INTO SPRING. TOM WOLFE'S NEW novel, *A Man in Full*, then with the title *Red Dogs*, was scheduled for publication in the fall. His publisher was selling the rights for a magazine excerpt, and on a call, the sub rights department indicated that it was expecting aggressive first-serial offers. "What number are you looking for?" I asked, as innocent as that cloudless April day. A million dollars was suggested as the starting bid. I did a colossal spit take with my Diet Coke.

Esquire had had about twenty legendary years with Wolfe, publishing, most famously, "There Goes (Varoom! Varoom!) That Kandy Kolored (Thphhhhhh!) Tangerine-Flake Streamline Baby (Rahghhhh!) Around the Bend (Brummmmmmmmmmmmmmm-mmm . . .)," a rollicking piece about custom-car and -motorcycle culture, and (at least) two great profiles: one about a stock car driver named Junior Johnson and the other about Robert Noyce, nicknamed the Mayor of Silicon Valley. Wolfe's nonfiction had opened up for me, as it had for countless other writers, the flashy ways in which voice, comedy, and satire could be used in journalism, and I was fascinated by the way he used dialogue. Although I *hated* the way he punctuated . . . and that whole crazy onomatopoeia thing—OMG. A gimmick that has not aged well. And was he too status obsessed, too lacking in pathos, and, frankly, not all that deep? But Wolfe was venerated at *Esquire*—one of the few old-school writers held in the highest esteem. The sense was, however, that he didn't want much to do with us. His work hadn't appeared in *Esquire* since the mid-eighties.

Red Dogs/A Man in Full was embargoed (the pages couldn't be reproduced or even discussed) in a highly theatrical—nay, dramaturgical—maneuver: the publisher summoned me, as well as editors from *The New Yorker, Rolling Stone,* and *Vanity Fair,* into its offices to read the manuscript. On a glorious spring day, I was led into a drab little office at Farrar, Straus and Giroux where, on a desk, the mammoth manuscript of *Red Dogs/A Man in Full* awaited me. It was a very odd experience, to be alone with this manuscript (which had been produced on an old-timey manual typewriter) for one entire day: here I was, twenty-six years old, and casting judgment upon the grandest of the grand old names. One of the main messages in a bottle I'd send myself: in order to do my job, I would need to maintain a serene confidence in my own taste and judgment. I had to believe in myself, even if few others did. As such, I was convinced that the novel was not actually very good—old, stale, out of touch. It also wasn't any fun. Wasn't Tom Wolfe supposed to be fun? (And when the book was published, most critics were aligned with my assessment.)

Back at work, I was candid. We wanted Wolfe back in the magazine badly, though, so I offered a fraction of the figure the publisher had proposed (still an absurd amount of money) for an excerpt I'd pulled together. I was too distracted to do much else the afternoon I waited for word back from the publisher and agent. When my offer was, predictably, declined, I found that I was a lot more upset than I'd expected to be. (Something needs to be said about how highly emotional these editorial jobs are, about how an editor can experience the entire repertoire of human mental states in about ten minutes at her desk.) *Rolling Stone*—the magazine with which Wolfe had been most closely associated for the past decade (it had published excerpts of *The Bonfire of the Vanities*)—got the first serial, and frankly, if I'd been shrewder, I'd have seen that this was a foregone conclusion. There were plenty of complaints around the office about how we'd most certainly been used as a stalking horse to get *RS*'s offer up.

I've never looked at *A Man in Full* again, yet I will say that I can recall scenes from it more vividly from that one day with it than I can many other books I'd deemed, in my exalted way, to be of higher classes.

Also, that spring there was another Norman Mailer event in the cards for me: a party for his book *The Time of Our Time,* an anvilesque collection of his reported pieces.

The party was held at the Rainbow Room, the splendid art deco landmark restaurant on the sixty-fifth floor of 30 Rockefeller Plaza. So long ago does that world now feel that this party may as well have happened in the thirties. Wasn't Bing Crosby on the record player, and weren't there Dubonnet cocktails and elegant ladies swirling around in cream-colored silk charmeuse?

I'd already learned my lesson and didn't attempt to speak with Mailer at the party, although I did somehow find myself talking to that twinkly old charmer George Plimpton, whom I'd never met before.

"Ah, the czarina!" Plimpton said, and kissed my hand.

Plimpton rattled off the subjects for a number of articles he'd written for *Esquire.* He mentioned a piece he'd done about Hugh Hefner.

"Now you *know,*" he said, "Hefner had *been* [pronounced like *bean*] in the *mailroom* at *Esquire* in the fifties."

This was not quite accurate—Hefner had worked as a copy-writer in the *Esquire* promotions department, but who's going to go around correcting George Plimpton?

"I *know,*" I said.

An *Esquire* journalist, one of these guys who seemed to know everyone, led me over to meet the writer Bret Easton Ellis, who was standing by a long, high window. The sun was starting to set; the sky was rosy. The suave *Esquire* writer seemed to think that I should want to do an excerpt of Ellis's forthcoming novel, *Glamorama.* (Everyone was always telling me whom and what I should publish.)

Ellis and I had a short and perfectly reasonable conversation, yet I will again admit that I had a hard time with these events. I hated performing at them: making frigid small talk, pretending to be amazed with someone—usually a man—when I was not. Most of the people I encountered were always pleasant enough, but what *was* it about dealing with people who had, or believed they had, some sort of power? You always had to play along and enact a charade. You had to meet these people in their illusions of themselves and pretend to see them as they wished to be seen. You had to pretend that the mask was real.

When a young woman at the Mailer party, a writer, said to me, "You're my hero," I was not self-deluded enough to think that she meant this fatuous remark by even 0.3 percent. Of course nothing real was there. Let's get to the truth: she wanted something from me. Multiple motives. There were always multiple motives. And since there were always multiple motives, everything often felt like a lie.

When I arrived at work the following morning, there was a voice-mail message from David, left in the middle of the night. He was wondering how the party had gone. David's line, when you were invited to return a phone call from him: "Call me any time. I'm in and out all day."

When we spoke, I mentioned that I had witnessed the following scene at the party the previous night: TV's own Tony Danza approached Mailer and Muhammad Ali (frail and seated in an armchair—the diminishment from Parkinson's was tough to see), got into a low crouch, and put up his fists. I died a little death when Mailer, age seventy-five, countered with an approximation of the same crouch, fists also raised.

"I don't know how you do your job," David said. "It's just like high school, and I *hated* high school. I would *not* have been able to handle your job at your age."

There were plenty of things I couldn't handle about my job, but they weren't the ones David was thinking about then. The main thing: I'd believed that if I got this job, or even if I got any sort of power, that I wouldn't be scared anymore. I had been hoping that power was the way to undo fear. But then you learn: the fear is here to stay. The fear was always there, except when I was at my desk, with a manuscript in front of me and a pen in hand.

The following Saturday morning, David called me at home at *eight* A.M. I was quite surprised to hear from him then and also, may I say, rather freaked out: Had he no sense of propriety?

At one point during the call, he seemed to think he heard me speaking to someone else in my apartment.

"Big *night*, huh?" he asked with unexpected sting.

And of course I lived alone, in my tiny West Village studio apartment, the one small space in the world I had to myself.

I explained to David that I was talking to my pet rabbit.

(I mean *obviously*.)

"Wait," David said, softening. *"What?"*

I related the story about how the rabbit came into my life: she had been a model bunny, purchased by a member of the *Esquire* art department to photograph for the artwork accompanying a fantastic short story I'd edited by the writer Elizabeth McCracken. Turned out: rabbits can't be returned to the pet stores on the Upper West Side from which they'd been purchased. No one else at work displayed any interest in adopting the bunny, so I decided to keep her in my office—for as long as I could get away with it.

"Aw," David said.

The rabbit-in-the-office experiment lasted three, four days, tops. The dream ended the moment Granger's excellent assistant (Fran was one of the few staffers who remained from the ancien régime)—a genuine "dame," in the classic Sinatraian sense of the term—declared, in the hard-boiled, hilarious way she had, in the direction of the editorial department's cubicles, "That thing has *bugs*." So the rabbit came home with me, living a cage-free, if not overly hygienic, lifestyle on Waverly Place. (A few years later, when I mentioned to the brilliant McCracken that thanks to her story, I'd acquired a rabbit, she said, "I hate to think of any animal in a cage." I was pleased to offer the reply: "Oh, she's *not* in a cage.") I loved that little rabbit a lot. Her name was Lulu.

"Aw," said David.

He got onto a riff about that ur-bunny novel, *Watership Down*. He could give me his copy of it but warned that I would make fun of his marginal notes of "wow!" and "neat!" I was promised a cycle of already-written DFW rabbit poems narrated from a canine perspective—"Rabbit Songs," as he called them, and an homage of sorts to John Berryman's *The Dream Songs,* an important influence on *Infinite Jest.* Jocularly, he recited a bit:

"We like rabbits / yes, we do / we like to break their heads in two!"

From my end, I was charmed by my sardonic, alarmingly quick-witted, and . . . *peculiar* new friend. I got a kick out of him, as we say in Ohio (or at least as my mother says). Which was exactly his intention, of course. Yes, I sensed that he was a person with poor impulse control and even poorer boundary issues, and without a doubt his sense of entitlement was extreme. And was it possible that this was just what he *did*—entertain ladies with his torrent of words? And was my number simply the one he happened to have in front of him?

Plus, and more to the point, didn't David Foster Wallace, this Tasmanian devil of energy and ideas, have anything *better* to do? Here was a man so varyingly engaged and multidisciplinary, so supernaturally productive—how did he even have the time? For Christ's sake, *I* didn't have the time. Again, "Adult World" wasn't actually the only story in the July 1998 issue. Did he have any awareness of that? Yes, of course he did, because I'd told him about some of the other pieces I was working on. I had even gone so far as to mention the header for the section: "RANDOM ACTS OF FICTION." (Dave Eggers came up with that one.)

"There is nothing 'random' about my fiction," David had said. And then he'd added a malicious little "I can't speak for your other authors, though."

"So why are you calling me?" I asked him at home one night. "What's this all about?"

I mean, I wasn't much of a conversationalist anyway. I didn't get it. Was he just bored?

"Because you're blood in the water for a shark," David said, with menace. And less menacingly, more charmingly (which is to say even more menacingly), "Also because talking to you is so incredibly fun. We should sit down in person someday with a pot of coffee and talk about all this stuff we've been talking about."

"Sure," I said. "Why not?"

On an afternoon in May, after three months of phone calls, a message awaited on my office voice mail:

"Hey, Adrienne. It's Dave Wallace. I believe it would be more fruitful to meet in person. If you happen to call me back—I hope this is not too presumptuous—it will be easier to talk in person. Thank you."

After letting him sweat it out for an hour or two, I returned the call.

"I'm sorry I left you that howlingly lonely message," he said.

"Oh, please."

"I didn't think you'd call me back."

"Oh, please."

He was coming to New York.

I actually wished he weren't, because even then I knew that this was a possible collision course—one that could very well end with twisted metal and broken glass, flames of woe, flames of wrath.

"We should go to a restaurant that serves fish that tastes like the underside of a dock!" he said.

I was getting my first glimmerings: to know David Wallace was to be involved in a constant process of interpretation.

16

The first engagement was to play tennis at the East River Park. It was a Sunday morning in the early summer. I had located my high school tennis racquet in my one and only closet, and know this: the racquet had rainbow-colored strings, a tennis fashion fad in the late eighties, and it was great. So I was set to go and trying as hard as possible to ignore one small issue. I'm terrible at tennis, just terrible.

David and I spoke on the phone before I left to meet him at his hotel.

"Would you mind picking up something for me to eat?" he asked plaintively. "I'm *starving*." His order consisted of a plain bagel (untoasted; no butter, no cream cheese—"as is," as the bagel shops say), a Caffeine-Free Diet Coke, and a bottle of water.

I must say that the food request peeved me, mildly, and in the taxi on the way to the hotel, I had a whole dialogue with myself about it. "Why can't he leave the hotel and get his *own* food?"; "He thinks women are there to *serve him,* does he?"; "He drinks *Diet Coke* for breakfast?"

The answer to at least one of those last two questions was a resounding yes.

David was sitting in an armchair in the hotel lobby. I went toward him, grinning (my peevishness had passed) and waving frantically. He saw me and stood. No freaking *way* he was six-two. He was in a state of great dishevelment, wearing an ensemble of T-shirt and cargo shorts and, in violation of all possible flag codes, an American-flag bandanna. He gave a quick leonine stare to my racquet and extended an arm straight, as if a semaphore signal. We shook hands. (Several years later, the last time I saw him, he held his arm out to me in the exact same way, as if we were strangers. Maybe we were.) The first thing you thought about him was that he was a warm person with a gentle manner. The second thing was that he was dreadfully ill at ease. But David's discomfort and clumsiness upon first acquaintance only made him more endearing.

He gathered his things—he had a canvas bag with a lot of stuff in it, and he had his tennis racquet, too—and we got a taxi. As we slid into the back seat, we were met with a scent: high, stinging, tough-to-ignore BO.

David gave an audible sniff. "Is that me?" he asked, smelling one armpit, then the other.

"It's definitely not *me,*" I said.

We each cracked our windows.

"You actually buckled your seat belt?" he asked.

"Of course."

He buckled his, too. We each scooted as far away from the other as we could get.

Shy understands shy, so I started chattering away—my preferred mode when I am with someone even more socially challenged than I. It's so embarrassing to recall this now, but I told David about my tenth-grade crush on a particular Scandinavian tennis player (I didn't like tennis, but I definitely did like this guy and the concept of Scandinavia—I've always been pro-Continental, I guess you could say; always tilting toward Europe), whose picture I had taped up on the inside of my locker door at school. Don't ask me why I thought David needed to know this. High school didn't seem so long ago then. It *wasn't* so long ago. I had graduated only eight years before.

"He's supposed to be really dumb," David said.

"Yeah, but he's pretty cute, though," I said, trying to keep it light, always trying to keep it light.

"When I did that tennis piece, they made fun of him on the tour for being so stupid." That tennis piece was the one about Michael Joyce that had run in *Esquire*.

David regarded me with hard eyes.

"Do you have a thing for older men?"

"Not that I'm aware of."

"You may have daddy issues."

"I don't," I said.

"You certainly have questionable taste in tennis players," he said with the smallest of smiles on the long, handsome DFW face. "But at least it wasn't *Agassi,* I guess." He volunteered his own celebrity crush: Calista Flockhart. "Her eyes are as big as *plates*."

When we arrived at the courts, there was a snag in the plan. No one told me that you had to reserve one in advance. For someone whose motto is "Measure twice, cut once" (for my eighteenth birthday, my best friend Michelle gave me a *This Old House* mug—the Bob Vila years—with this handy axiom on it), this was an atypical oversight. You can be sure that I did a lot of apologizing to David. He was fine about it, though, and my secret was that I was more than fine about it, because my mistake meant that we wouldn't actually have to play tennis. ("You're not 'bad,' *necessarily*," David would say later when we did knock the ball around. "You just seem like someone who hasn't played for a long time." And he would indeed mock, mercilessly, my racquet of the many-colored strings.)

We decided to sit on the grass outside the court and chat. We had a view of the East River and the Williamsburg Bridge. It was one of the first very warm days of the year and the sky was a high cloudless blue. But did David even notice? How much interest did he even take in aesthetic pleasures? David was Augustinian, self-punitive in tendency: his was a fallen, decadent picture of the world, a humanity that needed to be redeemed. That redemption did not, and would not, come easily, however.

"It's so pretty today," I said.

"I couldn't live in New York," he said. "I would feel as if I were living on some bombed-out, postapocalyptic *Blade Runner*–ish movie set."

"Oh, it's not so bad. New York is great, actually."

"Well, I don't know how anyone can live here." He said that he would find it odious to be just another writer in New York, jockeying for status along with everyone else. "At home, people are like, 'Duh, you write books? What are *those*?' No one there understands what I do for a living."

He noted that Bloomington was cheap, the people were nice, he didn't have to lock his front door, and he could exist undercover there. This was a very different assessment of his town from the one he would give me four years later, weeks before he moved to California: "I fucking hate *everything* about this place."

"You could make some new friends in New York," I said. "Most people aren't actually *writers*, you know."

Although, given the jobs I had, it actually *did* seem as if most people in New York were writers. Most people everywhere seemed to be writers, and the thing they seemed to like to do more than anything else was submit their work to me at *Esquire*.

"I don't need any new friends," he said. "I know enough people."

We picked at dandelions and crabgrass. We talked about our families. When I was in the middle of a very poor description of the kind of statistics my father did, David interrupted and said, "Yes, like W. Edwards Deming," citing the guru of whatever type of statistics this was. I found it impressive that David was able to extract a pearl from the sludge I'd given him to work with.

When I told David that I had no siblings, his response—traditionalist, conservative (this was David, too, a big part of him; he wasn't much of a radical, except artistically)—was "Why? Was this your parents' choice?" He did an impression of his mother, a writing professor, performing the Eudora Welty story "Why I Live at the P.O." and told me about some of the tricks he'd stolen from her when he taught his own writing classes. They were excellent tricks, they really were.

I asked him where he'd gone to high school.

A pause.

He would always seem surprised whenever I signaled that I didn't know such-and-such biographical detail about him—annoyingly, David was, in fact, a celebrity, a reality I always kept forgetting. (*He* never forgot, though.) At this point, I think he'd assumed I'd read whatever those articles were about him, but I hadn't read them and never would; all the data I had about David always came from David—and that was plenty.

"I went to a really shitty public school in Urbana, Illinois," he said.

Hey, I had a friend from college who'd graduated from his high school—did David know him?

He did not.

"Remember, I'm much older than you."

"You don't seem that much older."

"I'm very immature."

He said that he probably would have been better off in boarding school, but his parents couldn't have afforded it. He was contemplating going to his twentieth high school reunion, but all his friends knew he wasn't very reliable, so no one would be surprised if he didn't show. Actually, they'd be surprised if he did.

"What was your favorite book when you were a little girl?" he asked.

From the Mixed-Up Files of Mrs. Basil E. Frankweiler, obviously.

"Why did you like it?"

"Because it's fancy."

"How old were you when you read it?"

I wasn't sure, but I took a stab at an answer. At that age, David said, amusingly and calibratedly underselling, all he'd done was memorize every possible fact there was to memorize about dinosaurs.

"Your sunglasses make you look like a superhero villain," David said. "May I ask you to take them off? I'd like to be able to see your eyes."

"But I *always* wear sunglasses outside during the day," I commonsensically explained, and kept the shades on.

David rooted around in the plastic bag of food I had brought, had a little complaint about the brand of water (Evian), proclaiming it "too velvety," but drank it anyway. He dug into his canvas bag and showed me his battered address book, turning to the page with my very own name on it. "Look," he said. "That's *you.*"

He offered me the book, and I flipped through the many, many names, addresses, and numbers, all written in the spooky, spidery DFW hand. I noted that David seemed to know everyone—or at least seemed to have everyone's contact information.

What else was in his bag? He wanted to show me. Let's see—there was a secondary "head hankie," a white one, in case he perspired through the American-flag one he had on, and a yellow legal pad—"that's in case you say something witty." (This was David, too: a thief and a vampire.) There were some books. There were pens. There was an amber-colored container with pills in it. He showed me his Illinois driver's license. I showed him my license from Ohio. We shared the bagel. We exchanged "how I lost my virginity" stories (neither story interesting). He sang the Madness song "Our House." (He had a great singing voice. He was also completely stuck in the eighties music-wise.) He spoke French. I tried to speak French back. He held forth about the very important distinction between "I could care less" and "I couldn't care less." He told me when his birthday was, the name of the city where he was born, and his parents' ages, and he recited from memory the entirety of the Philip Larkin poem "This Be The Verse," whose first line is, of course (say it with me now): "They fuck you up, your mum and dad."

"It's odd. It's as if I'm here *offering* myself to you," he said. "I feel totally comfortable with you. And I'm never comfortable with anyone."

The important point so far about that morning, which became that early afternoon, was that everything was very sweet, and fast. I was about to say that everything was also very ordinary, but that would not have been true.

But.

"I need you to know some things about me," David said. "This is strictly dead man's talk. Do you understand?"

It was at this moment that a firm code of omertà was established—because David established it—in our relationship. The tacit "dead man's talk" agreement that would continue for the years I knew him. It was our thing, though it was his thing with plenty of others, too, I'm sure. "Dead man's talk?" he would ask. "Dead man's talk" would be the only possible reply.

"I am mentally ill," he said.

He spoke of a suicide attempt in college, said he had taken a year off school (graduated a year late and lied to the day about the reason) and had gone back home and driven a bus. Later, there were other attempts. He told me he'd been to McLean, the famous psychiatric hospital in Boston.

"I couldn't do anything right, not even kill myself!" he said.

Like so many other of David's most deliberately self-deprecating one-liners, this mordant comment had the character of something rehearsed, rehashed.

"I also need you to know that I'm a drug addict and an alcoholic," he said.

David said he had gotten clean a decade before and had dedicated his life since to his sobriety. There were stories about rehab, about his time in the halfway house that would become his model for Ennet House in *Infinite Jest*. When he was younger he'd gone through life thinking that he was better than everyone else, "but nothing breaks you down quicker than cleaning toilets in a halfway house filled with a bunch of terminal-stage drug addicts."

He said he'd found the only effective path to sobriety in AA. "The dumber it is, the better it works," he noted of the seeming simplicity of the AA ethos. He added that this was generally a good lesson for life, too.

David asked about my experiences with drugs. I explained that I was so squeaky clean in that department that I'd barely even *seen* any drugs; if I ever found myself in the unhappy situation of being at a party with drugs, my friends would always leave the room to do their substance-related activities ("Oh, God, *Adrienne's* here") rather than deal with my stringent disapproval face-to-face. In many ways, I was as *rasa* a *tabula* as there ever could have been. Maybe this appealed to David. Or maybe it didn't, who knows? This is my story, not his.

"I'm jealous that you don't need AA and I do," he said.

After we'd spent a few hours on the grass outside the tennis courts, we went for a walk. I could sense that he was silently freaking out about carrying his tennis racquet—his worry (that he was a spectacular self-parody of David Foster Wallace wandering the streets of the Lower East Side) emanated from him in waves—and I asked if he wanted me to hold it. He did, and wouldn't you know it, I was the one who carried that racquet (and mine) for the rest of the day.

When we were on Lower Broadway, David said quietly, "I have something to ask you, Andrea."

"*What* did you just call me?"

"What? I don't know. What did I say?"

"You called me 'Andrea.'"

"Oh shit, I did? I'm sorry."

Question: Did he even know whom he was talking to?

"You *do* know my name, don't you?" I asked.

"Um, *yes*," he said. "It's just that I've never known any Adriennes before. I'm a space cadet. Get ready."

Never did find out what he wanted to ask or who Andrea was.

We went to a restaurant—an upmarket diner, really, Time Cafe—on Lafayette Street. It was the sort of place where you could get lunch at 3:00, which it was. As we got seated at the table, David said, in that soft-spoken, guileless, nearly childlike way he had that could lull you into thinking he was less brilliant, and less dangerous, than he was, "I usually take first dates to the slaughterhouse near where I live."

Had I even considered this a "date"? I'm not sure. David ordered a turkey burger (his burger line in those days: "Well done. And I mean *italicize* 'well done'"). I got the pasta. Before our meals arrived, David pulled the amber-colored container out of his bag and took out a pill.

"What's *that* for?" I asked.

"Syphilis," he deadpanned.

I had a sip of water. I had a sip of milk. (I was then still an unembarrassable orderer of milk in restaurants.)

"I'm going to tell you the worst thing I've ever done," he said. "Please don't react immediately."

He told me that during a crippling period of insanity when he was trying to stay sober, he'd bought a gun and hired a hit man to kill someone. (Later, David's biographer would say that David had just considered buying a gun and hiring a hit man. I have no idea where the truth lies—David was, shall we say, an unreliable narrator.)

"I can see you scooting your chair back from the table," he said, wincing away. "I'm sorry. That's one of the things with being an addict. You can never tell when you're making other people uncomfortable."

This man sitting across the table from me had had a very different life experience from mine, I now knew. It seemed important to remember that.

"Can you even imagine *me* with a *gun*? I'm such a spaz, I would end up accidentally shooting *myself*!"

He placed both hands on the table.

"Dead man's talk?" he asked.

"Dead man's talk," I said obediently.

"Now maybe you can see how much I trust you," he said.

But he barely knew me. On what basis had he decided that I was to be trusted?

"Do you hate me?"

This would not be the last time he would ask me this question.

"No," I replied.

"I need you to understand that I'm a different guy now," he said. As he spoke, his hands tremored slightly on the tabletop.

"Your hands are shaking," I said.

He raised his hands, holding them out flat in front of him. "Do you see?" he asked. "I can't keep them still."

In addition to everything else wrong with him, he said, he was allergic to sugar. I held my hands up next to his. Still as stones.

"Do you want any of this?" David asked, pushing his plate toward me. The turkey burger really was appallingly well done. "It's yummy."

In my restaurant experiences with David, he was always trying to share his food with you. Also in my restaurant experiences with David, he never once ordered anything I would actually have wanted to eat.

"If you met my friends at home, everyone would be *very* confused: I never go out with anyone who's *appropriate* for me. 'Dave, who's this attractive, intelligent, *sane* woman?'"

He had created this whole fantasy relationship when he barely knew me? Didn't I get any say in the matter? Also, he wasn't being very nice to his ex-girlfriends. A note to the men of the world: when you speak ill of your ex-girlfriends, we know that we'll be next up.

"And you'd actually even be able to deal with my parents," he said. He added that I would like his mother, whom he described as tall, blond, highly theatrical, and a Meryl Streep doppelgänger. She'd recently won a national teaching award, he said, and placed a hand over his heart.

"I'm almost never attracted to a *nice* woman," he said.

Now whenever David described someone as "nice" in this tone of generalized blandness, you'd start to worry that the nice—but, in truth, not overly remarkable—other person held his interest just about as much as would a walnut. I had a bad feeling about this. Was he also suggesting that he'd already decided I was boring?

"If I'm presented with two relationship choices—one of them sunshine and flowers, and the other a flashing red light: *beep, beep, honk, honk, danger, danger!*—I'll see that red light, and I'll say, 'By gosh, that's where *I'm* going!'"

I wanted to know why someone would choose to becloud his own happiness. I was just some regular person, Adri, Matt Miller, the most regular person in the world, and as stoical as Seneca (sometimes). I didn't understand.

"Why do you *do* that?" I asked.

How did he phrase it, exactly? I wish I could remember, but the essence of his reply was that in order for him to function, he needed extreme highs and extreme lows. I do clearly remember this: "When you exist without the extremes, you *miss* them." And then: "I *always* make the wrong decision, in every area of my life. I'm defective. You will soon learn this."

The expected narrative would have gone this way: David would have presented himself as a survivor, as someone who had fought through the hopelessness of addiction and profound mental illness and emerged on that hard-won other side. But with David there would be no narrative of the expected answer—ever. Throughout the years of my relationship with him, David's psychological existence would be the principal topic of our conversations. The other topic, the one I was better at dealing with—and, I hope, better at understanding—was his work.

I tried to pay for lunch. As I opened my wallet, David took a look at my mass of credit cards. "It would scare me too much to have all of those," he said, and asked if he could pay. I'd never thought I had a lot of credit cards, but since he brought it up, maybe it *was* true that my wallet did sort of have a bulge in it like a meatball.

As he signed the bill, he asked if I wanted to have dinner with him.

Every Friday, I'd bring home a tote bag of reading material from work—submissions, review copies of books—and I'd set aside Sundays as my big reading day. I loved my reading time, and I approached each manuscript with such a crazy sense of expectation then; there was always the hope that maybe *this* story would be, say, the new "Snows of Kilimanjaro," the new "The Things

They Carried." It really is so true that editors need to be people of enormous faith.

"Haven't you got anything else to do today?" I asked.

He'd already set up several evenings of activities with me during his trip. Back in Bloomington, he'd (weirdly, for he knew me not at all) given me his American Express card number so I could buy tickets to a play for us to see (and went on to say that I could use his credit card to buy anything else I wanted for myself) and asked me to attend some other events with him.

"Not a thing," David said.

17

David wanted to go to his hotel and change clothes, and I acceded to a stop there. The room had ivory-colored wallpaper printed with blue-green palm leaves. On the high dresser in the room was an array of orangey translucent prescription bottles; on the desk, pointing toward the bed, was a black Vornado fan he'd brought from home. That fan took up one whole duffel bag.

I sat primly on the bed and watched David as he listened to several accumulated voice-mail messages on the room phone. He provided a caustic little commentary about each message and did an impression of one of the callers (OK, twist my arm—it was Jonathan Franzen).

As he placed the receiver back in the cradle, he said, "I'm just going to pretend I didn't hear any of those."

The substance of some of the messages had to do with a dinner party he was supposed to attend that night. He didn't want to go, he said.

This was of interest. I reminded him that he'd told me he didn't have any plans tonight.

"Yeahhhh," David said. "I may have told you a little fib."

The more he talked about the party, the more certain I became that it had been organized for him, as the guest of honor.

"I think you should go," I said.

"Eh. They always get sushi. And they know I *hate* sushi."

He went over to the TV and found the station showing the French Open. He asked if I would mind if he took a shower.

"Go for it," I said.

He left the bathroom door half-open (he later said he'd been hoping that I would come in as he showered), and I moved over to the floor, sitting in front of the TV. I turned the channel from tennis to golf, mostly to mess with him. The Memorial Tournament, always held at Buckeye golf legend Jack Nicklaus's country club outside Columbus, was on. I will admit that my grandparents were big golf people (for a couple of years in the late sixties, my grandfather had been the president of his country club, a position that had seemed to me just about as high prestige as being the minister plenipotentiary to France), and when I was a little kid they'd always come to visit us in Columbus on Memorial Tournament weekends. They'd go to the tournament with my parents, returning with humble gifts for me that immediately took on a totemic significance: a white-and-green Memorial Tournament visor, a pen with a floating golf ball, multi-colored golf tees. At another more recent stop on the PGA tour, the Firestone Tournament, my grandmother ("George") had been hit on the head with a wayward golf ball as she sat on a folding stool at the third green. (My parents continue to maintain that this accident was the beginning of the end for her.)

My point here: golf is the only sport I had any actual real feelings about. Do with that what you will.

The shower stopped. When David emerged from the bathroom, he was fully clothed, thank God (I knew he would be), and wearing a blue button-down shirt and cargo shorts. His hair was wet. He started hunting around the room for his glasses. I got up and started searching for them, too; found them facedown on the nightstand. He put the glasses on and squinted at the TV.

"You switched it to *golf*?" he asked.

The blue button-down shirt looked as if it had been wadded up for decades in a swamp of some sort. He could see me looking at his shirt with distrust.

"My clothes always get wrinkled when I travel," he said enlighteningly.

Well, I had just the perfect solution for him then: hang up those wrinkled old clothes in the bathroom, turn the shower on hot, and close the door—you've got yourself an instant steam clean.

"Wow, that is *so smart*," David said with just a tad too much gusto. "I've never thought of that before: *steam your shirts in the bathroom*. That's just *so smart*."

Seriously?

"How does suggesting that you *steam your shirts* make me 'smart'?" I asked. "It's like Hints from Heloise or something. It's just housewife wisdom—it's the opposite of 'smart,' actually."

David's gaze at me was sharp.

"Touché," he said.

He pulled an armchair over in front of the TV. He asked if I minded if he changed the channel.

"Not at all," I said.

He switched the TV back to the French Open and sat down.

I asked him again about the dinner party.

"They know I blow things off all the time," he said, glued to the televised tennis. "It's fine."

Now, I'm not saying I'm ever the smartest person in the room, but I do believe that I have the intuition of a Jedi, and I knew how the scene at the dinner party would go: the people there would be watching the door all evening, waiting, waiting, for David to walk through it. When it was eventually accepted that he was not going to show, the chatter around the table would go, "Welp, Dave disappeared with some *girl* again." It was with a quiver of horror that I recognized this girl was, in the present circumstance, me.

"You're not going to call them?" I asked. "You should at least call them. Don't you think you're being rude?"

"But I don't *like* them," David said, and gave me a small coy smile. "I like *you*."

He then went on to identify a couple of these people as his best friends (a Wallace specialty: saying mean things about his friends) and told me he'd been having an argument with some of them about Kant at dinner the previous evening.

"That sounds interesting," I said. "What were you talking about?"

"You wouldn't understand," David said tartly, eyes back on the TV.

Yes, yes, I appreciated that David was so intellectually brilliant that he could make *anyone* feel like the most junior member of an Attic society, but he needed to understand that he would treat me as an equal. He had placed me in the blanket category of "Woman." He was telling me that he didn't believe I was capable of playing with the big boys.

I stood up from the bed.

"You can't talk to me like that," I said.

He turned and looked at me in astonishment.

"What?" he asked.

Suddenly, I wasn't even sure that I liked him. He obviously didn't exactly hold me in terribly high regard. In an instant, the entire day spent with him collapsed, and everything was exposed as a sham, revealed as a toy town made of cardboard and plastic; if I were to take a closer look, I'd see that the walls were held up with scaffolding, the nightstand and chairs were props, and the phone was just a toy phone an actor uses. The weird candor or whatever it was David had been offering, and the relationship fast-trackiness, had merely been some sort of performance of intimacy. I could see that now. I could see it quite clearly.

"I don't know *who* you think you're talking to," I said. "Whatever assumptions you've made about me, David, are incorrect."

He winced and stood.

Would I stay in this room with him, or would I walk out? I would learn a lot from the very complex experience of knowing David over the years. For one: he helped me understand that anger is *active,* that it is a process and a decision.

"Look, I'm *really* sorry," he said, in what I believed sounded like genuine self-rebuke. He came a couple of steps toward me. "I'm an asshole. I'm a sexist asshole."

Anger is not just something that *happens* to you—it is a choice you make.

"You're not going to leave, are you?" he asked, and placed his hands square on my shoulders. We were about the same height.

It is a *choice* to follow your anger forward, step by step.

"Please," he said, "don't leave."

In this case, I would not follow my anger. I would choose to back down.

"Are we still friends?" he asked.

I would find it in myself to give him another chance.

"We are," I said.

"Excellent," David said, and lowered his hands from my shoulders. "I grew up in a house with strong women and I have a lot of experience with being told when I'm being a sexist shithead. You'll find that I've been trained to *always* put down the toilet seat, too."

I sat. So did he. We watched TV in silence for a few moments.

"Can I ask you a question?" he finally said. "Everyone says that I remind them of James Spader in *sex, lies, and videotape.*" Did I detect a soupçon of pride there? "Do you see that about me?"

Although it is true that there is little on earth as glorious as eighties-era Spader—the best of all possible Spaders—I couldn't have imagined that anyone had ever mentioned any sort of resemblance to the *sex, lies, and videotape* Spader, a louche vagrant who videotapes women talking about their sex lives, to David as praise.

"You do know that the whole thing about that character is that he's a pervert, right?" I asked.

"Oh, I know," he said.

David was sitting with his bare feet up on the seat of the chair, knees bent. It is a fact that he would continue, years after he wrote his famous essay about existential dread and the Caribbean cruise, to privately brag about how he'd won the Best Legs Competition on the ship.

He asked how my parents had explained sex to me when I was a little girl. (What he actually said was "the birds and the bees.") I told him that my parents weren't big talkers in that arena and that they'd given me the good-natured book *Where Did I Come From?*, written by Peter Mayle of all people, and illustrated with grimy-in-a-specifically-seventies-way cartoon people. He said he knew the book—a friend's child had a copy of it. He started speaking of his past habit of cruising AA meetings for emotionally fragile women ("It's hard for me to even go now because everyone sits around and talks about me"), of targeting married women and young mothers— that was but the beginning of the horror show, I would soon learn.

Somehow we got on to the monograph *Suicide,* by Émile Durkheim (I'd never read it, unsurprisingly—but who has?), and he wanted to know my thoughts about the ethics of suicide. I said this was a subject I'd given zero thought to. Next we were into a discussion of Ian Curtis, the singer from Joy Division, who, said David, had committed suicide at twenty-three by putting a noose around his neck and standing on an ice block as it melted. I was aware of the vague outlines of Curtis's end, but the ghastly method David described was news to me. (David's account was untrue, by the way, and I have to believe he knew this.) He said that he admired Curtis's ingenuity for coming up with the ice block idea.

"Can you imagine hating yourself *that* much?" he asked.

I said I could not.

I watched as David opened a tin of chewing tobacco, which he'd bought earlier in the day at a deli.

"Why don't you smoke cigarettes instead?" I asked. "Wouldn't it be less of a hassle?"

He replied that he wouldn't be able to play tennis if he smoked. He shook the tobacco tin at me and asked if I wanted to try some.

"No, thank you," I said.

"Are you sure?"

"No, thank you."

"Come on," he said. "Just try it."

He brandished the can again.

"No, thank you," I said.

He removed a bit of tobacco and put it in his hand. He stood. As he came toward me, he offered the extraordinary biographical tidbit that he'd dated a woman—actually, he said "female," just to make it extra creepy—who chewed tobacco.

"Always an attractive habit in a woman," I said. "And in a man."

I related how the only tobacco chewers I'd ever known were gigantic Ohioan rednecks. An image I'll never be able to delete from my permanent Rolodex: on the floor in front of my senior-year locker, a Mountain Dew can tipped on its side, brown tobacco fluid oozing out of it in really just the most atrocious way.

"Come on," he said, holding his hand out. "You know you want to."

I took the brown nubbin from David's palm. *"You,"* I said, "are a bad influence."

"Yes," he said, "I am."

I looked at David. David looked at me. His eyes were a rich chestnut flecked with gold.

I put the plug of tobacco in my mouth.

Item: wintergreen tobacco, in case you've ever wondered, has the mouthfeel of sulfuric acid.

I couldn't get into the bathroom fast enough. I spat the vile thing into a tissue, turned the water on, rinsed my mouth, and kept on rinsing.

"You're *gross,*" I shouted over the water.

"Hahaha," said David's voice from the other room. "Your teeth turned green. Hahaha."

He came into the bathroom. I considered his reflection in the mirror.

"People who make other people chew tobacco should be prosecuted for war crimes," I said.

I pivoted to face him. His hair was now completely dry.

"You're welcome to use my toothbrush," he said, and smiled.

LATER IN THE WEEK, THERE WAS A PANEL DISCUSSION FOR *HARPER'S* magazine. The subject of the panel was book-to-film adaptation, and David maintained that he was submitting to the thing only as a favor to his sometimes friend Charis Conn, one of his editors at *Harper's.* The story David told me was that Charis had asked to stay with him for a week or so in Bloomington so she could work on her novel. (This whole setup seemed very weird to me, but whatever.) The visit reached an unpleasant finale, said David, that involved shouting and slammed doors and an imperial directive for Charis (whom I also knew—she was a piece of work herself): *Leave at once, I say.* (David often did tend to exaggerate for narrative effect; he also liked to present himself as a comic—and semi-deranged—character in his stories.) His participation in the panel was atonement for his impetuous boy-king behavior. This was the kind of thing he'd try to do all the time—make reparations to parties he felt he'd wronged. David was always seeking absolution.

"Whenever there's a problem in a relationship," he once said, "I always assume it's my fault."

The *Harper's* panel was held in a university auditorium on West Twelfth Street. David had been complaining about the thing all day and asked me if I could help him get in a better headspace about it. He had a therapeutic stress-relief idea, he said: he wanted me to meet him in the empty theater a couple of hours early and have sex with him in the seats. This request completely blew my mind.

HIM: "But if we really hate it, we can stop."
ME: "What is *wrong* with you?"
(Reminder: he was thirty-six years old.)

I now understood that David was an outré character, and I was fine with that. I had no problem with outré. My professional life was spent dealing with outré, massaging outré. But who on earth did he think *I* was?

The event was standing room only, and I counted myself lucky to get to wedge into an alcove along the side of the auditorium. It was a total hipster crowd—lots of thrift-store clothes and hoodies, beards and barrettes. (Question: Was Mr. Facial Hair in the second row wearing that green John Deere T-shirt to signal an allegiance with the rural working class or to mock it?) Everyone in the audience seemed very amped up to be there, and the overall vibe was much more "concert" than "literary panel."

The panelists—David, two other novelists, and two film directors—came onstage. David ambled along in the middle, towering over everyone else, wearing a T-shirt with suspiciously tight sleeves—he always enjoyed a shirt that provided at least a subtle biceps reveal—and for some reason chewing a toothpick. Let's not put too fine a point on it: everyone in the audience had come to see him. David was the one they wanted. I got to hear a young woman with a better seat than I had say, "I'm going to marry him when I grow up!"

The panel was deadly, as these things always are (one of the panelists, Dale Peck, made the announcement that he believed all art should be didactic), but David of course managed to be witty, charming, and extremely interesting. The audience tittered knowingly when he made a sexual joke about slipping videotapes into his VCR. I couldn't decide which made me uneasier: the joke or the audience's reaction to it.

The plan, as laid out by David, was for me to stay in the auditorium after the thing was over, near the stage, and wait for him. The panel ended and the audience filtered out, going back to their real lives; I loitered creepily at the front of the theater. Another of the panelists, the movie director Todd Solondz—who was, inexplicably, a nineties indie-film darling (and is now enjoying a well-deserved professional oblivion)—slunk out from backstage. Solondz was probably about forty but dressed like a student: thrift-store-type clothes, sneakers, and thick black nerdlinger glasses.

As chipperly as possible, I asked him if he'd seen David. With cold eyes, Solondz gave me the once-over.

"You wait *out there,*" he said, and pointed to the exit.

I tried to explain that David had told me to wait for him here. I was merely following *his* instructions. I actually *knew* the guy!

My foil was having none of it. He shook his head.

"You can wait for your autograph *outside,*" Solondz said, "with *everyone else.*"

I had an ace up my sleeve, of course: I was in fact my own person and was not in need of any DFW-imparted legitimacy. I could still sputter the dread "Do you know who I *am*?" Yeah, that move was still very much available.

But the thing was I had done this before (and would do it again, alas), and I'd felt preposterously like the Person of Consequence in Gogol's "The Overcoat": *"Do you know to whom you are speaking?"* It's never pretty to see someone defending her illusions about herself. And anyway, to be honest, whenever I uttered my ponderous title, I always felt like an actor playing the part of Literary Editor. (This is not, however, to say that I didn't always take my job very seriously.)

So I decided not to put up a stink with this man. It wouldn't have gotten me anywhere anyway—he had made his judgment of me and that was that.

In high dudgeon, I stalked up toward the exit. Back to my point about how anger is a process and a choice.

But maybe someday, I thought, I'd be in a position to fire this guy—yeah, fire him from . . . *something*. Or maybe I'd be the head of some movie studio somewhere, and I'd cancel this guy's movie. Oooh, I looked forward to *that* one. Just when he least expected it: *canceled*. It would be so great. I mean, I hated Solondz's movies anyway, loathed their aesthetic and their nasty worldview. (I also knew that when you're consumed with thoughts of retaliation, you are probably not coming down on the right side of things.)

A male voice called my name.

David had his canvas messenger bag slung over his right shoulder, and he'd put on a sport coat, a big boxy one.

"Where are you going?" he asked. "Why are you leaving?"

He stopped a few feet in front of me and we faced each other. With one athletic hop, he jumped toward me. David moved like an athlete; his actions were always crisp, brisk, tight. He was not a spaz, never a spaz, despite those jokey avowals.

He grasped my hand and gave it a shake. His hand was firm, and soft, and warm.

"Hi," he said, looking me steadily in the eye. He drew my hand to his chest and placed it over his heart. "I'm Dave."

Although I knew the feeling was unreasonable, I was mad at him, slightly. I pulled my hand away. I half blamed him for leaving me vulnerable to humiliations of all sorts. I told him what had happened.

"I'd rather *die* than let someone think I'm some sort of *groupie*," I said.

I mean, who would even *want* to be a literary groupie? Most of the (male) fiction writers I knew were so odd and persnickety, they were always broke (and they were *always* talking about money), and, worst of all, *they were always at home.* Literary groupies really just had to be groupies of the lowest order.

"I wouldn't worry about it too much, sweetie," David said as we went through the door. He had just started calling me sweetie. "He's an odd dude. Can you imagine him in high school? I'm sure he got the shit kicked out of him, and it just so happens that you're the person on whom he decided to enact his revenge today."

As difficult as certain aspects of David's life had been (as I was just starting to learn) and as much pain as he endured, he certainly had never been made to feel so powerless and inferior, not in such a tawdry—let's be real: *sexist*—way. He'd never been made to feel as if his only identity in the world were as a leech, a parasite. No, worse than that: a silly little ephemeron trifler, a life lived only in relationship to another person. I couldn't have expected him to understand.

"Hey, did you notice that I kept trying to make eye contact with you up there?" he asked. "Every time I caught your eye, I'd stick my tongue out at you."

I had not noticed that. I found that I was more interested in watching the audience watch him than I was in watching him. I kept thinking about how, to them, he was unreal, a thing, an abstraction—when he was now so very unabstract to me.

"Nice joke about the VCR," I said. "Didn't know you worked blue."

If I didn't know that lewd material was David's favorite kind of material, I didn't know him too well yet.

Some Fanilow-type people were waiting for him out on the sidewalk. A woman said she was working on a scholarly article about him and said she'd send it if he gave her his address; in her notebook, he wrote his address at work. A bearded lit bro said that *Infinite Jest* had changed his life, asked David to sign his hardcover copy, and kept right on talking. I thought we'd need a Jaws of Life to pry the dude away. A couple of young women were idling and smoking, waiting for a glimpse of their man. I knew I was figuring this out a bit late, but people definitely had an odd and intense relationship to David's work and to his persona. And they so wanted to be recognized by him as *what* . . . as peers? As fellow travelers? As fellow humans? What even was their deal? I for one never had an interest in meeting an artist I admired. (Once at an event, I found myself standing right next to Sondheim, and was so afraid that I might have to talk to him that I ran off and found a paper bag to breathe in.) It seemed very important to keep your idols distinct from your actual people.

And I wondered what that was like for David, the terrible burden of always being expected to be brilliant (not that he had anything much to say to this particular group of fans), knowing that so much was demanded from him in each encounter. I'll never forget when an acquaintance of mine who vaguely knew Thomas Pynchon said, "He's never even said anything *interesting*." I thought then: *Well, no wonder Thomas Pynchon became so darn Thomas Pynchon-y. Who could possibly endure the weight of being him?*

I also supposed that a celebrity like David got to see humanity at its weirdest and most affected—everyone always performing for you, presenting false versions of themselves, trying to please you. But the celebrity was, of course, expected to perform, too, and so in each encounter everyone had to meet everyone else in their falsity and pretend that the masks were real.

But in order to write, and to live, the mask had to come off.

"I DON'T WANT TO HAVE ANY SECRETS FROM YOU," DAVID SAID. "I WANT to tell you *everything*."

He spoke endlessly of the grubby turmoil of his past, and I heard more about the dazed cycles of self-destruction and self-erasure that seemed to have prevented him from living. In presenting his raw and battered soul, David was, I believed, demanding total trust. I was starting to learn just how trapped in his own thinking and just how self-devouring he was. To know David was to take many walks down the DFW memory lane and to hear accounts—often of questionable taste—about his bizarre and disturbing history with women. Although, to be accurate, the women in his stories were never even "women," so much as phantasms of people, personlike ideas in the margins of his own story, expressed in relation to him.

He called himself a slut and a con man. He said that he'd always believed that it wasn't good enough merely to have women fall in love with him; he needed each woman to love *only* him and to never love anyone else ever again. (Never only a part, always the whole.) And for their love, after they'd been slept with, he said, he repaid them, in classic Orin Incandenza form, with a null set symbol (there are three; I never asked which symbol was his favorite), traced onto their bodies. "And none of them ever knew what it was," he declared. (In *Infinite Jest*, the evil Orin traces an infinity sign onto his women. A null set is so very much worse.)

"But don't worry, sweetie," he said, with various levels of irony, self-mockery, bitterness, and also tenderness—yes, there was so much tenderness, too. "I'm much more mature now."

I sure hoped so. I also sure hoped that every promise of love from him was not also a threat. Minimally, what if all of it was a foreshadowing? *If you want to believe the false version of me, go ahead, sweetie, but you've been warned. You will be thrown onto the pile, too.* I did not want to believe that the only possible outcome to any relationship with him would be, at best, betrayal, but would more likely be end-times-level annihilation—locusts descending from the skies, plague, famine, cities torched.

"And all of these people," David said, speaking of . . . what? The literary universe, those who believed him to be a perfect intellectual and moral model, those who expected him to be a fully integrated being, those who believed a false version of him? "They think I hung the moon. When it's actually possible I'm the devil."

Scene: After the two of us departed a meal ("supper," as David would have had it—*le petit prince* masquerading as country bumpkin) at a restaurant with a genial couple, old friends of his, I observed, "Well, they were nice."

"They *are* extremely nice," David said. "They're not like most people. They won't trash you as soon as you walk away."

"People don't trash you, David," I said.

"People don't trash *you*," he said. (Correction: yes, they did.) "*Everyone* trashes me. I am *hated*."

But how could that have been? The most important thing now was that I believed that David was a good person. I'd always considered myself an excellent judge of character, and I would not have had any interest in him had this not been my essential assessment. The David I wanted to see was the one who said that in college at Amherst, when he did his laundry, if he used a dryer that had someone else's clothes in it, he'd take the dry clothes out, fold them, and place them in a stack. He wouldn't just dump the other person's clothing into some unruly heap. That was the David I wanted to try to believe in, despite everything (although it is also true that I never did quite make up my mind about him, either): the good citizen, the gentle soul.

I WAS LISTENING TO THE BEATING OF HIS HEART AND THINKING IT WOULD have to always be this way. It would always have to be this way now. His hands were in my hair. "Can you help me?" he asked. "I need you to help me."

He said, "I look for the darkness in people. And when I find it, that's what I cling to."

He said, "I haven't had one honest day in my life."

He said, "I never thought I'd find you."

He said, when I asked why the bed in his hotel room had remained unmade for the day, "I slept all afternoon. This is what happens when you're not around. I need you with me all the time." He didn't want me to go to work that week, and he'd call me over and over again on the days I did go in. He said he'd delayed his flight home because he wanted to stay with me forever.

He said, "You're a china doll, made of porcelain. How can you be real?"

He said, "You'd be a stellar mother. I can just feel it."

He spoke of his desire to marry and have children, spoke of his love for a very young family member, repeatedly described as the world's most beautiful baby.

He said, "When I see you, all I can think is *Mount. Hump. Impregnate.* It's *terrible* being a guy."

He said, "But you wouldn't want to have a baby with *me*. I'm sorry I'm so defective. Our children would be reptiles."

He said, "This is what I've always wanted but never thought I could have."

He said, "I can't move to New York. You'd have to come out and live with me."

He said, "Never leave."

He said, "You are my resolution."

He said, "I've found her. I've finally met my match."

I was lying in bed, and David passed his hands over the length of my body without touching me. There was a current of electricity from his fingertips, and it's hard to describe or explain what happened or how it felt, but I thought, *This is a snake putting a spell on a mouse.* David pressed the air from his lungs into mine, and such was the power of his breath and his electricity, and such was the power of his stare, that we didn't need to talk about what he'd done. Something, I knew, was transferred then.

18

This was the message David left on my work voice mail when he arrived home in Bloomington:

"Well, *that* was the trip from hell. The man next to me on the plane had a mild heart attack and urinated on my leg. I couldn't change my pants until I got home. I miss you. I love you."

I loved him, too, but what my expectations were with him, I'm not sure. But I do know I presumed that he would always be in my life. Of course he would. It would have to be that way. The world looked different after spending five days with David; it felt different. The world *was* different. He now felt indispensable. Everything with him seemed so easy, beguilingly easy, in many respects.

David, on the phone when he was home, said, "I've been trying to think of the perfect word for you."

Oh, really now? I geared myself up for a superlative ten-cent word, something rich, something exquisite. This was going to be so great.

"'Willowy,'" David said.

Willowy. OK. I liked that fine. Willowy was fine, willowy was good. But I knew what a willow was. It was passive. A willow was a tree whose existence had everything to do with its bowing.

"My willowy, French-eyed girl," he said softly. "Please come to Bloomington."

But I couldn't go to Bloomington, not then at least. I wanted to, but I was terrified. That was all I wanted to do—to be with David and to be in love with David. But love, with him, was a danger, the biggest danger there was. And I already knew what would happen: I would go to him because he would never come to me, and I would slip into the intoxication and the seduction of being with him, and I would not leave. He would make me surrender my life for him. And he would, sooner or later, abandon me. There could be no other possible conclusion.

But David was terrified of being abandoned, too, and had erected fortresses of all sorts to guarantee his protection.

"I'll even pay for the plane ticket," he said.

Thomas Jefferson (a deeply compromised man himself), in one of his most famous letters, wrote to Maria Cosway, an English painter and musician then living in Paris whom he admired, "The art of life is the art of avoiding pain."

But I couldn't come to Bloomington. The following day, I was flying to Berlin, that exciting tinderbox of Europe, for a long-planned vacation with a friend from college, Adam, and his German mother.

I was not well traveled (though I was already better traveled than David, an inveterate homebody)—I'd been to Paris a couple of times and, improbably, to Russia (to this very day, I consider flying Aeroflot the single riskiest thing I've ever done)—and this weeklong German vacation was a big deal for me. I was really excited about it. I gave David the phone number for the house where we were staying—with Adam's mother's best friend, in a suburb of west Berlin. David promised he'd call. I hoped he'd call. I needed him to call.

David said, "I wish you didn't have to go. I wish we could keep talking."

That was all I wanted to do, too—I wanted to talk to David. If the trip to Berlin had not already been planned, I believe I probably would have gone to him. But at the same time, I already found him overwhelming. It was not impossible that I needed to take a little break so I could think some things over.

"I can't move to New York," he said again. He again added, "You'd have to come here."

I already understood that David would always define the terms of your reality. That's what he did, that's who he was. And I also already understood that I could never be a woman who slid into a man's premade life and claimed it as her own. I had a world. I had a job. It had taken a lot of work to achieve those things. And no offense to downstate Illinois, but I was from the same sort of place—"Midwestern born, bred, and educated," I used to say about myself, with pride, with self-abnegation, with a great big freaking chip on my shoulder—and there was no way that I was going back there already.

I thought about him constantly on the trip to Berlin. Mostly I thought about his stare, which was hard, and unearthly, and challenging, and took you apart at a molecular level. "You should ask for permission before you stare at someone like that," I said to him.

The Berlin trip, to put it in the most lenient terms, was not a success. Our host loathed me. She hated having me in her house. She complained about my bathroom habits (note: I have impeccable bathroom habits), she was appalled by my iced coffees (which I ordered, to make matters worse, at uncouth times), and in restaurants she was repelled when I placed my order in English or cravenly had another member of our party order for me in

German. Although this woman's English was excellent (so I was told), she made a big point of speaking only in German . . . and when a group of people at a table is speaking a language only *you* don't understand, of course you must assume they're all making fun of you, even though they're probably not. Rarely are you as important to someone else's life as you may wish to believe you are. We're always a part, never the whole.

Early in the week Adam and I went wandering along Berlin's linden-lined boulevards and through the lush Tiergarten to the Berlin Zoo. I drank my first Kir Royale, an elegant Continental potion made with champagne and crème de cassis, in an outdoor café in the Friedrichshain district, which was described to me by Adam thusly: "It's the East Village, basically." *That* was a reference I got. At the Reichstag, I knew I should have been thinking about fires. Hitler set a fire there and pretended to be a fireman.

Midweek, Adam's mother and our host went with us into Berlin. All four of us were making the journey on a commuter train from the suburb into the city, to do a bit of group sightseeing. That morning, on the outdoor platform at the suburban train station, Adam and I each bought a ticket from a machine. The women, however, did not buy tickets.

Vaguely, our host suggested (Adam translated for me) that the trains operated on a kind of honor system and that tickets were never checked. I found it unlikely that the Berlin mass transit system had such a laissez-faire approach to ticketing, but I gave the matter a languid mental shrug and assumed I'd never give it any more thought.

On the train, our group got a four-seater, two seats facing the other. Adam and I sat side by side, and his mother and our host (who had short, choppy blond hair and thin, pitiless lips) sat across from us. We settled in for our ride, and I nerdily flipped through my *Fodor's* Berlin guidebook. The train made one stop, two. At the third stop, the doors opened and two male voices said in tandem, *"Fahrkarten, bitte!"*

I twisted around. Two uniformed transit officers were working the aisle.

"Fahrkarten, bitte!" said the first cop.

"Fahrkarten, bitte!" said the second.

This was unexpected, but I was prepared, ticket clutched in hand. I privately congratulated myself for being so conscientious and law-abiding; it was also fun to think about how the ladies were going to talk themselves out of this one.

Our host, seated across from me, craned over to get a good view of the cops. She then considered me for a moment with bright little blue eyes, leaned over to me, and yanked my ticket right out of my fingers. Just seized the thing right from me.

Adam's mother watched as this happened. She paused a beat. She looked at me, looked at her son, her handsome twenty-five-year-old son whom she loved so much, and, deciding to follow her pal's lead, grabbed his ticket from him. Don't ask me what their motivation was. A last gasp at youthful orneriness? Fear? Both, probably.

The officers stopped at our seats.

"Fahrkarten, bitte!" said the first cop.

"Fahrkarten, bitte!" said the second cop.

The two women (one of whom was in her late fifties, and the other younger, both of them divorced) produced their—our—tickets. They showed the officers *our* tickets, the ones Adam and I had bought for ourselves.

Ticketless passengers are viewed dimly by the Berlin transit police. At the next station, Adam and I were summoned out onto the platform. The women followed along behind us, silent, unrepentant.

"Papiere, bitte!" said the first cop.

"Papiere, bitte!" said the second.

The mood on the platform went right to DEFCON 1. I had no papers, no passport, and (obviously) no ticket. I felt like poor old Timofey Pnin: "I haf nofing left, nofing, nofing!" I was reduced to sign language and finger pointing, overcome with an image of myself getting handcuffed by the police and hauled away in a vehicle that I now pathetically recognize as the dogcatcher's cart in *Lady and the Tramp*. When I started sobbing there on the platform, I'd like to think that it had little to do with my specific situation, but everything to do with the cosmic idea of injustice. (Sure, I was that principled.)

Adam talked to the cops. He's a beautiful man, Adam, and a smooth talker (smooth in German, too, I'd have to guess), and, frankly, one of those confabulators I've always enjoyed and, God help me, have always seemed to attract. (Why was it that I've always been so susceptible to those for whom reality isn't good enough, to those who want a different kind of theater?) Long story short: whatever it was Adam said was convincing enough for the transit police to let us go.

After that, Adam and I took our remaining trips into Berlin alone, without the ladies.

When Adam and I came back to our host's house one night toward the end of the trip, our host had something to say to me, the only words in English she spoke to me the entire week:

"*Day-fid* called."

She emphasized the word "David" unsavorily, as if this David person were the king of the swamp people.

When I got back home to New York, David's was the first number I dialed. I called him before I called my parents.

"I thought I'd lost you," he said.

Well, that was a rather odd, doomy thing to say.

"This is not possible," I said.

"I *did* call you in Berlin, you know," he said. "There was this weird honking sound, and then some *lady* answered. When I asked for you, she started yelling at me in German. See, I was *trying* to be a good boyfriend."

I noted again David's habit of announcing his intentionality and proclaiming how he wanted an action to be interpreted. He wanted points. Was he keeping score? *Why* was he keeping score?

During my time with him in New York, I had observed and experienced some weird stuff. There were strange examples of emotional illiteracy: a beautiful, tender moment might be followed by "Sweetie, I'm just trying to be nurturing" or "Do you see how vulnerable I'm trying to be with you?"—remarks that undermined the primary experience, when I wanted the primary experience to be the only thing. There were odd flashes of physical control ("your toes and fingers should always be painted the same color" was a most unwelcome comment and one of the tamer examples). Like a child, David had to be led by the hand through crowded rooms.

I had also developed the unpleasant sense that part of his impulse to talk about other women was to make me—or shall I be more general and say whichever woman he was talking to— possessive? territorial? jealous? *crazy?* He actually seemed to *want me* to be a head case about him. He actually seemed to *want me* to be anxious, insecure, and dependent. I was too self-contained for such nonsense, though. David and I were very different that way: I had a more fluid and (hopefully) more merciful idea of relationships. Weren't relationships, if they were worth anything, meant to be loose and fluid? Weren't they meant to go as they went?

"No one owns anyone," writes my hero Liv Ullmann in her superb memoir, *Changing*. "Together, we have each other and nature and time.

"It is as simple as that."

And did it occur to me, given my *job* and all, that any romantic involvement with David Foster Wallace might have been inappropriate, unprofessional, and, frankly, high risk? Yes, it did, of course it did. (But did it occur to him? And did he even care?) That was one very big reason for a lips-zipped approach. But more to the point: there was no neat, bright social shorthand to talk about him, and anything I might have said would have been reduced to gossip anyway. The more I talked, the more the thing would not be viewed as real.

Or maybe I've just always liked to keep things safely in cages.

In interviews, David would duck any questions about addiction and depression—mental health issues are more openly discussed now than they were then, for starters (although he still wouldn't have talked about any of it)—and the public image we had of him then didn't have much to do with the one we have of him today. From acquaintances of mine who knew him slightly (would they have taken issue with "slightly"? did they maybe believe they knew him better than they really did? wasn't there something a *little* too terribly self-congratulatory about their insistence on calling him "Dave"?), I heard him described as formal. I heard him described as courtly, as sweet, as shy. I heard him described as a really chill dude. I heard him described as human greatness incarnate. How, I would wonder, were we even talking about the same guy? Yes, David's theatrical constructed persona—stubbly Zarathustra in a bandanna?—did have something to do with the man I knew, but that was just one of the many diamond facets upon the glittering DFW diadem. It was always unclear to me how many literary-world people knew the swirling haunted-house aspect of David. Because if you did not know the swirling haunted-house aspect of David, you did not know David.

But for those who *did* grasp at least some of it: to know David was also to understand that he demanded full protection ("dead man's talk") and that you would help him be seen exactly the way he wanted to be seen. So was it possible that we were *all* joined in protecting him?

It was very confusing. Better not to say much at all if I could help it. Which of course added to the hermetic nature of everything.

"It's odd," David said. "I think we must share genetic material. I've never met anyone who has at least as many privacy issues as I do."

THAT SUMMER WAS ONE LONG PHONE CALL WITH DAVID. THE RHIZOMATIC conversations pinballed all over the place, and you knew a call was really on fire when he'd say, his words trying to catch up with his brain, "I'm trying to think what else, I'm trying to think what else." And you'd be off onto another topic. David was, at his Olympian remove, a tremendous gossip and enjoyed being provided tales of folly or excess from the so-called literary world. "OK, let's *dish,*" he'd say. But the sad truth was that I never had too many good stories—mostly they were secondhand, or not even that. But at least we knew a lot of the same people: "And how many times did he tell you where he went to college?" he'd ask; "You know, he *sounds* smart, and he has a smart-person *sheen,* but he's not actually that smart"; "Wait, was that the really hairy guy we were talking about?" He'd say, "Sure must hurt to be him," if he had a low opinion of someone. Declaring that an individual had "hard-core integrity" was high praise; the highest: when David said that a person was an "actual adult."

He was an aficionado of the prank call and really had me going with a couple of these performances: posing as an aspiring writer, inquiring about the status of a short-story submission called—get ready—"sex, lies, and bacon" (did David know the *Esquire* man or what?). David once pretended to be Salinger: "Miss *Miller,* this is J. D. *Salinger,* and I am about to *make* your *career.*" I'm remembering now how much David enjoyed the narrator's description of his wife in that excellent Salinger story "For Esmé—with Love and Squalor": "a breathtakingly levelheaded girl." All hail the exacting adverb.

Now, it is a fact that many writers of fiction like to brag about how they don't read too many new books or new authors. Not so David—the man read everything. Send him a book to read, any book, and he'd read it. And no matter what kind of time I was having with him, he'd often check in with writer recommendations: "Hey, I thought you might like this guy. He's really *good*." (Yes, it was *always* a guy. And about every third time the guy was William T. Vollmann.) More often than not, he'd provide the writer's address. David Foster Wallace: more connected than you would have thought. No, more connected than *he* would have wanted you to think.

And his literary aesthetic intersected *enough* with mine, I guess . . . although, in my view, he definitely could have stood to have been a bit more of an Anglophile, and although he did say, when taking a first gander at my home library, "We have the same books, although you sure have a lot more Martin Amis. Is everything OK?" So many conversations you have with people about books are so solemnly literary, but with David there was never any arrogance, never any pretentiousness. He never held forth; he was humble, he was modest . . . but no . . . that wasn't right. David wasn't humble. He wasn't modest at all. He had the arrogance of one who could *afford* to be modest.

Questions: If you "act" humility, what difference does it make that you aren't really actually humble? Maybe the appearance of humility is actually as good as humility itself?

David was finishing the manuscript for *Brief Interviews with Hideous Men* that summer and said he was trying to work on a novel, too. My impression then was that the novel had something to do with the porn industry. He was auditing a math class for novel research (but a math class related to the porn industry how exactly?); the course was once described to me as statistics and another time described as accounting. He'd leave his house mostly to go to AA meetings, he said. Drone's situation was stable, though probably not for long. I knew all about the heartache of loving a dog. As a child, I'd always dreaded the idea of turning eighteen, because our dog would be fourteen then. David said he'd always done the same thing—calculate the year of his future sorrow.

"I think I've found my twin," he said.

He sent pictures of his dogs and his house—"just so you can see what you're getting into." The house was a real "Jacqueline Bouvier Kennedy Onassis, where are you when we need you?"–type situation: "It's beyond all hope," I said. "Torch everything and start over." (And was that really *duct tape* holding his atrocious sofa together?) The truth: he had no visual sense whatsoever.

A call from David at work: "What's the definition of 'bivouac'? I was having an argument with someone about this."

Wasn't a bivouac like a tent or something? (And why the hell was he asking *me*?)

"Can you use it in a sentence please?"

Well now. He was testing me, I guess. I wasn't going to give him some plodding old declarative sentence ("the boy pitched his bivouac") or an unbeauteous something or other. I love the great poet James Tate—always have, always will—and his delightful poem "In My Own Backyard" was the first time I'd experienced "bivouac" not in its stolid noun form but, enchantingly, as a verb. I remembered that part of the poem, which I'd read in college. I showed off a little and recited for David: the sky and daisies, "bivouacked between worlds."

"The most intelligent man in the world would not know that," said David.

Flan, meet thumbtack. Whipped cream concealing swords. Everything was barbed, spiky with qualifications.

I think about this one a lot: *The most intelligent man in the world would not know that.* He'd said something similar to me before, when we were watching a talk show on TV. I'd made the comment about how, as unlikely as it seems, there was something slightly off with the proportionality of Gwyneth Paltrow's outfit (and I say this as G.P.'s biggest fan). "Wow," he said gallantly. "The smartest man in the world wouldn't notice that."

Another call:

"What female writers should I be reading?"

"Nice question, David."

"Was that sexist of me?"

"Yes," I said. "That was very sexist of you."

He did ten minutes on Cynthia Ozick and I did ten seconds on the somewhat obscure modernist poet Laura Riding, later known as Laura (Riding) Jackson, a crowd-pleaser whom David said he'd never heard of. I was then reading—or trying to read; she's a tough one—Riding's book *Progress of Stories,* and I attempted to explain to David her renunciation of poetry theory, which was exactly how it sounded: Riding, an abstruse yet highly original poet, associated with the Fugitives and Allen Tate and a major influence on her paramour, Robert Graves (particularly on his classic book about Greek mythology and poetic inspiration, *The White Goddess*), withdrew from poetry when she was in her thirties. Riding's framework for making sense of the world: toppled. The question to which I kept returning: How much can you give up and still be "you"?

"But do you know why I really called?" David asked.

"No," I said. Although I did.

"I needed an excuse to talk to you."

Why couldn't we just *go* to each other? Why did we still need *pretexts*?

That night, I believed that my apartment had been broken into (it had not: at fault was a complex set of misunderstandings involving my rabbit, my dry-cleaning delivery, and a loose door-knob screw). Not that David could exactly do anything about it from Illinois, but he was the person I wanted to talk to. David was always the person I wanted to talk to, then.

"You are clearly too freaked out to be at home right now," he said. "Do you have a friend you can stay with tonight?"

I did.

"Call me as soon as you get there, do you understand? I worry about you," he said. "We're the same, me and you."

How so? (And I always loved it when David would go all ungrammatical.)

"Our brains are our own worst enemies."

This was also a choice Wallace move: we shared genetic material, we were twins—no, even better, *we were the same person*. "I think I like your hair so much because it's just like mine," he said. "We even *look* alike." It was an irresistible mistake to make, thinking you and David were identical—but then when you got to know David better, you'd think, *Man, I am nothing like you at all*. At certain later points, if he'd told me he was literally a Martian and had been delivered to Earth via flying saucer, I would have nodded serenely and said, "Of course. It all makes sense now."

"And how *is* my brain my worst enemy?" I asked.

"You know," David said, "it's always so interesting talking to you because we use similar conversational tactics. Like me, you tend to deflect attention from yourself by asking a lot of questions. It's a way of controlling the conversation and a way of managing someone else's perception of you. It's also extremely manipulative. We're manipulative in pretty much identical ways, I think. I suppose I don't have to tell you this."

I didn't consider myself particularly manipulative, but David had a fixed perception of me already—a projection that may or may not have been connected to reality.

A couple of days later, I heard an unappealing story about David from a female acquaintance. I believed that this woman had taken a brief, intense interest in me because she'd seen "Adult World" in *Esquire* and had surmised that I'd been the editor for it. We went to dinner.

"Has David tried anything with you?" she asked. "You seem like the type of person he'd have a crush on."

David had a type? From what I now understood about him, his only "type" seemed to be female and, sorry to say, without power.

I took my usual mum's-the-word approach to him, but this woman seemed to need to talk—so I listened. I hoped that her story (another thwarted getting-laid attempt on David's part) wasn't true (I sensed that it was), and I hoped that David wasn't *that* much of a loser and a creep. Could he really have been *that* unutterably lame?

When I returned home from the dinner, I felt compelled to run her account by David for his take.

"*Not* true," he said. "Totally false." And he added an unconvincing "I ever see her again, I'm going to say, '*Girlfriend*, what'chu talkin' 'bout?'"

A few hours later, David woke me up with a late-night phone call: "Sweetie, it's possible that I may have lied to you. What you heard earlier about me is maybe seventy-five percent true."

Silence on both ends.

"OK, more like . . . *eighty* percent," he said, folding up like a rusty lawn chair. "Are you mad at me?"

I wasn't, but I should have been. He'd lied to me.

I asked him now if this woman knew anything about the really horrific thing he told me about the day we met—the worst thing he'd ever done.

"*Seriously?*" he said sharply. "Do you *think* I would tell her about *that*? Who else do you *think* I talk to like this?" He paused. "Is it actually possible that you really know me so *little*?"

But I was learning that you would never get the whole truth and nothing but the truth from David; his truth was always on somewhat of a sliding scale. You could be getting 20 percent, you could be getting 80—but you could be sure that the stories you heard from him were never completely told. What you had to do was learn to navigate within all those gambits and dodges, those omissions and erasures.

How could someone who seemed, in many ways, such an open

book also be so sneaky and furtive? The more he'd say, the more you'd notice that things didn't quite fit together, that there were versions of stories behind versions behind versions—and some of these versions were self-contradictory. I asked him once why, in his essay about tennis, tornadoes, and math, he had fibbed about the name of the town he was from. He wrote that he was from something called Philo, Illinois, but of course he was a faculty brat from Urbana. What did this little obfuscation even get him? Why did he always feel the need to throw everyone off his trail?

"Oh, you know *me*," David said. "I always have to wear my Groucho glasses."

Yes, it was always performance art, in a way. I understood that. I was a fan of the theatrical approach to life, too—when you're from northeast Ohio, you understand that you must invent whatever you have, because that was all you got. But there were a couple of problems with living in the theater, the first exemplified by these lines from the Yeats poem "The Circus Animals' Desertion":

Players and painted stage took all my love
And not those things that they were emblems of.

The second problem: you create the theater that undoes you.

19

At my high school, during gym classes or extracurricular sports games, students would cheer "Conducive!" when the team scored a point. The emphasis was on the second syllable, like this: "CON-*DU*-CIVE!" Everyone seemed to think that "conducive" (which surely has to be the worst cheer word ever) meant, approximately, "awesome." It's safe to say that I didn't really like my high school much. I didn't seem to find meaning in the things the other kids there found meaningful. I didn't seem to worry about the same things they worried about. Essentially, I guess you could say that we didn't live in the same theater.

"*Who* is oppressing you?" I once furiously wrote in my Spanish workbook, as I took an aggrieved gander at the classroom situation before me. The answer: the students were oppressing themselves. I'd always had this idea that people were pickled in some vague notion they believed the world had of them. The truth: *the world does not care*. So just be who you are. Simple as that, yes? Yes.

Fortunately, in high school I had a best friend, Michelle. We were both self-righteous teetotalers and, conveniently, we both found the same individuals and situations ludicrous. In classes, we would write each other these endlessly long, grotesquely self-aggrandizing letters, exchanged like throbbing hand grenades in the school hallway. In these letters, I regret to report that one of us once referred to our fellow students as "luminously dull"; the other one once referred to these persons as "mental cotton candy." We were intolerable.

Toward the end of our high school careers, Michelle and I did everything we could to spend as little time as possible at school or in our town. Our town wasn't much to write home about, really (that was our belief at the time; now I see that we missed a lot—or at least I did): there was a drive-in A&W, a real hot spot in town, as if eating French fries in your car and getting ketchup all over the place were some sort of prize; there was a Bob's Big Boy with a big dumb mascot that would inevitably come up missing whenever the high school *won* a football game, not when they *lost*. With these other kids, their lives seemed *right there*. Their worries seemed *right there*. Michelle and I, we wanted something else entirely—but what?

Our parental hand-me-down vehicles became A-to-B devices whose principal function was to spirit us away, on Friday nights (and occasional Saturdays), to the Cleveland area and back. The first stop on our northerly journey: a Saks Fifth Avenue, where we'd stalk around and jabber about how we wished we could buy this or that. The second stop: a coffee shop in Cleveland Heights called Arabica, where we'd engage in some serious people watching. These drives took about an hour each way, and during them Michelle and I would listen to the Sisters of Mercy or Bauhaus (Andrew Eldritch and Peter Murphy, I will love you always) or maybe the Elvis Costello album *Spike,* which we found too dense, too busy, although we did both enjoy the little dig at Andrew Lloyd Webber in one of the songs. But mostly we'd recite lines from the Martin Amis novels *London Fields* ("You don't need much empathic talent to tell what Keith's thinking. He doesn't do that much thinking in the first place") and *Money* ("I saw myself as an idealistic young corporal in the Thought Police"). It seemed to me then that very few writers were able to use the English language to greater effect than Amis (and, of course, my beloved Anthony Burgess). It's now of interest to me that Michelle and I were both possessors of such a rigid, particularist aesthetic and that that aesthetic was unfortified by anything resembling actual information. Is there wisdom without knowledge? We were also untroubled by the self-evident fact that we were interested only in art by men, art whose intended audience was also, probably, men.

Yes, it was troubling to me that the writers I loved also didn't seem to have all that much interest in female characters. I didn't know how fraught I should have been about that. Should novels be evaluated morally? Only aesthetically? Both? My struggle with this matter was but in its nascent phase.

NOW, MY SENSITIVITY ABOUT THE WAYS IN WHICH MALE WRITERS REPRE-sented female characters—or, in the case of male journalists who wrote for men's magazines, how they represented actual women—was ever increasing. It was a very complex matter to deal with, because I also felt that I shouldn't really be reading ideologically—how could I possibly do my job if I did? How could I possibly work at a men's magazine if I went around applying what might be called a postcritical analysis to everything? I ought to read aesthetically, not morally, yes? It was not my job to be a censor. But I also knew that I needed the women in what I read to be as clever and as dumb, as noble and as wicked, as any man. Was this asking too much of our literature?

I posed this question to David.

"Have I got the piece for you," he said.

He'd been thinking a lot about misogyny in fiction, he said, and had recently written a review of a John Updike novel for the *New York Observer* addressing this very topic. He'd send it to me.

That sounded super. Super duper. I'd look forward to getting the piece. I was, I mentioned to him, reading *Infinite Jest* again, and I had some things to say about his *own* female characters.

"Oh, God," said David.

Briefly, very briefly, very lightly, I asked whether he didn't feel that the two principal female characters in *Infinite Jest* (there are very few others)—Madame Psychosis (aka Joelle Van Dyne, the P.G.O.A.T.: Prettiest Girl of All Time) and the evil matriarch Avril Incandenza—were not hypersexualized and perhaps grotesquely objectified? Indeed, Madame Psychosis is such a figure of male fantasy, so beautiful (so deformed?), that she keeps her face hidden behind a veil, and Avril—sexually promiscuous, twisted, generally out of her freaking gourd—is certainly one of the most stupendously awful mothers in the history of American literature.

"I don't even disagree with you," David said. "I'm trying to do better."

He said he was thinking a lot about misogyny in his own writing, too, and that in the manuscript he was working on (still *Brief Interviews*), he was trying to deal with his sexism.

Sounded good to me. My preference was for him to deal with his sexism himself so I wouldn't have to.

He would also send me a copy of his first novel, *The Broom of the System,* he said (and did), which, he suggested, had a female protagonist who might be more up my alley. But then he warned that the novel wasn't very good.

"That's what happens when you're a reasonably intelligent college student trying to rewrite *The Crying of Lot 49*," he added.

(Hilariously, David, in interviews, would deny *any* Pynchon influence on his work.)

And I wasn't sure if *The Broom of the System* was any good, but at least I was certain that the central female character, a young woman worried that she may exist not as a living person but only as a creation in a story, was David in drag. He also said he wanted points for setting the book in (a surreal version of) northeast Ohio. He'd even name-checked my humble little town, Tallmadge. "It was as if I were conjuring you," he said. "I'm pretty sure I must have been."

An envelope arrived in the mail with a caveat he'd written on the back: "WARNING—TOXIC UPDIKE MATERIALS ENCLOSED—Read at Risk." Inside was an essay, *that* essay, a printout from DFW HQ of "John Updike, Champion Literary Phallocrat, Drops One" (later retitled "Certainly the End of Something or Other, One Would Sort of Have to Think"), David's boisterously pious evisceration of the Updike swan-song novel *Toward the End of Time* and the Great Male Narcissists of the Updike generation. Thanks, David, by the way, for introducing that useful term in the essay: the Great Male Narcissists, the postwar trio of writers—Updike, Roth, and Mailer—whom he characterized by their solipsism, their machismo, and their swinish attitudes toward women. They were all still in the world then, the GMNs—and Wallace, too—all of them gone now, gone where the goblins go.

David's Updike hatchet job was an instant classic, although I didn't believe the rowdily hostile tone was consistent with the David I knew, or believed I knew—*that* David was as generous when speaking of writers and writing as anyone ever was. Updike, a superlative prose stylist and a true artist-critic, ought to have been granted a bit more reverence, I thought. It was impossible to imagine what twentieth-century American literature would have looked like without him. (Although he was indeed also quite problematic in all the ways David observed.)

"Geez, David," I said. "You could have a little more respect for your elders."

He conceded that Updike was a titan and that his prose was gorgeous, and he added a terribly gross and impeccably Wallace-ian comment about how some Updike sentences made his sphincter pucker. He offered his number one favorite Updike line, from the short story "A & P": "You never know for sure how girls' minds work (do you really think it's a mind in there or just a little buzz like a bee in a glass jar?)."

"OK, that's actually terrible," I said.

His favorite sentence from Updike was a misogynistic dig at female intelligence?

"*Bzzzzzz,*" David said evilly. "*Bzzzzzz.*"

I also had to wonder how much the judgment of a young hooligan like Wallace—Updike's replacement, in fact—actually mattered to a writer like Updike. Certainly, the piece had to hurt the old man—the marginalization of Updike (which, by the time of his death in 2009, was nearly complete) was already very much in motion: Gore Vidal had been going around describing Updike's novels as "Biedermeier" (I mean, *oof*), and Mailer had, in his outrageous "Norman Mailer versus Nine Writers" piece in *Esquire* in 1963, compared Updike's prose style to stale garlic. But David's essay would certainly help speed the late-career Updike demotion along.

There was something else about the piece. Its sanctimonious, high-minded moralizing about the novel's central character's use of women for his own gratification didn't exactly track all *that* well with what David had described to me of his own life. But he *did* keep insisting that he was, in every way, a changed man—so maybe the essay was illustrative of the new, improved David? This was the hope. Lord, this was always the hope.

But the main thing that stuck in my craw was the essay's insistence that women readers didn't, or couldn't, make critical evaluations about books, only emotional ones. (Don't even get me started about the casually patronizing line about the fruitlessness of arguing with these female "readers" about the aesthetic merits of Updike's writing.) The operating principle of the piece seemed to be that women detested the GMNs because they—or their authorial stand-ins—were incapable of love. And a love story, really, is all women—and women *readers*—want.

Closer to the truth: we want a respect story. We merely want to see what we understand of the human estate represented on the page.

Less crucially, I needed to know which of David's female "friends" were included as the supposed speakers of the essay's hilarious and, yes, emotional (not critical, not literary or learned) mosaic of Updike insults: "Just a penis with a thesaurus," etc. This was of interest to me because in my observations, when David talked about the women he knew in his actual life, he tended to boast (that's not right: it was half boast—see, the bonny princeling David could coexist with the regular folk!—and half ridicule) about how they were not, to put it charitably, big readers. (I know, believe me, on every possible level, I *know*.)

Now, it's of course important to recall that with David you never knew what to believe—that old sliding scale of truth—but the claim to me was that his sometimes friend Charis Conn from *Harper's* had made a comment that vaguely suggested one of the lines. But he'd made the quotes up (of course he had), appropriating her voice—sort of.

"But please don't tell anyone," he said. "Dead man's talk?"

My other takeaway from the piece was that it was inwardly directed, a note to the self. I suggested as much to David.

This was a conclusion, an obvious one, I'd already reached about a lot of David's work. Despite the opulence and majesty of his writing, much of it was just such a note to the self.

"Yeah," David said. "I guess that's right. I just never want to become one of those old fuckers who writes about his genitals and who teaches his own stuff in class."

It was also clear that this was just the sort of grave-stomping nightmare review that David so feared of his own work. If I'd been smarter, I would have seen that David believed he already inhabited the position of the Great Male Narcissist himself and that every sentence in the essay bespoke the terrors of the king, dying or otherwise.

THAT SPRING, DAVE EGGERS HAD BEEN TALKING ABOUT PUBLISHING A journal. As I understood it, this project, possibly called *Timothy McSweeney's,* would be democratic, all-embracing, and celebratory in spirit. It would have little to do with good taste; *energy* was the thing. It would be, as Dave described his vision for it, text only and would publish weird and adventurous work that perhaps would be (or maybe already had been) rejected by a mainstream magazine— rejected, that is to say, by a magazine like *Esquire* and, probably, by an editor like me.

The first issue of *McSweeney's* was produced, in large part, in the *Esquire* offices. We had brand-new iMacs at work, and I watched the initial issue come to life on Dave's new computer, and that egg-shaped, ice-cream-colored beauty just added to the thrill. I helped write a couple of small pseudonymous pieces for that issue and proofread some others. I thought this *McSweeney's* of Dave's was creative, bold, gorgeous, and hilarious. (And the best pieces were the ones Dave had written himself.)

In the after-work hours that summer, I witnessed some guys, the same niche demographic as the HoJo guys—the literary urban hipster, I guess the stereotype would be, although these guys were more benevolent than that stereotype would suggest—moseying on into the *Esquire* office after everyone else had gone home, to help Dave with that first *McSweeney's.* The fellows would settle into the empty editorial cubicles (has there ever before been an editorial office with *too much* physical space? we actually had too much space) and would get industriously to work proofreading whatever it was Dave had given them to proofread. Dave worked with a printing company quixotically located in Iceland to produce that first issue; a rep from the company came into the office one afternoon to meet with Dave. Why did this guy also meet with me? I have no recollection, but there he was. I can still see his soulful face as he sat in the red velvet chair across from my desk and spoke of Iceland's stark beauty.

Dave had it in mind to do some sort of future event for *Mc-Sweeney's,* and I toured some possible venues with him. Would it be funny to have the party at the Hooters by our office? A Hooters manager—yes, she was wearing one of those shirts—took us on a tour of the place. We quickly concluded that a *McSweeney's* party, or indeed any party, at a Hooters would actually not be funny at all. That first *McSweeney's* event ended up being held in the back room of a Belgian beer bar with the congenial name Burp Castle. There was no guest list, and there were no young Byzantines waiting by the door with scary clipboards. Those early events had a sprightly egalitarian ethos, and even if you were only nominally a *McSweeney's* contributor but you wanted to read or perform, all you had to do was state your case to Dave. He'd probably let you go on. This was Dave's genius—he really did include everyone.

Smartly, Dave had opened up the evening to people outside the world of books, and the event at Burp Castle had the feeling of an ersatz variety show at a summer camp. It was emceed by John Hodgman, then a literary agent and a phone buddy of mine (never has there been a greater gap between such an outstandingly hilarious person and such a humorless job; he'd have me in stitches on every call), and everyone onstage seemed to be some kind of comic or musician. The whole DIY ethos of the thing stood in conscious opposition to a gatekeeper-controlled literary culture—the culture that *Esquire,* for better or worse, had once represented. It is true that most of the Burp Castle performers were boys—clever, clever white boys—but it is also true that there wasn't much machismo to the undertaking, either. And, most important, there were no oldsters yammering on about their books. Writers who talk about their books: intolerable.

David's story "Philosophy and the Mirror of Nature," which, before David went the Richard Rorty title route, was called "Yet Another Example of Porous Borders (XIII)," was published in that first issue of *McSweeney's*. I edited it. I'd sent David a short, witty book about predatory insects I knew he'd like (*The Red Hourglass* by Gordon Grice), and he composed the story in a sort of response to it, and for, as he wrote to me, my amused information about the dangers of giving him a riveting spider book when he was finishing a manuscript; there's a wacky peripheral backstory in "Philosophy and the Mirror of Nature" about a lawsuit and a black widow farm.

(He had considered including the story in *Brief Interviews* but decided against it and would place it in *Oblivion* instead. When he was putting together the manuscript of *Oblivion,* he said he couldn't find a copy of "Philosophy and the Mirror of Nature" around anywhere and asked me to send him that first *McSweeney's* with the story in it. Which just goes to show you, I guess, that even, and probably especially, geniuses don't always have their shit together, either.)

Embarrassingly, I was tasked with the job of asking David if he would consider a sort of videoconferencing situation for that Burp Castle event, and I got a moderately miffed "I think you know that is *so* not me" in response.

Later, there would be another *McSweeney's* event at a BBQ place on the west side. (I was supposed to find out how to rent a Mister Softee ice-cream truck for it, but I didn't get too far with that one.) These early events felt unusually noncompetitive, and I think we all felt part of the same team. I guess we all knew we were witnessing the birth of a movement of some sort.

AMONG THE MANY CHALLENGES OF LIVING WITH AN UNCAGED CITY rabbit: she will chew your baseboards and electrical cords to bits, and large hunks of your weekends will be spent doing touch-up work to your walls and slapping black electrical tape and/or plastic tubing onto the cords she'd gnawed through the previous week. (The bitter apple spray David sent as a rabbit deterrent did nothing.) So I had no home answering machine that summer—the rabbit had eaten the cord—though I did still have a phone.

It was a Saturday afternoon, and the phone was ringing, just ringing away, but at this particular moment, I did not feel like talking.

The cycle appeared to be: the phone would ring for a minute or so (seemed like ten) and the caller would hang up, call back, and let it ring for another minute (or ten). I sat on a straight-backed chair in my infinitesimal apartment, timing the whole show on the digital clock on my microwave.

I felt the first pulse of a headache and considered all the ways in which I was simply not equipped to handle the dazzlingly complicated person on the other end of the line. It was hard to imagine how anyone ever could be.

"Where were you?" David asked, his voice expressionless, when I finally did pick up.

I lied. "At the gym."

"Why do you work out so much, Adrienne?" he said with flat affect. "You sure seem to spend a lot of time at the gym. Are you afraid that you're going to become obese?"

I loved him, but, man, was he *so* exhausting. I was terrified of his need for me. It also frightened me to admit how emotionally yoked I felt to him now. Not to get too mystical about it, but sometimes it seemed that my emotions, which apparently were no longer mine alone, became—sometimes, not always (I was still an autonomous entity, and I wanted to keep it that way)—undulations of his. (It was never the other way around, of course.) Whenever I'd think, *Something is going on with David,* I'd be right. His drama became, to a certain extent, your drama, too. You'd cry right along with him. Who knows how David was able to work his voodoo, but I'm telling you that it was real. I think he probably had some form of ESP. And I think I had a form of it, too, at least regarding him. (I know how that sounds.) I'm certain that those who knew him better than I felt his telepathy with significantly more force.

One night, I could feel that something was happening with him. We spoke, and he sounded peculiar, dazed almost. He said he'd been driving as slowly as he possibly could without actually getting himself killed, listening to a Carpenters CD while repeating, "I am the most boring person in the world. I am the most boring person in the world."

I always worried about David and cars. A couple of years later, when I was reading a manuscript he'd sent me of his story "Good Old Neon," which has its terminus in a fiery vehicular suicide, I went into my bathroom and threw up. That was the moment I knew he believed he was doomed. It was always so hard to imagine David's third act.

But there's a problem with communicating with a person who's combatting some sort of darkness in himself, or at least there was a problem for me: I always felt that I was speaking in generalizations and repeating conventional wisdom. I always felt like Polonius, in other words—cliché, cliché, platitude, platitude. *David, you're doing great. David, your life is golden. David, we all love you and admire you.* All of which was true, of course, but essentially it was all the lazy cliché "you have no *right* to be unhappy." When I'd talk to him, I'd often find myself thinking about how not everything can be distilled down to common sense. I'd also consider how resistant depression is to interpretation and how inadequate our language is to deal with it. (And from his end, I'm sure David was like, *You just don't get it at all.*)

A bit later in the summer, David was calling from a hotel in Arizona, where he was visiting his family. He had finally finished *Brief Interviews with Hideous Men.*

"I don't have anyone to dedicate it to," he said, in lonely-boy mode.

Where was *this* going?

I said nothing.

"Oh, *I* know," David said, performing just a little bit too much for my taste. I'd hoped we were beyond the routines, the acts, by now—but no, we never were. "I'll dedicate it to *you*."

He would? Well, that would be slightly . . . odd. I mean, he'd sent me a couple of stories in the book for me to give friendly notes on, writing that he didn't want to send them to his editor if they were so bad or off-the-wall that they would hurt his credibility (and while also wanting points for being "vulnerable" with me). But I hadn't read the whole manuscript and obviously hadn't known him during the composition of most of the book—he'd written some of the stories in grad school, for God's sake.

Throughout the rest of the summer, he dangled the prospect of a *Brief Interviews with Hideous Men* dedication before me like some kind of book-dedication worm. I was of many minds about this. On one level, I was flattered. Of course I was. We liked each other. We loved each other even, maybe, I hoped. But a book dedication at this stage would really have been pushing it.

Here was another feature of the well-oiled DFW act: he'd say and do outlandish things just to see what your reaction would be. He'd poke you and prod at you and try to get your goat. And so, looked at from this view, David could certainly have been screwing with me. Jesus, did he really want me to *ask* for it? The more I thought about this as an explanation, the more infuriated I became. I would never be a beseeching woman.

Yet on another level still, the book-dedication thing made me so crushingly sad—this beautiful, difficult, suspicious, paradoxical man was so emotionally barricaded, such a colossus unto himself (the guy was his own mountain), that he had no one close enough to whom to dedicate a book.

But *no*. No, that couldn't have been right. That *wasn't* right. There were many, many people in David's life, many people who loved him, many people who were, or considered themselves to be, close to him—to the extent that anyone could ever be close to David.

He said he was going to send the entire manuscript of *Brief Interviews with Hideous Men* for me to read. "It's weird," he added, "but I usually keep my stuff away from women I'm going out with."

He remarked that not only did he make a general rule of keeping his stuff away from girlfriends, but he would break up with a woman immediately if she dared to peek at his work. I disrespected him for this. I also disrespected him for having dated women he did not value intellectually. Also, how dysfunctional and dreadfully compartmentalized was that, to keep the most important part of himself away from the people who were, theoretically, closest to him?

He paused, his tone shifting again, going from vaguely malevolent to sweet as marzipan. "You know, we *like* each other."

"Sure," I said. "We do."

"I still can't believe it," he said. "I still can't believe how much we *like* each other."

Back in New York, he'd remarked that when he'd been photographed for the *Esquire* contributors' page for "Adult World," he'd worried that I'd see the contact sheets from the shoot and would think he was ugly.

"Do you know how many people I meet a year?" he asked.

No, I didn't. I hadn't given the matter any thought.

"A *lot*," he said.

OK, so what? I met a lot of people, too. Big deal. The difference was that I wasn't meeting people because of anything inherently to do with "me"—people were interested in me only because of my job. But everyone also wanted something from him.

"And do you know how many I actually like?" David asked. "Maybe two."

"Well," I said, "I'm *thrilled* that I'm one of the two for the year. This is *very* exciting."

"I wish I could *bottle* you," he said. "Sometimes you smell like lemons. At other times, you're the world's most delicious vanilla cake. I wish you were here in this hotel room right now."

I wished I were there with him, too. That was all I wanted. But I knew something about David. I knew that being close to him meant that, sooner or later, you'd be forced to discover what you were made of.

But *why* was I so terrified to discover what I was made of?

The art of life is the art of avoiding pain.

A pause.

"You'd just better never hate me," he said. "Do you understand? Never hate me."

IT'S HARD TO EXPLAIN HOW MUCH *BRIEF INTERVIEWS WITH HIDEOUS MEN* hurt to read. A damp cloth on the solar plexus was the least of it.

So many of the stories—"Forever Overhead," the intimidatingly brilliant "Octet" (one of the greatest stories ever), and "On His Deathbed, Holding Your Hand, the Acclaimed New Young Off-Broadway Playwright's Father Begs a Boon"—were just stunning . . . though I *would* gently suggest to David that "Tri-Stan: I Sold Sissee Nar to Ecko," a painfully unamusing mock-Homeric, John Barth–esque pastiche set in seventies-era Hollywood, maybe not be included in the collection. (It could possibly be the worst thing he ever wrote. Although he believed that his book about rappers took that particular prize.) I was hugely disturbed by what would become the collection's most illustrious story, the so-called "Granola Cruncher," in which a woman's rape somehow becomes, through an act of empathy with her attacker, no longer a rape. And I hadn't been expecting the savagery of the title stories. I guess I'd anticipated something interrogating sexism rather than confessing to it. Maybe I'd expected the female "characters" to be granted something approaching full humanity.

"I can't *wait* for the feminist critique of this," I said to him on a call.

"Well, do *not* send it to me when it comes out," David replied.

An unnamed female interrogator, whose questions are represented only with a "Q.," "interviews" the hideous men about their grisly sexual histories, and they rant back at her. The whole enterprise felt awfully Spaderlike to me, I told David, Spader-sense tingling. (David admitted that there might indeed have been some subconscious *sex, lies, and videotape* thing happening with the conceit, but let's not make too much of that.) But unlike the creepy, prying Spader of the movie, in *Brief Interviews,* the female interviewer's questions are never heard.

I pointed out the obvious to David: the woman is not given a voice. She is muzzled, silenced, erased.

His reply: It was fine because he stole the whole "Q." thing from DeLillo.

(This had also been David's response, by the way, to my complaint that the interminable Eschaton sequence in *Infinite Jest*—Eschaton is a game of global warfare played by students on the courts at a tennis academy—was one of the most self-indulgent wankfests ever put to paper. "Don't blame *me!*" he said, and went on to explain that he stole the idea from *End Zone.* DeLillo. The source and the absolver.)

The unnamed male characters in *Brief Interviews* are grotesque parodies of the Updike/Roth/Mailer narcissists David had attacked in his GMN essay. Visions of those already entombed—liars, manipulators, con men, abusers—they are all stuck, like so many Wallace characters, in pernicious cul-de-sacs of thought. Thinking is unconstructive; thinking is paralysis. Were they able to experience happiness? Were they able to experience love? Wait a minute—was *David*? And what about that GMN essay? Was the concern expressed in it merely an artfully constructed mask?

Not to put too fine a point on it: I was worried about him.

"David, you weren't one of those little boys who set insects on fire, were you?"

"No," he said. "But I *was* one of those little boys who put insects down the backs of little girls' *shirts*!"

I needed him to explain to me: Why was there so much abuse? Why were all the relationships—or "relationships"—in the book so pathological? Why were the men all such sociopaths? Why were the women all such victims? Why was everyone so *trapped*?

"Yes, the characters *are* trapped," David, a control freak about everything, especially about the interpretation of his work, said. "But you have to understand that they are all totally self-aware."

About "The Depressed Person": he rather rhetorically wondered what it meant that he was able to look at the parts of himself he most despised only if he portrayed himself as a woman—just as, he then suggested, he'd done with another psychotically depressed character, Kate Gompert in *Infinite Jest*. He said that in "The Depressed Person" he'd tried to confront his own narcissism in a more direct way than he'd ever done before. He'd been, he added, an ass to everyone in his life when he was writing it.

Regarding the interview chapters of the book—there was the small, dark chuckle (it always indicated any number of malfeasances)—he said that some of the interviews were "actual conversations I had when I had to break up with people." That doom-laden "had to" was not an easy one to forget. Neither was the fact that he characterized the interviews, in which men talk at, not to (never to), their anonymous female interrogator, whose voice is never heard, as "conversations."

I realize this could come across as a facile interpretation of his work, by the way. David would in fact caution us against doing exactly this—poking around a writer's life in search of "personal stuff encoded in a writer's art," as he wrote in a scolding review of a Borges biography, in which he warns against the syndrome of "psychological criticism." I agree that this sort of literalism is a crude way to interpret an artist's work. But what am I supposed to do here?

David later claimed that one of the interviews, #2—the female interrogator's own breakup, in which her boyfriend preemptively dumps her so he may be spared the hassle in some indefinite but inexorable future—had been conceived of as an imagined breakup conversation with *me*. This was not intended as flattering information, and it was not received as such. And this is the interview that sets everything in motion, by the way: after the interrogator's bewildering breakup (she and the boyfriend actually seem to like each other, and "liking each other," amid the profound relationship dysfunction in David's fiction, is about as good as it gets), she henceforth embarks on the project of trying to understand what makes these various hideous men tick. (Yeah, good luck with that one. And does it ever occur to our nebulous lady that none of the men would ever begin to grant her the same level of analysis she grants them?)

Occasionally, when you'd read David's fiction, you'd notice that he had used a bit of you or perhaps a suggestion—sometimes more than that—of a thing you'd said or written. Your reaction was never "Oh, neat, look at that!" It was always a queasy *"Ew."*

Yes, I know: again with David's point about the dangers of rooting around for extra-literary clues to a writer's work. But this is my life, too.

(And anyway, my biggest editorial gripe about this chapter: in the book version, David changed the hideous man's shrink's name from the outstanding "Mr. Chitty" of the manuscript to the far less excellent "Mr. Chitwin." For my money, there can never be any improvement on the line "As Mr. Chitty would put it I am just not a *closer.*")

But maybe, I thought then, we expect too much of our literary artists. No writer has a perfect corpus—I'm in agreement with Martin Amis's assessment that when we say we love a major writer's work, we actually really love only about half of it. I intensely disliked parts of *Brief Interviews*. Still do. I accept that. It's a dangerous, defiantly experimental collection, and each story takes its own risk. Some of those risks aren't successful. But David was also the genius who had written the searing "woman who said she'd come" chapter in *Infinite Jest* (an addict waits for his dealer to show up at his place with enough drugs for one final binge), and if there's a more virtuosic sequence anywhere in American literature, I'd like to know about it. How fitfully the rest of us perceive our interior worlds.

David would often speak of his growing ambition to write with, as he said, greater clarity and urgency and of his desire to develop more trust for the reader: "More respect," he'd say. "More respect, and more trust." He brought up "Cathedral," the classic Raymond Carver short story, a couple of times. "These aren't people like us," he said. "No one *writes* about people like that. That's what *I* want to do."

David believed in fiction—"our lone outpost of civilization"—and there was no more persuasive advocate for it. "Fiction is a lie," he said to me and to anyone else who'd listen (his own proto–TED Talk), because most of this stuff can't be talked about directly. But we believe fiction because, unlike everything else in this world, it tells the truth.

But with *Brief Interviews with Hideous Men,* I couldn't see how his stated goals for his fiction were in any way compatible with what he was actually writing.

I KNEW THAT I HAD BEEN PERMITTED TO WORK IN AN EXTRAORDINARY world, and I knew how privileged I was to be permitted to do the thing that enlightened me and the thing that I loved. My happiest moments came when I'd give a writer an editorial suggestion, and the writer would go off and return with something glorious. Of course, the accomplishment was always the writer's, but when an author took something I'd said and soared with it, I'd believe that I actually had some sort of role in the world.

Regarding the work submitted to me, I would try to assume, with varying degrees of success, a generous attitude: *Don't resent it. Try to appreciate it. Even if it is sublimely bad, it is well intentioned.* I had to reject far, far more than I was able to publish, and the odds were not in anyone's favor. The influx was astonishing, and I had to reject pretty much all of it. How many short stories did I have to reject every day? Think of a number and put an exponent on it.

And would there be a psychic toll, I wondered, for my having to come up with some half-baked run of reasons that a piece of writing, which had been created in a spirit of generosity, was getting a great big old "pass" from me? Now, as a career reader, I had to think about what this story/book/proposal failed to do, had to analyze how it *went wrong.* But the "it's not right for us"—the "it's not you, it's me" breakup approach—was always my preferred sort of rejection.

One of my most prolific renowned submitters was none other than Ray Bradbury, the sci-fi giant. He was in his late seventies then and still admirably writing away, writing, writing, writing, and submitting to *Esquire,* via his agent, what seemed like a story a week. Was it a weird experience to send continual pass letters (*Esquire* didn't publish sci-fi, but his stories were always cool and interesting) to the great fantasy author whose supreme novel, *Fahrenheit 451,* I'd read in eighth grade? It was.

Indeed, there really were plenty of writers who didn't let rejections get to them too much—they just kept slugging away. Slugging and slugging. I had lots of regular slush-pile authors who did not stop submitting, who *could not* stop submitting; I would ultimately come to respect their amazing defiance (and, frankly, their amazing self-regard). So here's to you, you aspiring authors who would routinely call me to check in on the progress of your submissions. (And let's not forget those among you who would leave voice-mail messages asking if we could meet in person! Thank you for telling me you were in town.)

But usually I worried that all I was doing was canceling people. All I was doing was taking things away. And if you take things away, you have to give them back elsewhere.

THERE WERE NOW SOME SIGNS OF TROUBLE IN MY RELATIONSHIP WITH David.

A friend showed me a letter David had written to him in which David had taken a potshot at me, suggesting I wasn't sophisticated enough to understand his work.

More trouble. On a call, David said, "I don't get any work done on the days we talk."

He actually had the gall to suggest that I was a Porlockian person, a mere *interruption,* a bumbler blocking the artist from his art. That really hurt.

"And then when we do get off the phone," he continued, "I *think* about you. It is *very* disruptive."

That hurt even more. I *wanted* David to write. I wanted him to work. It did not need to be explained to me that if he didn't or couldn't write, his world would collapse like an avalanche. David was an artist rare and true, and we needed him to write. We needed him to hold a mirror up to ourselves and tell us who we were. The question was: How much did we really want to see what he showed us?

And more trouble still. Once when I called with a check-in, I was greeted with the choice Wallace brush-off: "I'm *fine.* I'm a big boy."

After he'd come back from a dinner with a woman, or women, he'd deemed perilously middle-aged, he said, menacingly, "I've been thinking: it's going to be very hard for you to get older. You'd better *watch out*."

(Similarly, he had yelled at me once when he believed I was looking at myself in a mirror [it's maybe possible that I was], when I ought to have been looking at *him*.)

"Don't worry," I said. "I have a little too much going on for that."

"Oh," David replied. "Sorry."

Another time, David: "I wish you were older."

"*Excuse* me?"

"I would prefer it if you were older, that's all."

("Please say you're not doing that younger woman–older man thing," he would say at a later date, irritated by a mildly toadying remark I had made.)

I started receiving tastes of the small acts of gratuitous cruelty of which David could be so dreadfully fond:

"I was trying to actually *talk* to you," he said, "but you were making these excited little squeaking sounds that could only be *confused* for human speech."

As I've noted, in my experience with David, after some offensive thing he did or said, I'd often be presented with a series of choices: Do I walk away from him now, or later? Is the time now, or now, or *now*, to yell at him? Should I hang up on him now, or should I wait? How angry do I allow myself to become at him—now, later, and forever? How much forgiveness does he even deserve?

Eventually—it would take a long time, but I would get there—I would begin to understand that in adult life, in the adult world, one had to learn to control not only the expression of anger but also the emotion itself.

Toward the end of the summer, David said, in regard to *Brief Interviews with Hideous Men*, "You know, I've always liked pseudonymous dedications."

David's fondness for coy pseudonyms was well known; he used one for his piece "Neither Adult nor Entertainment" in *Premiere* and would later deploy a female pseudonym (yes, a *female* one) for his story "Mr. Squishy" in *McSweeney's*. David, of course, always had to mask everything.

"I've always hated 'personal' dedications," he added, and said that he liked to keep his "personal stuff" away from his work—which was really just such a gas, given how patently autobiographical his fiction so often was, a charge he'd both concede to and deny.

"So the dedication will be pseudonymous," he said. "But it will *really* be dedicated to you."

He told me that I should consider it a little in-joke for classicists and said, in a house-of-mirrors spirit, that he had given "me" the sizzlingly assonant pseudonym "Ms. Nicolette Fiss"—the name that appears on the dedication page in the manuscript draft.

"Sounds like steam escaping," I said to David, quoting, naturally, Dom DeLuise in *Blazing Saddles* and trying to sound amused.

(In the published book, the fake dedicatees are "Beth-Ellen Siciliano" and "Alice Dall.")

I had been wondering when and how David was going to shove the old dedicatee snake back into the can. Now I finally had my answer. Shirley Hazzard wrote of Graham Greene that he regularly invited you to step on a rug, which he would then pull out from under you. David said it would be our little joke—a joke that was so very unfunny.

"Do you hate me?" he asked.

20

One night when Dave Eggers and I were disembarking from a taxi (blast from the past: we were seeing the Jesus and Mary Chain, but they were a nostalgia act even then), he opened his wallet to pay, and a bunch of receipts and papers and whatnot came fluttering down to the floor. One of those pieces of paper was his pay stub. I reached down to pick it up and noted with astonishment that Dave's salary at *Esquire* was twice mine.

Men were prioritized. Men were always prioritized. My only option, as I understood it then: I'd have to develop a thick skin. I'd have to take my knocks; that was to be expected, of course. I was also learning what I had always known but had never really *known*. Power is always an ephemeral event, subject to ebb and flow. Power is never absolute.

The truth was that I always felt as if the benefits that came along with my job were rather generalized. Anyone who had the job would have gotten the same prizes. And it would have been self-deceptive indeed to think that any of the fluff on top had anything to do inherently with *me*. Plus, I was from the cornfields, from the Rust Belt, and being pandered to was not my natural mode. Whenever anyone showed me any deference or somewhat aggressively attempted to be my friend, I always assumed they were lying.

This is why power must always be mistrusted: the narcissistic self is not "in" the world; the narcissistic self does not consider itself a part of the whole. The amount of power you have (or believe you have) shapes your demands of life and your demands of other people. And you'd better have an unshakable moral core if you always get what you want—otherwise what, exactly, *is* the incentive to behave decently?

"All men would be tyrants if they could," wrote Abigail Adams to John.

Quick story: A couple of years ago, my husband and I went to a cocktail party at a town house, hosted by a CEO of something or another. As my husband, Joe, attempted the sociological experiment of chatting up the CEO ("That dude is the human embodiment of an Excel spreadsheet," Joe later said), I silently considered the room, the paintings on the paneled walls, and found myself thinking about that Balzac (or Mario Puzo, if you'd rather) line: "Behind every great fortune lies a great crime."

The oligarch, surely one of the wealthiest—and luckiest—people alive on the planet, was grumbling to my husband about the increase (as he preposterously saw it) of homeless people in the neighborhood.

"But you just have to wonder," Joe said, "about the circumstances in their lives that led them to where they are."

The oligarch's eyes narrowed into little black slits. He was a simple, simple man, the oligarch (oligarchs, you find, often are), not much given to introspection.

"I've never thought about them as 'people' before," he said. "I've always thought of them as cockroaches."

I've come to understand the most dangerous individuals are always the ones who are completely devoid of issues of the self—they're the ones who have never had any reason to examine themselves or their own subjectivity. David's commencement speech "This Is Water" is a rather modest call to live the examined life: try to control your biases about people and try to be lenient when interpreting someone else's behavior. It's a fine speech (and is another entry in David's note-to-self cycle), but it's come to be regarded as his *Walden,* albeit an aphoristic, self-help-y version. It is of interest that the speech has resonated as profoundly as it has with people. Have we actually really not given any thought at all to what it might be like to be someone else? And what does this say about the total absence of empathy in our culture?

A MAN SAID TO ME, "I'VE ALWAYS WONDERED WHY IT IS THAT YOUR sisters aren't better writers."

A man asked me, when discussing the work of a female author, "Is she a 'big' girl?"

A man asked, "Why is there always a scene in every women's novel with a female character making snow angels?"

A man asked me why it was that women writers seemed to be capable of only two things: *sensation* on one hand or *attitudinizing* on the other.

A man told me that he didn't believe I'd read enough books to be able to do my job effectively.

A man told me that only someone with an M.F.A. should have my job. (The real answer: someone with an M.F.A. definitely should *not* have had my job.)

A man, someone probably actually lower on the status totem pole at *Esquire* than I, took a story I had acquired and had already edited—and did his own (very poor) edits to it, returning it to me as if he were some sort of conquering hero.

A man said that no one would take me seriously until I won a National Magazine Award for Fiction.

A man told me that he couldn't believe the literary editor of *Esquire* had never read anything by Anna Akhmatova.

A man seemed to believe that he needed to routinely explain my "mission" with regard to the literary section of the magazine: "The stories can't be perfunctory," he'd say. This was his trademark word: "perfunctory." Naturally, my private code name for this guy became Perfunctory Man. And was he ever. As Simone de Beauvoir put it: "The most mediocre of males feels himself a demigod as compared with women." (And, indeed, I was one happy individual when Perfunctory Man was finally fired.)

A man—OK, *men* were Hobbesianly snaking around, trying to get in their own short-story submissions. There were always men after my job, and I would come to feel as if I were constantly whipping a lit torch around to protect my territory. But had these men ever actually read any of the fiction published in the magazine? Unclear.

A man referred to a woman who worked at the company as a cunt.

A man said to me, "I wish my groupies were of a higher caliber." Me: "You have *groupies*?"

A man told me that I should "fucking spit" on a notoriously demanding female media professional.

A man brought a coffee-table book of high-end pornographic art to me at a work lunch.

A man said, at another work lunch, "You're not so young anymore, you know." The man was my father's age. My age: twenty-eight.

A man asked, at the end of a professional drinks appointment, if he could kiss me.

A man asked me, after he'd moved my hand close to his crotch at another professional drinks appointment, if something he'd done had made me seem so close to crying.

A man—one of the most celebrated writers in the country—sexually assaulted me. After a professional drinks appointment, when we were standing together on a sidewalk waiting for a light to change, he put his hands down my pants.

(After that, I pretty much stopped doing professional drinks appointments with men.)

A man rated, in terms of purported attractiveness, the women—the brilliant and judicious women—who read our unsolicited short-story manuscripts.

A man said that "everyone wondered" whom I had slept with to get my job.

It would go like this: I'd find myself at an event, standing or sitting next to some man, illustrious in this or that sphere; another man, unknown to me, and assuming an air of importance, would come up to the first man. I would note how often the second man would look through me, around me, over me, to something much more important. People are ghosts until you actually have to start taking them seriously.

My view: these men were, as Kate Millett wrote of Mailer in her masterwork *Sexual Politics*, "prisoner[s] of the virility cult," and their chest-thumping machismo was, more or less, a pose—even if they didn't know it. It's always hard to gauge how self-aware other people are, but the overall sense usually seems to be: not very. We are unknown to ourselves. (Recall, in an extreme but useful example, that Mussolini wanted his epitaph to read: "Here lies one of the most intelligent animals who ever appeared on the face of the earth.") So I attempted to take a nuanced view, even when the actions of the men were abhorrent. I tried to approach the behavior with a spirit of irony, leniency, and good humor . . . when good humor was musterable.

The truth: my career had been built around protecting male egos. This was the world I lived in. This was the world I knew, and I never believed this world could, or would, change. It seemed incomprehensible that the system could ever collapse. So I started trying out a new approach. I would change *myself. I* would become unattackable. I'd train myself not to let other people's—men's—opinions of me penetrate. I'd become a fortress to be approached, a Soviet tank of the spirit.

This was a strategy. This was a deeply antisocial strategy, in fact, and philosophically in direct conflict with the central precept of my job. When you're trying to cultivate appreciation, you have to maintain an open heart.

HAROLD HAYES ONCE SAID THAT NOT ONLY WAS HE APOLITICAL, HE WAS *apersonal.* His tactic: to keep his distance from his writers. And the English book editor Diana Athill wrote in her classic publishing memoir, *Stet,* "Very rarely someone from my work moved over into my private life, but generally office and home were far apart." All of this now made a sort of sense to me. I came to understand that an overly close editor-writer relationship presented all sorts of risks—the editor did not want her personal feelings about the writer to impact her aesthetic and literary judgment on a piece, for example. (And then things could get rather awkward when an editor rejected something a writer friend had submitted. And I had a hard enough time—emotionally, I mean—rejecting submissions anyway.) Maybe it wasn't a bad idea to keep your distance and to become even more of a fortress than you already were.

"WHAT IS THIS?" DAVID WAS ASKING. "*THE* FUCKING *RULES?*"
He had been annoyed that I hadn't come out to visit him—or maybe he was just performing annoyance?—and now it was too

late. The questions: How real was anything ever with him? What was a dream, and what was reality? What was true, and what was fake?

"'Oh, I'll just let "my man" take care of everything.' Why are you so *passive*?" he asked.

Did I actually believe that David was "my man"? I wanted to, but I suppose I couldn't let myself. I wasn't sure that was the way I worked. I wasn't sure that was the way *love* worked. No one owns anyone. Love isn't proprietary.

But more to the point: David was used to being fought for. Everyone fought for him, fought over him. This was not an experience we'd shared.

"David," I said in a small, sad voice, "I just think you're the most."

"*Horseshit,*" he said. "You think I'm the *second* most. You think I'm the *third* most. You don't even *like* me."

I felt it in my throat—I always feel grief first in my throat.

He said, "I have always been extremely clear about this: *I cannot move to New York.* Living there would eat me *alive.* And I find it difficult to imagine that you would want to come out here and be my *nurse.* I find this *very* hard to imagine."

Drone was getting sicker—that was a part of it—and I had not provided what David needed. I was good at my job and good at dealing with words on the page, but it was possible that I was otherwise a mess. I had little mastery over my emotions or my tongue, and I didn't yet understand that the most important thing in the adult world is to keep your cool, keep your mouth shut, stay in your own lane, and state an opinion only when you know which side is winning. I still didn't understand that most accepted "intelligence" is merely the stock intelligence of popular opinion. I still ate cookies and sliced deli watermelon for dinner. I had too many credit cards. I could barely take care of *myself.* I was certainly no caregiver, not then, and David needed—David demanded—a caregiver. But I loved him, and that was what I should want, to help him and to take care of him. Maybe I didn't understand what love was. I was so confused.

But what if I ever needed *him*? Would he ever take care of *me*? I was pretty sure I knew the answer.

"And what do you *expect*?" David asked. "Practically, how would this *work*? That we'd have really intense sex a few times a year? I've seen how long-distance relationships destroy people. Do you understand?"

"I can come out to Bloomington," I said.

"Too late," he said. "Too late, Adrienne. I've met someone."

My stomach churned.

"I feel as if I've been betraying you," he said.

"That's because you *are*," I said.

"But at least it's not some *student*. We're the same age!"

"Wow, congratulations!" I said. *"Progress."*

He told me about the woman's job and background. He said she was not very bright (but, to be fair, I'm certain he said that about me, too) and had never read a book in her life. My response was classist, petty, obnoxious. (Remember that our behavior is rarely equal to our dream of ourselves.)

"Not literary," I said. "This person is totally inappropriate and you know it."

"Wow," he said. He gave a little cough. "That was mean."

"You are a child," I said.

But I was a child, too. We were both so very childish and would become even more so. We weren't through with being children yet.

"Could you do me a favor?" he said. His voice had dropped an octave. "Could you destroy the manuscript of *Brief Interviews*? Just throw it away right now. I want to *hear* it go into the wastebasket."

"You are such a bastard, you know that? Why have you even been bothering me all this time?"

"Oh, Adrienne," David said, a catch in his voice. "Don't you understand what we *have*?" Was this the only kind of intimacy we could have—intimacy at a distance? "You don't understand. You have *never* understood what we have. It's *higher* than that."

This was precious—really just so precious—he was breaking up with me because *I* didn't understand how important our relationship was. That was good stuff.

"Men just don't like complicated women," I said. (I always hoped he forgot this little comment.) "And it's *fine*. I understand this now. It's taken me a while to figure it out, but thank you for finally being the one to explain it to me: *it's just the way it is*."

"Some men don't like complicated women," he said quietly. "*I* do."

"Yes," I said. "*Obviously*. Of *course*. I'm hanging up on you now."

"OK, well then fuck you, Adrienne," David said.

He was crying now. So was I.

When you get thrown back into who you are, you'd better have something there.

In Elizabeth Jane Howard's novel *The Long View,* a character has the following devastating insight: "there were only two kinds of people—those who live different lives with the same partners, and those who live the same life with different partners." David, I now understood, with a terrible spasm of recognition, was one of the latter. And I was, and would ever be, I knew, the former.

God, I hated David then. Just loathed him. It had been a mistake, I decided, to think that anything with him had been real—it had been fake intimacy, a fake relationship, and everything I had believed about him or about "us" (whatever that even meant) had been completely self-generated. He was precisely as manipulative as he'd threatened. He'd warned that every woman got thrown onto the pile sooner or later. Should have listened. A woman is a woman is a woman is a woman is a woman, as Gertrude Stein said, or ought to have.

Several days later, David called me at work. He was crying. His dog, his beautiful stray, Drone, had died.

"I loved him with a purity with which I've never loved anyone or anything else," he said.

And I was crying, too, and we were two unhappy people crying together, separated by a distance of nine hundred miles.

ALTHOUGH ONLY THE NOVELIST IS PERMITTED TO ASCRIBE MOTIVATION, I believe it's fair to say that Dave Eggers was feeling restless at *Esquire*. He sold his memoir proposal and left the magazine to write the book. At one point when he was working on *A Heartbreaking Work of Staggering Genius* ("Terrible title," I said, "you'll be destroyed"; though it was better than the title runner-up, *A Heartbreaking Work of Stunning Genius*), he made the remark to me that he'd always thought he'd be able to fit the entire world into a book and that in a book he'd finally be able to say everything he'd always wanted to say. But he now understood that a single book wasn't much room at all.

I went with him to help hand-sell the inaugural print issue of *McSweeney's:* we visited a few independent bookstores downtown (remember when there were lots of independent bookstores downtown?) and, interestingly, a map store. I made one solo trip, to the late, great St. Mark's Bookshop, and tried to recite Dave's sales pitch to the staff at the counter, but I ended up babbling something about these crazy kids today and this hot, new, and super-creative literary journal.

"Just leave the copy with me," the guy instructed. He told me to check in with him the following week.

Gamely, a week later, I made my return visit.

Number of copies of the first issue of *McSweeney's* I was able to convince St. Mark's Bookshop to take: zero.

On a warm early-fall afternoon, Dave and I sat across from

each other on benches in a playground on Mercer Street and read excerpts from the Starr Report in the *New York Times*. We were both repelled by the existence of the "report" (drafted, as we now know, by a team of bad elves that included everyone's favorite future Supreme Court justice Brett M. Kavanaugh), and we were both horrified by smarmy Bill Clinton's grossly exploitative sexual relationship with a young woman our own age. Dave was the only other Monica defender I knew then, and I mean the *only* one.

"This is pure porn," said Dave, glancing up from the paper. "But there's one good thing about it and I'm going to tell you what it is. Are you ready?"

"Sure," I said.

"Now every president is going to have to have a perfect moral record."

ALL I'VE EVER REALLY WANTED TO DO WAS TO DISAPPEAR INTO SOME room with great wallpaper (de Gournay if possible), read my little book, listen to Mozart, and be left alone. I'm a quiet, placid, harmony-loving person, and I was unprepared to discover that I had become, for a time, and for reasons of romantic and professional anxiety and control (mostly control), a D. F. Wallace irritation object.

He seemed to want to remind me how irrelevant I was to him but also to remind me that he still had power over me. Although he had a new girlfriend, we were as emotionally enmeshed as ever. David, of course, was interested in simultaneity, which he explicated in his art and in his life, and everything was always a two-level game with him; there was always a double movement—you had to understand that he was never in one place or the other, and neither were you.

During a call after he returned home from a vacation to the Caribbean with her (the details of which, I recollect with a shudder,

I actually had to hear *all* about), he said, "I've been making fun of you to a bunch of people." I certainly did not want to know what he'd said about me, and I tried to convince myself not to worry too much about it—anyone who knew David surely understood that he was not exactly the most reliable character witness when it came to women. And I'd been trying to train myself not to care about what people thought of me anyway. A Soviet tank of the spirit, a Soviet tank.

When his girlfriend was preparing to move in with him, he asked me, "Can you give me one reason why this shouldn't happen?" I offered no reply. In a letter he wrote that he'd been feeling "stupefied and irritable as hell—only one of which is a disadvantage when it comes to trying to Live With Somebody." There was a call during which he uttered the astounding sentence "You may know more words than she does, but she's better at cleaning my underwear." He said he wasn't getting any work done because he was watching TV all the time (the woman brought her giant TV with her). He was in a persistent bad mood, he said. He was unhappy, he said.

Good, I thought. *Enjoy your unhappiness.*

I started dating a man, also a writer, whom David happened to know. When he learned of my involvement with the other guy, his response was "You *slimehead.*" And then he hung up on me. He called right back, said, "You *manipulative* slimehead" (pinching the loaf, as it were), and hung up again. Another time, when I was in mid-answer of some inoffensive question he'd asked about the other guy, he said, as pitiless as an executioner, "I *hate* you. I *hate* you. I *hate* you. I *hate* you. I *hate* you."

I was about to say that David—with his ridiculous nicotine patches that kept coming detached from his sweaty, sweaty skin (a fruitless new treatment for his tobacco addiction), his bad attitude, his joyless writing of his beautiful essay about dictionary usage wars and the English language, and his non-writing of his novel—was a real can of worms to me for about a year. But, no—

that's not quite right. We could still talk about writing . . . about *his* writing, I mean. And we were still, improbably, able to work together as editor and writer.

I took a very short voice piece of his, "Yet Another Example of the Porousness of Certain Borders (XII)," for Snap Fiction. The story ran in one of the greatest months of *Esquire* ever, the "heroes" special issue, which also contained Tom Junod's justly celebrated profile of Mr. Rogers. Although it is also true that Woody Allen (yes, *Woody Allen*) was included in this issue, too. *As a hero.*

It was always fun to read David's appropriation-of-voice pieces, though whenever he ventriloquized an unsophisticated character, as he did in the "Porousness" piece (see also, if you dare: the failed voice experiment of the infamous "Wardine be cry" sequence in *Infinite Jest,* written in some sort of horrible pidgin dialect—though David offered to me, by way of explaining away the lesser quality of the Wardine pages, that he wrote them in grad school), the situation always did bring somewhat to mind the case of Sondheim and the Maria lyrics in *West Side Story*. What happens when a hyper-intelligent upper-middle-class guy who went to Williams College and who later studied with the avant-garde music theorist Milton Babbitt attempts the voice of a poor Puerto Rican girl? You get "I Feel Pretty."

David also agreed (after a lot of hemming and hawing and also an aggrieved "But I don't want to be a *journalist;* I want to be a *novelist*") to write a piece for me about Thomas Harris's then forthcoming novel, *Hannibal*. The idea was that a critique of *Hannibal* would lead into a discussion of the aims of literary fiction versus commercial fiction. But the manuscript of *Hannibal* was under embargo and I couldn't get a copy. I went through the appropriate editorial apparatuses—publicist, editor, literary agent—but got nowhere. Then I tried every trick in the book, including some queasy-making name-dropping, and, still with zero progress, I asked some unscrupulous-seeming assistants at the publishing house if they'd sneak me the manuscript (really should not have done that). Still nothing. David's essay would have been something else.

He said he was disappointed that it didn't work out, and I believed him, sort of—until he wondered aloud if I'd been using him all along the past year just to get his name in the magazine.

ON THE SURFACE, EVERYTHING WOULD HAVE SEEMED TO BE GOING pretty well for me that year. Actually, had I been seeing more clearly, I would have understood that things *were* going pretty well. But it's hard to see anything straight: the closer you are to something, the harder it is to have any perspective.

In the late winter, on the evening of Monica Lewinsky's TV interview with Barbara Walters, I held a fiction reading with young authors I'd published at a bar on Orchard Street. I created the guest list and I hosted the evening. (You might even say that, for this night at least, I reigned over an absolutist system.) A male writer in the audience told me that another male writer in the audience was mad at me because he'd heard that I believed Martin Amis wrote better prose than Don DeLillo. Some nerd-fights are worth having and other nerd-fights are not. This one, I decided, was not. A few months later, in celebration of the 1999 summer fiction issue— which would turn out to be the last-ever summer fiction issue—I organized a party at Elaine's, the clubby restaurant on the Upper East Side favored, for better or worse, by a certain specific type of midcentury male writer—the GMN type, let's say. (There's a famous story about how Mailer had once sent Elaine an epical letter of complaint; she wrote "BORING" at the top of the letter and sent it right back to him.) On the walls of Elaine's were framed book jackets from the most celebrated of the writers who'd eaten and drunk there—on a tab. These authors were men. Yes. Elaine's seemed to be a fine place at which to be a man.

An uninvited yet very welcome Steve Martin showed up at the

summer fiction issue party, standing by the bar, distributing business cards drolly noting that the recipient had met Steve Martin.
The passed hors d'oeuvres were just terrible, but everyone knew
about the food at Elaine's, and no one had come to our party to
eat anyway. At 8:00 sharp, Elaine herself—and what an unnerv-
ing individual she was—flicked the lights in the bar area off and
on, off and on, the none-too-subtle sign for the *Esquire* celebrants
to skedaddle. With that flick of the switch, the place, like magic,
transformed at once from party scene back to restaurant.

I'D BELIEVED I'D EXPERIENCED DAVID'S RAGE BEFORE, BUT I WAS WRONG
about that. I had tried to do what I believed was the responsible
thing and told him on a call that I had assigned a short review of
Brief Interviews with Hideous Men to Greil Marcus, a writer David
admired and whose work he'd written about. I also felt I needed to
emphasize to David that I'd have nothing to do with the content
of the review. (No one ever talked to me about the ethics or the
standards and practices of any of this, by the way. No one had
ever told me jack crap about anything. I was just trying to figure it
all out on my own.) David was on a mailing list for *Esquire* comp
copies and was unfortunately sent an issue of the magazine with
the review in it.

A letter arrived from him—a self-serving sockdolager of rage,
entitlement, and self-pity. David was furious that he'd been sent
the magazine. He believed the short Marcus review in *Esquire*
was a pan of *Brief Interviews* (it was not). (And by the way, as for
David's constant public claims never to have read criticism of his
work: untrue, and as an e.g., I can confirm that he had swathes
of a spookily perceptive DFW career summation by A. O. Scott
in *The New York Review of Books* memorized.) David's letter took
the stance of an apology: he confessed that he'd been mad at yours
truly—plexusly kicked whenever he thought of me, in fact—and

had been going around saying mean things about me behind my back. He divulged that he'd also written a hostile letter about me to the writer I was involved with—but that he regretted the letter, he really did. This guy, it must be noted, revered David's work and would have chosen David over me any day. (And the guy, quite charitably, never mentioned the letter to me, and I certainly never asked him about it, God knows.)

"I will *never* cross you, Adrienne," David wrote. "Another lesson learned." He went on to suggest that our relationship had been little more than a sham of mutual professional self-interest, which really was the worst possible thing he could say to me. But David was an outstanding student of human nature (of course he was; recall: *I look for the darkness in people. And when I find it, that's what I cling to*) and understood the fissures at the center of your soul—and knew exactly how to cleave them apart.

David, in the letter, declared me venomous, mocked me, and wrote that I'd hurt him "way, way" more than he'd hurt me. We were engaged in a contest of pain, evidently. The letter climaxed into an extraordinary threat of blackmail about our relationship—because apparently the moments of truth we had experienced together were now to be considered shameful—and he instructed me never to contact him again. His offer: he would stop "bitching" to people about me if and only if I agreed to never again speak to him.

The closing:

"All success w/ all endeavors whaever [sic] they may be & c.,"

The signature:

"Snidely Whiplash"

So David Foster Wallace was the dastardly mustache-twirling cartoon villain. Which meant, I guessed, that I was the hapless damsel he'd tied to the railroad track.

But no, no, that wasn't right—that wasn't right at all. I knew what his rage was about, even as he tried to reformulate his position into a version more to his liking. He hated me because I had power over him.

I needed him to understand that the letter was unacceptable. So I did what any rational person would have done: I picked up the phone and called him. He had changed his number—a classic Orin Incandenza move (in *Infinite Jest,* the odious Orin ditches his bimbos by writing them a letter and changing his number). This was a thing David did all the time: he would, with cruel surgical precision, drop people from his life forever.

The trouble I'd feared was always in store had finally arrived. Misery, which had previously visited my life only in gusts, became, for a period, constant and unvaryingly severe. I listened to Mozart and Cole Porter, and I read *Pale Fire* again, but none of the old tricks worked.

Whom could I talk to about it? What would I even have been permitted to say? Was my story even worth telling? He was David F. Wallace (as some of his cute little return address stickers had it) and I was not. He was a man and I was a woman. He was thirty-seven and I was twenty-seven. I was just some regular person, and he was David F. Wallace, that supreme genius, that towering colossus unto himself, the famous evangelist for empathy and for heads beating heartlike. But he was also a wicked Snidely Whiplash and quite the hideous man ne plus ultra. (Not to mention *very* touchy about his literary reputation.) This was tough information to relate. Would anyone even want to hear it? He was ferociously protected on all quarters. I was dreadfully exposed. Any way I looked at it, I'd lose.

I kept thinking: *His life is actually worth more than mine.*

I kept thinking: *He can treat people any way he wants to, and there will never be any consequences.*

The world spun emptily. I had no interest in flowers. *How ugly everything is,* I remember thinking at a grocery store on University

Place as I considered its bounty: cherries; I was holding miraculous fresh cherries, then out of season. I cried at work. I cried at home. I cried on the subway. I cried at the gym. I woke up crying. (Hadn't even known that was possible.) I thought I was finally seeing clearly, to the dark heart of the matter, to that place, previously hidden from view, where everything actually happened. I believed that reality had finally opened its door and showed me what it was. But the truth was that I wasn't seeing more—I was seeing less.

Had I actually been involved in an emotionally abusive relationship with David? Was *that* what it had been? I knew that I was still very young, and I worried that I would now be emotionally damaged, in some vague indefinite way, from David, forever.

But I also understood that pretty much everything David ever said was self-negating and that he was fundamentally incapable of making a forward statement without also making the backward one. Forward, backward—and at the same time. Which is to say that I knew the letter was also a plea. He needed reassurance that I still loved him.

We made up a couple of months later. Letters were exchanged and apologies were accepted, though it was David who needed to apologize, not I, and when he correctly wrote that my letters were better and more articulate than his, it was the absolute least he could have done.

I wrote to him about how during a particular recent phone conversation with him I had experienced an existential "I am a fraud" moment—a line he repurposed (to my biliousness) in the first sentence of his celebrated tour de force "Good Old Neon." He in turn wrote that he no longer believed that I was an *L. mactans,* a black widow spider. (In *Infinite Jest,* Latrodectus Mactans is the name of protagonist James Incandenza's film production company—a reference to Incandenza's venomous, and very tall, wife, Avril.)

But I knew David. I knew the game. Back to my point about how he proceeded by paradox and contradiction and about how nothing could be accepted on its surface. Each story was a cover story that pointed to its inverse.

So now I knew, I decided, what he had thought of me— possibly always. (I was . . . *Avril?* You always had to be prepared to get into a lot of very weird areas with David.) Finally, everything was explained. A workplace voice-mail message, weenie-ishly left after-hours, appeared with his new number, in case I needed it. I did not call him.

"WHY," I ONCE ASKED DAVE EGGERS, "IS BEING IN OUR TWENTIES SO hard?"

His response: "We're unsettled. We don't know where our next meal is coming from."

I STARTED DATING A CHARMING YOUNG MAN—A NON-WRITER, WHICH was an improvement—who lived in London, an eerily precise replica of the singer Davy Jones from the Monkees and about as tall. Anthony had gone to Eton (verified), was a titled lord (verified), and claimed to be closely related to Virginia Woolf (unverified). He took one look around my very tiny, rabbited apartment and quipped, "Well, *this* isn't much of a dowry." It is not impossible that my restaurant demands, in both London and New York, were a touch on the extravagant side. Once when Anthony came to New York to visit, I ridiculously insisted that he take me to Daniel, perhaps the most expensive restaurant in the city at the time. Maybe I should have offered to pay for something? And why did I think that dashing around London with Anthony on the back of his motorbike was such a capital idea? (Loved how he said "motorbike," however.) These were questions.

More significantly, Rust Hills was let go from *Esquire* that year. Or maybe it's simpler and more polite to say that Rust's emeritus position was eliminated. There was no Veuve Clicquot send-off for him or for anyone who got fired from the magazine in that era. *Esquire* wasn't really a Veuve Clicquot kind of place (*Esquire* did not have a Veuve Clicquot sort of budget, but fewer magazines did now). Rust just disappeared. I sent him a short, feeble note that should have been better and never spoke to him again. No one in the office even ever mentioned him, not once— although writers did, frequently, for if an editor is remembered at all, it is only by his writers. But for the rest of my career at *Esquire,* Rust Hills drifted ghostlike over me, a regular Banquo at the fiction department feast. Or famine, as it would eventually turn out.

Early on, the evil part of me—the icky, ambitious part; the callow youth who was always looking out for number one— experienced a slight little buzz whenever I heard myself say that *I* was the fiction department now. Just as quickly, though, I'd think: *My God, I actually* have *become Al Haig* ("*I am in control here*"). Plus, it wasn't as if Rust had ever been in my way or any- thing; he'd actually only ever tried to be helpful, with his long author lists written on legal pads and with the occasional short- story submission he'd pass along to me. In truth, Rust hadn't ac- tually edited anything at the magazine since I'd been there, and it was unclear whether he had the authority to do so.

It was a tough business—not a smidgen of respect given to a guy who'd devoted most of his working life to *Esquire.* I wasn't the noblest person in the world, not by a long shot, but the whole thing made me deeply uneasy—one minute, you were the red-hot center, and the next you weren't even a memory. But how many people are ever remembered for their jobs anyway? We all believe we should be more loved and respected, professionally and otherwise, than we are (we've all watched too many celebrity awards shows), but most people leave no legacy. Most of us are wiped off the face of time.

A colleague had once told me, during a period when several

people were fired, "There are no tenured positions at *Esquire*." (Indeed, this dude was eventually fired.)

I naturally also took this as a warning. There were no editors for life left here, or anywhere. (But why *should* there have been?)

And of course I understood that Rust's dismissal had little to do with "me"—this was just the way life went: the young replace the old. And the young can be had cheaply.

Remember, remember, I'd tell myself, *whatever power this job provides is an illusion.*

Remember, remember, I'd say, *when you get thrown back into who you are, you'd better have something there.*

Another lesson: I had to remember to quit before I got fired. I didn't want to become a Japanese soldier-holdout in the fifties, hiding on a Polynesian island, believing I was still fighting the war. I also knew this was an entitled approach to working life I couldn't afford; I was no aristocrat, but I *could* be an aristocrat of the spirit, at least in theory. I could try to transfigure myself into that mind-set, maybe somewhat. I wanted to write. I started working on a novel.

Writers take an idea, and they make a world out of it. They dream up a different drama. This seemed important. It wasn't power if you'd been granted it through someone else. You had to create your own power, your own stage, and, if I may say, your own reality.

The mind must be free and incoercible. Only when the mind is free can you live your life as if something is at stake.

21

In the spring of 2000, a submission of "Incarnations of Burned Children" arrived in the mail to me from David (original title: "Incarnations of Burned Children [IV]"—there was a Burned Children *cycle*?). The attached letter—friendly, chatty—felt as if it were in the middle of a conversation we were apparently already having, and it contained no indication that he had any awareness that nearly every encounter I'd had with him for the past year had been like getting zapped by a cattle prod. In the letter, he asked about the writer I'd been seeing. Right on cue. David was always so predictable. I thought, *What does he want from me now?*

A rapprochement, or the reconstitution of any sort of functional relationship with this guy, seemed unlikely. How could we move beyond that abysmal period when everything was black and red, the color of venomous spiders? Working with him would inevitably mean that, at minimum, we'd become emotionally entangled again.

Yet on David's end, I had to grant that the submission was a gesture of faith. "Incarnations of Burned Children" was a gift: an immaculate 1,100-word prose poem that had the stature of a classic fable. It seemed as if it were that had always existed. Scalding water from an overturned pot pools in a baby's diaper, and the mother and father don't know the cause of the—possibly fatal?—trauma. The parents' attempts at rescue only cause more pain, and they become unwitting accomplices in the harm of their child, for this is what human beings do in David's fiction: they fail each other and themselves. The story gutted me then, and now that I am a parent, it destroys me in a whole new way.

I wrote to David to say how much I loved and admired the story and to tell him that we wanted to publish it. "Incarnations" was an easy sell at the magazine. I'm not going to lie: its brevity helped.

Throughout the years, David would leave for me, as he did with other editors, ramblingly amusing office voice-mail messages, delivered safely in the middle of the night, when there was no possibility he'd actually have to talk to anybody. Whenever I'd amble into work in the morning and see the red voice-mail light on my phone (no calls in the publishing industry happen before 10:00 A.M. at least), I always knew the message was from David. (From him I also learned that the voice-mail system would cut a message off after two minutes; thus, David would deliver a multipronged series of two-minute messages.) In response to my note to him that we wanted "Incarnations," David left a set of those 3:00 A.M. voice-mail messages and the typical sign-off—"Call me any time. I'm in and out all day." He again provided his new number. Yeah, that was the way it was so much of the time—beckoned, yet kept at arm's length.

Unless he was expecting a scheduled call from you, he rarely answered his home phone, and you'd have to babble into his answering machine until he picked up.

"I had to write you something you wouldn't reject," David said.

How tenuous, how wholly tenuous, our relationship always was.

"I needed an excuse to talk to you," he said.

"I know," I replied.

"I never have as much fun talking to anyone as I have with you," he said.

A question I often had: Was I granting David, who of course had an unusually wide skill set and who was so very extraordinary in so many ways—here was a man who wrote some of the best sentences in the English language, a true sui generis phenomenon, etc.—all sorts of allowances I wouldn't have given anyone else? Because otherwise I was pretty tough on people.

"I miss you," he said.

All I'd wanted from him for the past year was for him to say that he missed me, and now I had it. He had said it.

I caved immediately.

"I miss you, too," I said. It probably shouldn't have been as easy as it always was to pick up and become friends again with David. The fact: I was never really ever able to stay mad at him for long. Looking back on it, that was probably a mistake. "So what are we going to do about it?"

He was coming to New York, he said.

So now here he was again, setting the terms of our reality. Always David's terms, always David's reality. Of course it was.

He asked about my pet rabbit.

"I'm sure that everyone who sees you walking Lulu outside on a leash is both overwhelmed and impressed," he said.

"You are *always* getting me wrong, David," I said lightly. "I have *never* walked my rabbit outside on a leash."

(Although I did take Lulu with me on airplanes sometimes,

and it probably *was* quite the spectacle to behold. You could actually take your rabbits with you through airport metal detectors pre-9/11.)

"Oh," he replied. "Sorry."

Should I remind him how incredibly unhappy he'd made me? Should I tell him that I woke up crying nearly every morning from August 1999, when the dread Snidely Whiplash entered my world, through November, when we finally patched things up? I had a terrific run of grievances, but I mentioned only one of them.

"You sent me a really mean letter," I said.

"Oh, that was like fifteen things ago," David valiantly replied.

That letter was not "fifteen things ago" for me. But he was thinking of himself, as always, only of himself. (It was also really just so fabulous to know the number on which I fell in the Wallace schema. That was just great.)

"Not a good answer," I said.

A pause.

David asked if the guy—*that* guy, the writer—and I had broken up yet. (He just had to get that "yet" in there.)

We had.

"I *knew* it," he said. "It was like watching an egg timer."

"Yeah, well," I said. "What can you do?"

I mean, what did he *expect* me to say? It wasn't any of his business, actually.

"You sure seem to have a real cavalier attitude toward relationships, don't you, Adrienne?"

David was incorrect. I wanted to be in love and I wanted someone to love me. But it now seemed just about impossible to get that balance right. I'd believed that David and I had something approaching that balance, but I was wrong. I was just starting to wonder if anyone could ever love me.

"You know, I've been thinking a lot about something," David

said. "Do you have incredible four-hours-long conversations with *all* of the writers you edit?"

Words on the page have always been my safe space. When I look at words on a piece of paper—even and especially David's—and try to solve them, I am finally in control. And all I really wanted to do was dig into "Incarnations of Burned Children" like some little burrowing animal looking for its hiding place.

I always felt that I could ask David anything about his work—dumb question, smart question, whatever. I actually always found him to be rather transparent as an artist, by which I mean there was nothing I at least *felt* I couldn't ask him about his craft, process, motives, etc. I would ask him what he meant by something he wrote, and he would tell me, pretty much.

"Incarnations," I told him, felt as if it had emerged into the world whole, like Athena sprung from the head of Zeus. Had it originated in an anecdote he had heard or read?

David claimed he did know a couple whose baby had been burned that way—scalding water in a diaper—and added that he had been thinking about using the anecdote as part of a backstory for a character in the novel he'd been working on—the mysterious thing I'd been hearing about in starts and stops for two years now.

"Wait," I said. "There's a eunuch in the novel?"

"Possibly," he said.

"Weird."

The mind boggled.

So: How *was* the novel going?

Not well, he said, not well at all. He remarked that he was having a hard time distinguishing what was irritating in it from what was not.

But David was such an insanely productive person and had such a puritanical work ethic, so it was always unclear to me how seriously to take any of his novel-related fussing and fretting. Mostly, I'd just think: *There's Wallace being Wallace again.* I'd just think: *There's Mr. Negativity.* But my main observation then was that his talk about the novel did not develop; there was no progression; it was the same old record, the same old loop, over and over, like a Yule log video. And I never got the sense that he was having much fun with it.

By contrast, he did tend to reminisce about the composition of *Infinite Jest,* though mostly these stories were centered on the conditions in whatever lachrymose little room such-and-such sequence was written in—e.g., the story went that when he was writing the section in which the character Hal Incandenza describes his initial unconscious reaction upon entering a suicide scene (the family patriarch has cooked his head in a microwave), David found the line "golly something smells *delicious*" so funny that he laughed so hard, and for so long, that the person in the apartment next door had to bang on the wall and yell at him to shut up. But he'd also talk about how much energy he had when he was writing *Infinite Jest.* He'd talk about how much younger he'd been then.

"You're still so young, David," I'd say.

"No, I'm not," he'd reply. "I *used* to be a very young writer. Now I'm a very old writer."

Sometimes you'd also feel compelled to remind David that he'd *already* written the novel that had changed the world. How many of the hundred billion human beings who've lived on this planet have actually ever made any kind of real contribution to civilization? *You changed our language, David. What else could ever be required of any person's life? You've done it. You wrote* Infinite Jest. *Hang up your hat and call it a career already. Enough.* Nunc dimittis.

"Yeah," David would say. "Well."

What an odd and hellish existence it must have been for him, to know that he'd changed the world, but also to know that changing the world wasn't enough. But it was better than the alternative, I suppose, for someone like David. Alexander the Great wept when there were no lands left to conquer, after all.

And where "Incarnations" went emotionally, I said, felt very new. Was the new novel similarly, uh . . . raw?

He said that he'd been trying to evolve from what he called his "annoying verbose persona" to something new and again mentioned, as he had a couple of years before, the Raymond Carver story "Cathedral" as a model. ("Cathedral," by the way, was not published in *Esquire*, alas. Lish was gone by the time the story ran in *The Atlantic* in 1981 and was then Carver's editor at Knopf.)

Superficially, maybe it's hard to see much Carver in "Incarnations" or anywhere in David's maximalist fictional world—he railed against catatonic Carver wannabes in his famous essay "E Unibus Pluram: Television and U.S. Fiction," for example—but he and Carver were kindred spirits in so many ways. For one, both always took the side of the little guy—the marginal, the heartbroken, the left behind. In the ending of "Cathedral," the narrator, an inarticulate man, a man prosaic from the ground up (an idiot savant, almost), draws a picture of a cathedral for a blind man. The narrator's eyes are closed as he draws, and the blind man places his hands over the narrator's hands and follows along. They are two people communicating deeply, without words. "It was like nothing else in my life up to now," says the narrator, for whom the act of drawing a church without seeing it, and with another human being, inspires feelings of awe and of hope. It is a transcendently hopeful ending.

David said, "I want to give us something that makes us happy we speak this language."

IN THOSE YEARS, WHENEVER DAVID WOULD PLAN A TRIP TO NEW YORK, I'd get a series of late-night voice-mail messages, and we'd set up a plan to "break bread," as he had it. He was coming to New York for the *Harper's* 150th anniversary party. We'd see each other at the party, and there was also a plan to get together during the trip.

The party was held in a majestic room at Grand Central, now

a European-inspired upmarket food hall. Who knows how many people were there that night. Three hundred? A thousand? I'm bad with guesstimates like that. I suppose the event was suggested as black tie, but there wasn't much of a Venn diagram intersection between this particular quadrant of publishing (high prestige, low profit) and formalwear. (David once remarked that I was too quick to make fun of people's clothes, so I'm going to just stop myself now.)

David was standing with a group of people—writers and editors—some of whom I knew slightly. His hair, I regret to report, was styled in a high man bun. (This occasion also marks my first-ever sighting of a man bun.) He and I saw each other, and I witnessed what appeared to be a full-system collapse: his eyes widened, he looked away from me, and a big strained grin came to his face. With too much enthusiasm, like a bobblehead on a dashboard, David nodded at something someone said. He stood there grinning and nodding, grinning and nodding, the ridiculous man bun bobbing away.

My reflexive response to seeing him, it turned out, was not to go toward him but to turn away. This unforgiving public setting was not perhaps the ideal environment for a rendezvous, and I needed a moment.

Naturally, the DFW routine was working its magic on the assembled group. He sure was a slippery one. He could be the sweetest person in the world, but he also had that addict's easy charm—he was brilliant at having you believe that you were the only reader whose opinion he really valued, that you were the only writer whose work he really liked, that you were the only person he'd really ever cared about. This light phoniness was a trick you couldn't help but slightly admire, I supposed—making people question your intentionality at least had the effect of keeping everyone thinking about you. And in the way that readers now feel an ownership of David's work, his persona, his memory, his legacy, people then were also fiercely possessive of David the man. (Which was exactly the way he wanted it.) I'd observed that even individuals who'd had but an oblique connection to him often seemed to think, to some degree, *He's mine.*

Well, let them think that, I thought then in Grand Central. *Bra*-vo.

Did they know that David was not to be trusted and that he in turn trusted *no one?* Had they considered how much of the act was real, and how much of it was prop furniture, frayed rug and peeling paint, cardboard and plastic?

I was thinking: *Let his bullshit work on everyone else.*

I was thinking: *He always gets what he wants from everyone— especially women—but he's not going to* get that *from me.*

Maybe ten seconds had passed when I turned around.

David was gone. He'd left the party. He'd fled the scene, slipping out like a ghost. I didn't hear from him during his trip.

Of course all of my least charitable thoughts about him had been proved true. And again I was reminded: You simply could not believe how ungentlemanly, how socially incompetent, and how cold David could be. You could never get your hopes up that any Marquess of Queensbury rules might be decorously observed—he would always do exactly what he was going to do.

The truth: in order to survive a relationship of any sort with David, you'd better have built up a massive arsenal of internal resources. Because, really, you were completely on your own. Thus it was, and thus it would ever be.

A call from him when he'd returned home.

"I *think* I saw you at the party and I *think* we made eye contact," he said.

"You 'think' we made eye contact?" I said. "David, you saw me and you ran away."

A pause.

"Your interpretation of events is somewhat different from mine."

Silence upon silences.

"O-*K*," I said.

"Well, you looked galactic!" he said.

What on earth *was* this relationship—or non-relationship?

I told him that he'd hurt my feelings. It was now clear that all this guy could do was bring pain—pain and more pain. Often I'd find myself wishing he'd just go away. But he never did, not entirely.

"Someday when we're really old," he said, "we'll be sitting together in rocking chairs on a porch with our glasses of lemonade, and we'll hold hands and laugh about the whole Dave and Adrienne saga."

SOME VERY FANCY WRITERS WON'T ACCEPT ANY EDITS. (PLENTY OF non-fancy writers won't accept any edits, either—these people always blew me away; as any editor will tell you, the authors who say they don't need any editing are the ones who need the most.) I've worked with writers of varying talent and stature levels, and I can tell you that David was the absolute best one to work with. No one was more playful or more fun. His fiction submissions were always object lessons to other writers about how to do their jobs. The manuscripts were always delivered immaculate and imposingly typo-free (and always in an irksomely microscopic font size) and usually included a note to the copy editors, instructing them to "STET EVERYTHING." (David's weird little editorial habits were just the best; I also loved how he would type, penguinlike, his FedEx shipping labels for the most urgent of printed material, and also how he'd both seal *and* use multiple pieces of tape to keep his envelopes shut, a worst-case-scenarioist as always.)

And yet, as much as a perfectionist and as exacting as David always was about his work, he was also open, engaged, and really incredibly generous with edits. I also appreciated that David, despite everything, took me seriously as a reader, as an editor, and as a thinker, when I had my worries that maybe not too many other people did. (I've been condescended to by far lesser men [and women] than David.) I know that various editors' opinions of him differ, and I certainly appreciate as well as anyone what a nightmare he could be (and he in turn could often be very mean about editors, most of whom were, in his view, always fucking with his stuff: "I think all he does is masturbate in his office all day," he said of one), but in my view, he was, professionally, a dream.

Although, looking back on it, I have to admit that I would have been rather blind not to note a mildly erotic component involved in our editorial exchanges: for instance, when he said, after "Incarnations" had closed, that I was his fantasy reader; when he thanked me in a letter for going through the story "so slow & careful"; and when he cryptically said that he wrote the line "If you've never wept and want to, have a child" for me. I had no response to that one.

In "Incarnations of Burned Children," the child expresses his pain and terror by the frantic moving of his hands. David and I had some hand logistics discussions—would the hands be *there*, or *there*, or *there*, and for how long? David once remarked to me that his mother, the brilliant writing teacher, had taught him that an action in a piece of writing must be able to be performed physically: Does the written description of the activity track with the real-world movement? The example he used as he stood in front of me then: he pretended to spread peanut butter on a slice of bread. In the draft of "Incarnations," I believed that there were not enough descriptions of the baby's hands: in fact, there was only *one*—"tiny stricken motions"—and it appeared late. I suggested that it be moved earlier. "Nein," he wrote, but added the very necessary "the toddler still made little fists" early on.

We discussed how the action and the timing of the events in the story needed to be flawless. (He had made an outline to help with exactly that, he said.) In the draft, the hot water collects in the baby's diaper for three, four minutes, which I believed was too long a period. David reduced the time to one, two minutes—although as he noted to me, the passage of time was the *parents'* perception.

The body is always a problem in Wallace fiction. David surely had to have been as great as Tolstoy, his closest peer (though his preference was for Dostoyevsky), in depicting how emotions are displayed on the body, and it was fascinating to see how "Incarnations" dealt with the expression of bodily pain. In the line "a high pure shining sound that could stop his heart and his lips," I had wondered about adding an adjective to "lips"; David plumped for "bitty." (We did both wonder if "bitty" was just slightly too cute, though, but "bitty" it was.) His biggest act of faith regarding my edits, he said, was changing the original spelling of "cigaret" (who *wouldn't* have queried it?) to the standard "cigarette" everyone knows and loves. According to David, "cigarette" is, or can be, or was (but what era are we even talking about?), spelled "cigaret" in the mid-South, the setting of the story. Up until that point, I hadn't known that "cigaret" was a thing.

In the end of "Incarnations," the baby floats above itself and experiences a soul death, described in the story as the sun falling and rising like a yoyo (or, in the original version, yo-yo). I recalled the very same description of a sun going up and down through a window like a yo-yo in *Infinite Jest,* although the perspective is from the character Don Gately, an addict mid-binge, not a gravely injured child. I did what any close reader would have done and brought up the repetition with David.

"This is horrifying," he said.

What, I shouldn't have told him?

"Of course you should have. If you hadn't, it would have been as if something neon had been hanging from my nose and you'd been too polite to say anything about it. But please don't tell anyone. Dead man's talk?"

This was classic David, trying to manage his own projection. And it was never a great situation whenever he sensed that your perception of him was not consistent with the one he wanted you to have, whenever he sensed that you had not accepted his self-inventions . . . but he was like all of us that way, I guess—we want to be observed only when we can control the image. Social media thrives on our hysteria to manage other people's opinions of us, obviously.

"You always seem to know when I'm ripping myself off," he said. "You've really got my number, don't you?"

Oh, no. No, no, no, I didn't think *that*—not for a minute.

David finally decided that using a hyphenated "yo-yo" in "Incarnations" looked, as he said, too prissy and anal for a story set in southern Indiana and written in a voice he characterized as "hillbilly," and he decided to do it as one word. So: "yoyo" in "Incarnations" and "yo-yo" in *Infinite Jest*. This was just the kind of thing I found a little too fatally interesting and could talk to David about forever.

Oh, and hey, David, does the baby die at the end of the story?

"I don't *think* so," David said, in perfect alignment with his resistance to closure. "Do *you*?"

David sent a picture of his new dog, Werner Whimperer—named for the actor Werner Klemperer, famous way back when for his role as the bumbling, monocled POW-camp commandant Colonel Klink in *Hogan's Heroes* (and, interestingly, the son of the illustrious German conductor Otto Klemperer), and we entered a more easygoing relationship phase, thank God. I was preparing to go to a writers' conference in Colorado, and David suggested that I try to relax a little bit there. He told me to take it easy for once. He wrote that I should drink a lot and bask in having people butter me up. "You deserve it," he wrote. Often he'd say that he and I both seemed to have a hard time letting people be nice to us, and he was probably right about that. He wrote, "I think you're a really good editor, better now than *Esquire* deserves, and f.y.i. I've told Franzen and G. Saunders and other people this . . ."

Well, thanks for that, I *guess*? (I mean, at least he wasn't still going around bitching to people about me.) I really did hope I was getting to be a good editor. I knew I had more confidence than I used to. But David was always so negative about *Esquire*—that "apelike *Esquire* reader" comment of his back in the early days was just the beginning. *Esquire* was too corporate for David, too mainstream, not sufficiently literary.

"Hey, what do you want?" I'd ask him. "The *Partisan Review*?" I'd remind him *Esquire* was an excellent magazine (minus its woman problem) and would also gently ask him to recall that he'd agreed to pose for an *Us* magazine photo shoot in the eighties, and a writer who'd agreed to pose for *Us* magazine was not exactly allowed to grandstand about literary prestige. A part of David always believed I was a sellout for working at *Esquire*. That was the kind of thing some of us used to worry about.

"So why do you even submit your stories if you don't want to be published here?" I asked.

"I don't 'want to be published' in *Esquire*," David said. "I want to be edited by you."

And now we get to the issue of his IRS audit. David claimed that the Hearst accounting department (although in truth he also seemed to kind of blame me) had sent him the incorrect tax form two years before for his "Adult World" payment—a personal tax form was sent to him directly, he said, when it should have been sent to his agent. This alleged mix-up, he contended, had helped trigger an unpleasant audit then under way. He was extremely freaked out about this audit.

"Someday I will have my revenge," he said ominously, although it was unclear whether his revenge would be exacted on the IRS, on the Hearst Corporation, or on me.

That summer, David had a residency at a writers' colony in

Marfa, Texas. The purpose of the residency was to get work done on the novel; afterward, he admitted that he didn't accomplish one thing there and that all he'd done was torture people with his off-key singing and take someone else's dog on walks.

He said he had been invited by the writer Lewis Hyde to read that fall at Kenyon College (where he would, five years later, deliver "This Is Water"), and it was on that trip when he would read "Incarnations of Burned Children" aloud for the first time.

"People seemed to like it, although I have no clue why," he reported back. Afterward, "Incarnations" became a staple in the DFW read-aloud repertoire.

Later, he would remark to me that the story was the only good fiction he wrote the whole year.

"I worry that my fiction is good only when I'm using it as a means of seduction," he said seductively.

Was he actually saying that "Incarnations of Burned Children," a story about the horror of parenthood and the death of a human soul, was his version of a love story?

DAVID HAD REMARKED THAT AFTER *INFINITE JEST* WAS PUBLISHED, HE'D temporarily believed that he would never again have any of his work rejected for publication. *"Wrong again,"* he said. He could feel his students watching him, he said, could feel their eyes on him, could feel them thinking how easy everything was for him. What they didn't understand was that nothing really ever changes and that everything was still a struggle, but an even worse struggle: "Now everyone's waiting for me to fuck everything up."

He was not incorrect. Of course I knew plenty of Wallace fanboys, but I also knew lots of Wallace opponents (both factions = unbearable; unoriginal observation: fanboys were younger than David, opponents were older). The criticism lobbed around most frequently about David's work then: "too cold," "too intellectual," and "ugly." (I heard "ugly" applied to his work rather often.) His adversaries, wet-lipped and beady-eyed as they were, always brought to mind the rival artist in *Sunday in the Park with George,* who says of Seurat's paintings that they're all mind and no heart, that there's no life in his art.

It was also true that negative energies seemed ever more on the ascendant in this, the literary world, where, at its least lovable, the worst parts of academia and the worst parts of celebrity culture merged into one hard-to-take package.

It was getting to be just a bit too much sometimes. The competing for slots. The whole who's-up-who's-down of it all. The masculine idea of competition. The hell world of the literary star system (it was *Esquire*'s Literary Universe all over again, all the time). The ranking, sorting, pigeonholing of authors. Who's in the red-hot center? The heartburn created among the people I knew whenever a new batch of names of the very most exciting youngish writers came out in a magazine. "Everyone is worried that this list is going to be seen as a correction to the last list," said a writer friend upon the rumors of the latest magazine list, concerned that if he didn't appear on the new one (he had appeared on the last one), his career would be over. (*"The list is life."*) To watch these brilliantly talented—and even occasionally dignified—adults be put through the processing machine. I wanted to tell them not to care too much about the opinions of people who had jobs like mine.

I actually almost sometimes wished that people didn't care about books anymore, or at least not like this.

Questions: Is there any more tenuous, insecure, and impossible job than a writer's? Are there ever any judgments more unforgiving than literary judgments? Why do we, or did we (back when we, for better or worse, cared a little more than we do now), insist on evaluating a writer's career—the career which is the life—so much more ruthlessly than we do other jobs? We don't say of an engineer, "Obviously, she's not too bright—she's *never* been able to combine quantum physics and general relativity into one unified theory." Or of a schoolteacher, "Poor thing. He'll never be Aristotle." We don't need our plumber to have won the Most Famous Plumber in the World trophy. But it's just perfectly fine to dismiss the whole of a writer's life and career with "His work is *not* going to survive in fifty years." The bar for literary achievement is remorselessly high—and so are the stakes.

I was twenty-eight years old. I had been at *Esquire* for three years. I was still frequently reminded that people would kill (kill *me?*) for my position. I was still frequently reminded that I had a dream job. But something was happening. I could feel the world changing around me.

The fiction we published was often formidable and important, but my big secret was that I didn't have much confidence that many people actually read it. People of course still read and even talked about the fiction in *The New Yorker,* but *Esquire?* And when I started at the magazine, I would acquire a short story, and it would be published with reasonable promptness. Now it was taking longer to schedule my pieces. I was also having a harder time getting long-form book reviews into the magazine, and there was limited interest at *Esquire* in most literary critics . . . but the thing was, I must say that I didn't even disagree with the thinking: it really *was* starting to seem as if the critic didn't have all that much to say anymore. Maybe everything was going the way of the star system—a world governed by star ratings. Maybe people no longer believed they needed an authority to tell them what to think, and maybe the culture of expertise was on its way out.

I was a rationalist, a realist (in some ways at least), and I tried to take a pragmatic view: the industry was evolving and budgets were shrinking. What practical value was actually brought to the magazine by my sections? I used to make the hilarious joke that I edited the "Please Don't Read Me" parts of *Esquire*—nothing to appeal to advertisers, no celebrities, no boobs, no bespoke suits, no handmade wingtip shoes, nothing newsworthy, nothing crudely relevant.

I still found so much about my job meaningful, but I now worried that it wasn't enough. I had always found my salvation in great writing, and I got to work with the remarkably talented people who wrote the literature I loved. I'd learned so much from them. Less nobly, I could get anyone on the phone if I wanted to (whether I wanted to is another question), and I could also be useful helping with an emerging writer's career . . . but that also wasn't enough. I had a very nice regular table at Aquavit, and I'd been to far too many cocktail parties and dinners. (Whenever I told David about an event I'd attended that he gauged a little too obnoxiously insider-y—meaning: I had an encounter with someone more famous than he—he'd say, "Why, you little *shit*.") I will admit that I now knew how it was to think you should be admired at least for getting in the room—whatever room that was. But what did any of it actually mean?

I WENT TO A DINNER FOR THE WRITER JOHN BARTH. THE DINNER WAS A publicity event in the campaign for his new novel, *Coming Soon!!!*, and its three frenzied exclamation marks. It had been a number of years since his last book, and Barth, then in his seventies, was being "relaunched" as an author, I guess you'd say, reintroduced—or *introduced*, as the case may have been—to a new generation of book reviewers and book-review editors. In a private room in a restaurant at a downtown hotel came the tapping of a spoon on a water glass. The room quieted down, and Barth's publisher gave a nice speech about the great man's virtuosic talent, his titanic stature in the world of avant-garde literary fiction, and his enduring influence—there would be, she said, no David Foster Wallace or Dave Eggers without him.

It's certainly true that Barth was a Wallace forefather, a major influence on him as a very young writer, but David's maturing view of Barth's work, as exemplified in David's weird, convoluted, and extremely boring earlyish novella (written, incidentally, in the late eighties, at a moment of Peak Carver) "Westward the Course of Empire Takes Its Way," is ambivalent at best. "Westward" is a direct confrontation with Barth's famous story "Lost in the Funhouse" and a harangue (*sort of*—it's complicated) against the deficiencies and limitations of clever, academic metafiction. John Barth and David Foster Wallace both appear in "Westward" as characters: Barth as the famed writing professor and metafictionist Professor Ambrose (Ambrose is also the name of the protagonist in "Lost in the Funhouse"), and David as two characters—an M.F.A. student (and competitive archer) in Ambrose's class, who is "hotly cocky enough to think he might someday inherit Ambrose's bald crown," and as a character in a story ("Dave") who murders his "neurasthenic," "mildly wacko" girlfriend. (Nice one, "Dave.") Or maybe David is *three* characters, if you also count the intrusive narrator (I said "Westward" was convoluted), but the point is that Barth/Ambrose, though affectionately drawn, served as patriarch in this particular patricide.

The story in *Coming Soon!!!* has to do with a rivalry between an older avant-garde novelist (character name: Novelist Emeritus, and he looks a lot like John Barth) and a younger novelist (character name: Novelist Aspirant; let's just think of him as the David Foster Wallace who wrote "Westward"), who wants to reinvent the older man's first novel (which happens to be Barth's first novel, *The Floating Opera*) in hypertext. Every sentence of this exhaustingly self-referential book burbles with the terrors of the once king, no longer absolute in his powers, and I will admit that I've been trying to read it for nearly twenty years.

The night of the dinner, Barth had on a black beret, worn at a jaunty angle upon his bald crown, and looked just like John Barth. He made the rounds to each table, and when he took a seat at ours, he talked wittily about hot-air balloons, which was just the sort of thing you'd expect John Barth to talk about. As he charmingly held court (unlike a lot of writers, he was very good at talking), I was thinking about how weird it was that John Barth was seated *right there,* performing for us. (Who were *we,* relative to *him?* Who was *I?*) Here was the novelist emeritus who once stood at the vanguard of American postmodern fiction, a truly innovative artist who had produced an original, hilarious body of work (although in truth a lot of it was also pretty bad), and still it wasn't enough. Each book is always a starting over, for every writer. I was thinking then about how I had always been so terrified of this line from "Lost in the Funhouse": "There ought to be a button you could push to end your life absolutely without pain; disappear in a flick, like turning out a light," because someone who could write that was someone who knew a lot about despair, and I was thinking about how Barth, with his jauntily angled beret perched upon that great big bald crown, was being reintroduced to whippersnappers such as myself, and about how we all become self-parodies in the end, and about how the whole Barth project concerning the internal problems of narrative in literary fiction maybe didn't even seem all that pertinent anymore.

Barth wrote a short "review" of *Coming Soon!!!* for *Esquire.* At a later date, someone at his publishing house said to me with a weary sigh that his piece in the magazine was the only good review the book got.

More and more often, I'd have an encounter with some veteran publishing professional who seemed to perhaps be nursing some vague cosmic grudge, as if something in life had eluded him—but what? I now understood that there was a huge fatigue risk with these publishing jobs; people would eventually reach a point of burnout—or maybe "malaise" is a better word—and then they would become resistant readers. I was always reminding myself never to become like that, reading suspiciously, my formerly lively mind ground to purest power. (I also had to make sure, no matter what, that I didn't become one of those ghastly voices who writes in rejection letters, "I found much to admire about his work, but, alas, I'm not the perfect champion for this one. I'm afraid I must step aside, but I'll be cheering from the sidelines. . . .")

One of the great things about David: conversations with him about books were always so uncynical. I really needed that in my life. And talking to David about writers and writing—what could have been better? The topic remained, I think, his most consistent source of optimism. Even though he was of course rabidly competitive, and even if he didn't like the work, he was always on the writer's side—never on the publisher's, never on the reviewer's; for example, you *so* did not want to say to David about another writer's "long-anticipated" novel, "Hey, what took him so long?" He'd be sure to scold: "Now you're sounding like one of *them*. And you do *not* want to sound like one of them."

Always good advice. (But also rather controlling, wouldn't you say?) I'd already been giving it to myself for as long as I'd been in New York, with varying levels of success. But was I even following my own warnings to self? It was possible that I was not. The worst of it—I now *knew* that I was starting to read suspiciously, at least sometimes. Was it possible that I was not quite approaching each new manuscript with the cheerful sense of expectation I once had?

One of my biggest mistakes as an editor: I rejected an excerpt from J. M. Coetzee's novel *Disgrace,* a stone-solid masterpiece (and with the world's most heartbreaking dog) by a writer I think the world of (I mean, who doesn't?). The excerpt may as well have been delivered to me on a golden platter: it had gone through an early-stage edit at another magazine and was submitted as a perfect stand-alone story. But I couldn't accept what I then viewed as the central character's sexism. The novelist is not responsible for the views of his characters, though. Would that I had had a higher appreciation for nuance with that one.

I didn't want to be a foe to writers. I wanted to be an ally. But I was, I knew, a little of both. Sometimes a little more of this, sometimes a lot more of that—but there was always that double movement. It was always both.

IN HIS SPECTACULAR MEMOIR, *FINISHING THE HAT*, SONDHEIM DESCRIBES an evening he and the composer Jule Styne had in the sixties with Cole Porter. Sondheim and Styne, who were writing the musical *Gypsy*, went to visit Porter in his apartment at the Waldorf Astoria Towers. Porter was despondent and in severe physical pain. (Both of his legs were by this point amputated—the tragic final outcome of a fall from a horse decades before; miraculously, some of Porter's best work, including his late triumph *Kiss Me, Kate*, was to come after his accident.) Sondheim and Styne played "Together (Wherever We Go)" from *Gypsy* for Porter, because what could cheer a guy up more than:

> *No fits, no fights, no feuds and no egos—*
> *Amigos. . . .*

When Sondheim and Styne arrived at the word "amigos," Porter gave a gasp of delight. He hadn't been expecting the shock of that fifth rhyme, the ravishing anomalousness of it.

This is the story I think about when I need to be reminded why appreciation is important, and brave, and heroic, and why you need to hold fast to it: it's the only thing that can triumph over the abyss. If you don't have your appreciation, you've lost your life.

22

When I was a child in Marysville, Ohio, I spent my afternoons with a babysitter, a small, stolid gray-haired lady named Mrs. Albrecht. She lived with her husband in a modest ranch house across from us on our rural road. Mr. and Mrs. Albrecht seemed about eight hundred years old, but they were probably only about half that then. Mrs. Albrecht made her own dresses, made her own wine, and, of most interest to me, made her own egg noodles. Every Friday, ribbons of powdery noodles dangled down from wood drying racks placed around the kitchen counter. It always seemed such a disgrace, concealing those glorious noodles within the inelegant mass of each Friday night's tuna noodle casserole, but on the upside, at least she'd always top the casserole with a few inches of potato chips that had been deafeningly pulverized between two sheets of wax paper with a rolling pin.

Mrs. Albrecht's husband, the mute, balding, and craggy Mr. Albrecht, worked as a clerk at a state store, an Ohio-run liquor outlet—a holdover from old Prohibition laws and also, we may assume, a continuing boondoggle for the state. They were German Lutherans, Mr. and Mrs. Albrecht were, and given that my mother is Welsh/English Lutheran, their overall approach to life always felt familiar to me. Mr. and Mrs. Albrecht were, however, demonstrably more biblically inclined than anyone in my family and attended services every Sunday and Wednesday at their small country church. They took me with them a couple of times, on Communion Sundays, but I'd always have to hang back at the pews as they went up and received the sacrament. I hadn't been properly baptized, I guess. And while I didn't join them for dinner too often, I do recall that Mr. Albrecht, being the man of the house, was the designated giver of grace at the beginning of each meal. We would join hands around the table and he would recite the Lutheran dinner prayer: "Come, Lord Jesus, be our guest. And let Thy gifts to us be blessed. Amen." Still to this day, on the rare occasion I'm asked to say grace before dinner, the one and only prayer I've got is Mr. Albrecht's.

Dinner would commence and, in potent contrast to my parents' more spirited table, would continue in silence, except when Mr. Albrecht would ask Mrs. Albrecht for a second or third helping: "Is there extry, Mother?" (He called her "Mother"; she called him "Father.") The obstacle of Mr. Albrecht's left thumb would serve as knife substitute to assist food from plate onto fork.

Mrs. Albrecht and I didn't talk much—she was supposed to be supervising me, I guess, but I didn't need much supervision, and she was always busy cooking, cleaning, or doing whatever other various household chores consumed her life. My mother was also always a bustle of activity at home, of course, and my grandmother was, too . . . and so was pretty much every other adult woman I'd ever known. This, it seemed to me, was what being a female was about: a body in motion, but deeper energies unexpressed. I was concerned about this already.

Every Friday evening, during the rite known as the Drying of the Noodles, my mother would come to pick me up and, while standing at the Albrecht front door, attempt to pay Mrs. Albrecht for the week's babysitting. The process always took an exceedingly long time; the ritual was that Mrs. Albrecht would refuse the money the first hundred or so times my mother would try to give it to her. Stagily, Mrs. Albrecht would wave the cash away, saying, "No, no, Lord, *no*"; there would be solemn shakings of the head. My mother was tall and rangy, with freckles and long red (*"strawberry blond,"* as she'd insist) hair, and might have been wearing her Navajo poncho, denim skirt, and oxblood boots; Mrs. Albrecht was small and gray, shrinking, fading to nothing, and would certainly have had on a homemade polyester-based housedress with a row of buttons down the front. Finally, the exchange would reach its inevitable conclusion as Mrs. Albrecht, contrite (but why?), accepted that filthy lucre.

Mrs. Albrecht called disabled people "crippled"; she had a shoebox full of small, eerie old dolls with delicate painted faces and another box with beautiful marbles in it; and she owned exactly two books, a Bible and a title in the Mole and Troll series. In her living room was a black-and-white TV on which *The Lawrence Welk Show* and *The Little Rascals* could be viewed, and upon the odd, mirrored cornflower blue of the coffee table top sat an emerald-colored glass candy dish, which, if you really studied it, you could see was embossed with moons and stars. She would feed me ice pops that came in dubious plastic tubes she'd snip open with orange-handled scissors, homemade rhubarb pie, and a regional candy specialty called a Buckeye—a milk chocolate–dunked orb of the most glue-like peanut butter, with a pound or two of sugar added to it for good measure. These dense little insulin bombs are fatally ubiquitous in rural Ohio, Buckeye State.

One afternoon, Mrs. Albrecht took me with her to visit Mr.

Albrecht at work at the state store. Before he knew we were there, I spied him in the stockroom, through a window on a swinging door, and watched as he stood peering down at some boxes. His face was downcast, and his shoulders were stooped from some unseen accumulated weight, as if the very embodiment of injustice. I recall having some vague, very vague, thoughts (but, man, I *felt* them) about the pathos of each individual life, about how most people seemed to have—or was it that they believed they had?—very little control over their own being.

I wondered: Did most people ever expect their lives to change? Did they even want them to?

When Mr. Albrecht wasn't at work, he could be found on the rocking chair on his patio—the rocking back and forth of the chair was the only sign that he was actually alive—watching the traffic, as Mrs. Albrecht weeded the garden, raked leaves, hung the laundry up on the clothesline (securing Mr. Albrecht's white undershirts with the beguiling wood clothespins onto which I always had an intense urge to draw fancy little old-fashioned ladies or flowers), or else he might be mowing their patchy, uneven lawn. (The Albrechts, as should now be clear, weren't the sort of people to invest in lawn chemicals.) In addition to the rocking of the chair, Mr. Albrecht's other projects on the patio involved packing down tobacco in his pipe with his fingers and cleaning his fingernails with the blade of the folding knife he kept in his overalls.

Often, and always in silence, I'd sit with Mr. Albrecht on the patio, watching the rural road for sightings of tractors and Amish carriages. Occasionally, you'd get a vintage auto out on a joy ride or, on the most auspicious of days, a truly splendid kit car. Mr. Albrecht would rock away on the chair as I'd sit cross-legged on the concrete patio floor, amusing myself by balling up blades of grass and stuffing them into the mouths of the beautiful pale-colored snapdragons I'd plucked from the Albrecht flower bed. You were always aware of the faint scent of garlic chives.

One summer afternoon when I was seven, I was sitting on Mr. Albrecht's lap, in their living room. The chair was a recliner. Mrs. Albrecht was not home. An old show I disliked enormously, *Family Affair,* was on the TV at a low volume. Mr. Albrecht was reading the Mole and Troll book aloud to me. He'd never read to me before and didn't seem to know that I was expecting an actual performance. Where were the voices? Where were the sound effects? The back of his neck was wrinkled like a peanut (or a mole's neck? a troll's?) and his skin smelled like pipe tobacco.

Unexpectedly, in the middle of a sentence, he stopped reading. He leaned back in the recliner. He looked at me, unbuttoned the fly of his overalls, and exposed himself.

I had a series of varying thoughts about this, but I kept them to myself—and I would continue to.

I got up from the chair.

"Now don't tell Mother," he said as I walked away. "She would be cross."

Mrs. Albrecht remained my babysitter for two more years, until we moved up to the Rust Belt. After what happened, I don't recall that I ever actually spoke to Mr. Albrecht again. He was always elsewhere in the (not large) house when I was there. I'm sure I never again watched the traffic with him out on the patio.

Years later, when I was a teenager, my parents and I went back to Columbus for a weekend trip. We visited Mr. and Mrs. Albrecht. Mr. Albrecht didn't say a word the whole time, and he looked extremely ancient as he sat immobile in a straight-backed chair, grimly pinned to the wall.

I actually really loved Mr. and Mrs. Albrecht.

People. What can I say? They'll break your heart every time. I suppose we're all more profoundly vexed, all more deeply shadowed and shaded, than we otherwise let on. "This thing of darkness I acknowledge mine," says Prospero in *The Tempest.* It's impossible to see anyone straight, I guess. You never get anywhere near a full picture of anyone or anything, and the deeper you try to get into something, the more illegible it becomes. The more you try to know, the more you find that the thing proliferates, and changes, and assumes new forms, growing starfish tentacles that take you deeper into something else.

23

In 2001—before the world cracked open and everything changed forever, back when our biggest problem was still the installation of an illegitimate president by the Supreme Court (remember hanging chads and the dirty Floridan secretary of state? remember when we all became experts in election law?)—*Esquire* was finally nominated for a National Magazine Award for Fiction. These awards, the Oscars of magazines, for better or worse, are the industry's raison d'être. It makes no difference that no one outside of the publishing world has ever heard of them. *Esquire* hadn't been nominated for the National Magazine Award in Fiction since 1994 and hadn't won one since 1991.

The lunchtime award ceremony was held in the grand ballroom at the Waldorf Astoria for an audience of fourteen hundred editors, media executives, and VIPs. Rosie O'Donnell, then the figurehead of a short-lived self-titled magazine, served as emcee. She came on-stage dragging a prop IV pack and cracked jokes about a recent staph infection, the gory aftermath (the audience learned, whether they wanted to or not) of an incident with a fishing pole. *Esquire* had received two nominations that year for the feature writing category but lost to *Rolling Stone,* for David Foster Wallace's article about John McCain. The McCain piece was long but slight, and its real subject was David's anxiety about being less of a man than John McCain. When the winner was announced, some guys at my table wondered aloud if the elusive DFW was in attendance. Of course he was not. "I hate him for not being here," said an *Esquire* writer to me. "I guess he's just too *good* for this, isn't he?" I had nothing to say about that. (Later, of his prize, David remarked, whether bullshitting or not, "I'd never even known these awards existed before. Are they a big deal?")

Esquire ended up losing the fiction award. ("You was robbed," said the journalist seated next to me when the winner, the upstart *Zoetrope,* was announced.) I disliked that I was so irritated we'd lost, and I knew I really had to watch myself and make sure I didn't become someone I didn't want to become. You have to be vigilant with yourself, of course. You have to be on the lookout for the first signs of psychic collapse.

Helpfully, the men's magazine could always be counted on to locate the first signs of a woman's *physical* collapse. That year, *Esquire* produced a special issue around the theme of the "Aging Woman." The cover lines:

HOW WOMEN AGE
A MAN'S SURVIVAL GUIDE
The Science, the Facts, the Photos
How She Gets from 20 to 60

Sigourney Weaver, who appeared on the cover, was reduced to the headline "Sigourney Weaver Is Fifty-Freakin'-One." The ludicrous section "How a Woman Ages" divided the "female aging process" into decades and had a photograph of a naked female model representing each number: 20s, 30s, 40s, 50s, 60s. As gormlessly stated in the introduction: "The aging of your own battered frame is confounding enough; her machinery is a complete mystery." Not to make too obvious a point, but the men's magazine's paradigmatic man was governed entirely by fear: fear of the loss of potency, the loss of relevance, the loss of power—yet the judgment was always applied to *women*.

I felt so bad for men sometimes. I had spent the entirety of my adult professional life dealing with men's magazines' profound anxiety about women—their need to "define" women and reduce them to their "machinery"—and it was really getting exhausting. But it had always been exhausting: just the same damn record, played over and over again, forever. I deserved hazard pay for all of it.

But lest you think that unexamined sexism and a fear of women's bodies were alone driving "How a Woman Ages," please know that there was real "science" behind it. Behold the illustrated diagram of young skin versus aging skin, the sidebar "Why Do Breasts Sag?," and the chart "Average Weight Gain by Age (In Pounds)"! And in the cover story, the clueless (male, of course) interviewer actually asked the fabulous Sigourney Weaver her feelings about the riveting topic of menopause.

Two examples of the prose quality we're dealing with in "How a Woman Ages": "By now, if she did not use sunscreen regularly in her twenties or if she smoked or swabbed decks on a swordfish boat for years, much of the skin damage is already done. (She can mitigate the results with exfoliation and moisturizers.)"

And: "But [fat] will soon start building in her abdomen, too, as it does with men . . . and this is bothering her, you'll soon discover, perhaps when she starts bringing home great numbers of grapefruits."

The copy department at *Esquire* was very good, and I can only imagine that they at least tried to rewrite those howlers.

Here's the thing that most enraged me: the men who made decisions at *Esquire* were better than that. And the magazine was better than that, too.

When this issue arrived in my office, it was so very difficult not to throw back the judgment. You judge us, we judge you. That's the way it works. I mockingly read that line about swabbing decks on a swordfish boat for years to one of my excellent interns, emphasizing "for years," and making a snarky comment about how some writers really just have no ear whatsoever. (Then I read the grapefruit line. "Great numbers of grapefruits"? Can we actually say that "great" and "grapefruits" *rhyme*? If so, a rhyme of what type? Assonant? Oblique? *Identical?*) This was my big rebellion. How toothless, how pitiful. How inconsistent I was in my opposition.

But yet: I also had the best job in the world. I was publishing stories by Don DeLillo, T.C. Boyle, Tim O'Brien, Jeanette Winterson, Richard Powers, Joanna Scott, Aleksandar Hemon, George Saunders, and Arthur Miller. I ran early stories by Nicole Krauss, David Means, Tony Earley, Heidi Julavits, and Adam Johnson (then a student; he would go on to win the Pulitzer Prize for Fiction). I published a piece by young Jonathan Nolan (now one of the brilliant minds behind *Westworld*) that became the movie *Memento*. (And for reasons now unclear, I dragged young Mr. Nolan, who was a great sport about the whole thing, to a rather awkward *Esquire* party at a pool hall.) I was also editing front of the book columns, and I was running an *Esquire* reading series at the Union Square Theater.

And as reprehensible and embarrassing as the "Aging Woman" section was, this particular issue of the magazine also had a great short story in it by the novelist Richard Russo—a very long story, I should add, at a time when it was becoming increasingly difficult for me to get fiction through, especially *long* fiction. The Russo story had gotten a nice cover line, too. And the magazine was, in general (minus the sexist stuff), really good.

So maybe it all evened out? Was one thing recompense for another?

The questions:

Was working life a zero-sum game?

How many moral compromises was a person required to make in her job?

I posed these queries to a male colleague once, essentially pointing out the various dissonances I felt I had to deal with at work, and he replied, "I think you're overthinking it."

But in my view, I was *underthinking* it. I was underthinking everything.

Said David of the "Aging Woman" issue: "When I saw it, I was imagining your face turning various shades of pink and purple, and I started laughing really hard."

Say what you want to about David, but he appreciated the manifold nuances, the many crippling paradoxes and challenges, of my particular job situation. He got what drove me nuts about it.

He had, he offered, the ideal title for a memoir he predicted I'd write someday: *Is It Sexual Harassment Yet?*

This was already the title of a novel by the experimental writer Cris Mazza—who, incidentally, devised the term "chick lit," though in her meaning, the phrase was meant to be ironic.

But *Is It Sexual Harassment Yet?* was better than *The Sorrow and the Pity,* I reckoned. (And *Humiliated and Insulted* was taken, too.)

"God, it must be so weird to be a woman," David added.

But had it ever really occurred to me before that moment that the term "sexual harassment" could actually be applied to me? The challenges and struggles of my professional life, such as they were, collapsed into that one unpleasant category: sexual harassment. Jesus. I wanted to be better than that. I wanted life to be temples and monuments; I wanted the Adagio of Mozart's Piano Concerto no. 23, Thomas Jefferson's letters to John Adams. But what I usually got was just so discouragingly earthbound . . .

no, *body-bound*: "Is she a 'big' girl?" and "Veal? You *are* veal." I wanted to be pure reason, pure intellect. I wanted to be pure essence. (I wanted to be a brain in a vat, basically. I didn't even want to have a body.) I wished I didn't have to think about boring things like sexual harassment.

"You're sort of stuck," David said.

I was twenty-eight and stuck.

I knew he was right, but I needed him to tell me why.

"Not only is it too late for you to go to grad school now," he said, "but it's also almost too late for you to get any other *job*."

"But I don't *want* to be stuck," I said.

"I don't think you appreciate how well I *know* you," he replied.

Did he? I was never so sure about that. But it was OK. I didn't even mind too much. Eventually you understand that that's just the way life goes: everyone is always getting us wrong, but we're always getting everyone else wrong, too, so I guess you can say that it all evens out in the end. He would use some vague idea of me, a phantasm unconnected to reality, for an unnamed character, the executive intern, in his story "The Suffering Channel." The character, last seen at the gym, is killed off in a sentence: "She had ten weeks to live"—dead, along with the other vain, frivolous young women who'd wasted their lives working meaningless magazine jobs, back when meaningless magazine jobs were something to even have an opinion about, in the dying days of the golden age of print.

"And I know," he said, "that you're never going to let anyone else tell you what to read, or what to think, ever again."

I asked David to explain to me why it was that magazines were always just so interminably "magazine-y." Why was everything of the same formulaic template, and why *did* everything have to be put through the same grinder, as he had so memorably put it?

"It's a question of stimulation versus narcosis," David said. "And it's not clear how much you can fuck with that."

"Sometimes I just feel so inconsistent, you know?"

I wanted to be engaged in meaningful work. I wanted to be a fully integrated person, and I wanted to feel that there was purpose to my work, to my life—which, if we are to believe Maslow's Hierarchy of Needs (which we must, because everything we understand about the human spirit is there), is all anyone ever wants. We all make compromises in our jobs. But how many compromises was an endurable number?

"We are all corporate products whose jobs are to be dishonest," David said. "We lie in order to capture a certain audience, but that's the price of being alive."

The one thing I knew was that I did not want to live a life of ambivalence and tension. It now seemed so very difficult indeed not to become the sort of person you didn't want to become.

THERE WERE ONLY TWO NEWS STORIES THAT VENAL SUMMER OF 2001: the scandal involving Lizzie Grubman, a publicist/socialite/party gal who'd allegedly shouted, "Fuck you, white trash!" before backing up her Mercedes SUV into a line of revelers at a Hamptons nightclub (the Conscience Point Inn; I've always enjoyed that detail), and a significantly less amusing scandal involving Congressman Gary Condit and a missing intern, Chandra Levy.

Then 9/11 happened. Then the chyrons started running across the bottoms of the TV news screens—and haven't left since. We were shell-shocked, we felt vulnerable and exposed, as if we'd been shorn a few layers of skin. We found that in our shell shock we were formal and restrained, but we were all joined in the same thoughts: *There is a profound darkness in human nature; there is something deeply unresolved and malign at the center of people.*

"We don't make time or space for grief," as Hilary Mantel has said. "The world tugs us along, back into its harsh rhythm before we are ready for it, and for the pain of loss doctors can prescribe a pill." The world of the practical wins because it always does—because the practical, the quotidian, is the essence of life. We didn't know what else to do, so we did what we always do: we got back to work. In doing so, we found that we were all everyday-minded midwesterners at heart: let's get on with it—let's get back to the prosaic, back to the routine.

Seated at our desks, finally, several days later, a week, we were confronted with our prop telephones, prop computers, all of us thinking in some vague way about how vexed and strange it all was, about how nothing would ever be the same again—but that wasn't deep enough. That didn't get at the center of the mystery at all.

Finally, someone at work made a low joke, a low joke about the real world: "You know who the luckiest man in America is right now? Gary Condit."

David liked to say, paraphrasing Lewis Hyde, that irony is the song of a bird that has come to love its cage, but in this instance I will respectfully disagree. Irony, this time, was just what we needed. Irony was a sign of life.

I HAD NOT EVEN KNOWN THAT I HAD NO IDEA HOW TO BE IN A RELATION-ship until I met the man who would become my husband. I knew it was love when Joe said, "You're not going *anywhere*." (I didn't even know that I *was* trying to go anywhere until Joe pointed it out. Had I, early on, been trying to get out of the relationship with him, a man so obviously perfect for me in every way? Had I always been trying to get out of *every* relationship? Was I actually *that* messed up?) For my thirtieth birthday, Joe took me to see a cabaret show at the Café Carlyle, because he understood, even when we were just beginning, that all I've ever wanted to be is Elaine Stritch. So of course Joe was the man I would marry. (There were many more reasons to love him, of course.)

When I mentioned to David that Joe and I had moved in together, David said, "Well, make sure to give him my *love*," in a sneering tone that I did *not* appreciate. But that was OK. David and I were friends. With David, you took the good, you took the bad. That was the way it worked. Those were the rules of the game. He turned forty, writing in a letter that he was now very, very old.

"For what it's worth," he said on a call around that time, "when you get to be my age, you start to feel that culture is passing you by."

He'd accepted a new teaching job, at a college first identified to me only as a small liberal arts school in California. He was going to stay in Bloomington for one more year to teach, but mainly he needed to stay put so he could finally get some work done. The previous year, he'd been to a retreat in France, for the purpose of (as he told me) clearing his head about work. When David talked about "work," it was always understood that he meant the novel. Work was *always* the novel.

On a call: Dare I ask how the novel was going now?

"It's turning out to be my *Finnegans Wake,* unfortunately."

"Oh, God," I said.

"Yeah, no shit. If you saw it now, the experience would be like going through my laundry and examining the pee stains on my underwear."

He said that at the rate he was proceeding, the novel would probably end up being about four thousand pages long.

"I'm going to need your help with it at some point," he said.

When I think about it, David and I almost never spoke about his nonfiction work (which, as Tom Bissell correctly notes in his excellent foreword to the twentieth-anniversary edition of *Infinite Jest,* "got better and funnier—the funniest since Twain—while the fiction got darker and more theoretically severe"), except when he'd mention the various feuds he was having with assorted magazine editors, or when he'd say that he'd taken on such-and-such magazine's assignment for the money. The nonfiction always came more easily to him than the fiction; thus it always seemed that David (Calvinist, self-punishing, school of hard knocks) did not respect his talent for it.

Throughout the years, David would say to me of some rival fiction writers, "I worry that his prose is better than mine."

    ME (WEARY): "It's not, David."
    HIM: "OK. Good."

I'd think: Were we really having this conversation again? How could we even have been having this conversation? I knew, he knew, we all knew, that he had no equal. He outclassed everyone.

From time to time, he'd send me manuscripts of in-progress stories for notes. "I really need your help on something," he'd say when he'd ask me to read a piece. "I've lost all perspective." And then, because he trusted no one, because he believed there was global interest in everything he did, because he was a total pain in the neck, he would inevitably write the admonition "FYEO" in a note included with the story and instruct me to destroy the manuscripts after they'd been read and discussed.

A menace and an eerie somnolence hung over the ones I saw: "Good Old Neon," "Mr. Squishy," "Another Pioneer," and "Oblivion." These pieces were darker even than the stories in *Brief Interviews*: all examinations of minds on the brink, and the characters again entombed, though this time the men were not hideous manipulators but emasculated emotional isolates. All the stories seemed part of the same general project, part of the same cycle, but I couldn't figure out how they all fit together. Again, I worried about him. I told him that "Good Old Neon," in which the supposed narrator (though the narrator could also be the narrator's ghost or also a character named David Wallace) is so tortured by the fear that his life has been a preposterous farce that he commits suicide by driving his sports car into a bridge abutment, was too upsetting for me to talk about with him.

"Is it any good?" he'd say, after sending me something to read, anxious as an undergrad. He was always candid about what of his fiction he felt was weak. (He wasn't so sure about "Another Pioneer," for example.) While it is true that I regarded David not merely as a great writer but as one of the greatest and most uncompromising artists of all time, it was important not to bow before his writing as if it were the Ark of the Covenant. I suppose that the overarching feedback I'd usually give him could be summarized as: *it's overegged, David; pull back; tone it down, please, for the love of God, too much.* As I saw it, my job as a reader, and as his friend, was to try to help save him from himself.

Example: In the draft I saw of "Mr. Squishy," a creepy, "thunderingly unexceptional" (I love that) focus-group facilitator obsessed with the idea of injecting ricin into a brand of prepackaged snack cakes fantasizes about having what is described in the draft I saw as "moist, slapping, semiviolent" intercourse with a married coworker. I had a major objection to the adjective "semiviolent."

"You're gross," I said.

"I guess you'd know," David replied.

"The 'semiviolent' is so horrible," I said. "Ugly and rape-y."

"I didn't think of that," he said. "But you're right, sweetie. Thank you."

(He did cut the awful "semiviolent" from the book version of "Mr. Squishy.")

I would have loved to publish any of the stories he sent me to read (even "Another Pioneer"), but all but "Oblivion" had already appeared in literary journals by the time I saw them. And there was a problem with "Oblivion" for *Esquire*: it was thirty thousand words long.

My strategy these days was to annoy Granger so much when

I wanted to buy a story that he would eventually just give in so that he wouldn't have to deal with me anymore. Granger did let me acquire "Oblivion" for *Esquire,* but it would have to be cut, by a lot, like by almost half. But even at fifteen thousand words, it would still be far longer than any fiction we'd published since we'd been at the magazine. We had options, though. Maybe we'd run the truncated version of the story as a folio insert in one issue, or maybe we'd break it in two halves, serializing it over the course of two months. We'd figure it out.

The sentences in "Oblivion" can run hundreds of words, and the paragraphs can run pages. As in all of David's work, everything in "Oblivion" feeds into everything else, echoing, proliferating, expanding—becoming something else entirely . . . or else replicating self-similarly, and we would have to work out a way to compress it without severing any of its many starfish limbs. David was ready and willing to embark with me on the process of cutting the story. We would solve the puzzle. Of course we would.

And it was just so thrilling to think that I could bring *this* story into the magazine. "Oblivion" is one of the best stories David ever wrote, and I adore and admire it so much that I still can't even believe it exists or that I had the chance to burrow into it with him as deeply as I did.

"I understand now why you still work there," David said. "They *listen* to you."

They did? Well, I wasn't *so* sure about that. When I'd arrived at *Esquire* four years before, we were publishing, say, ten feature-length short stories per year; now it was maybe half that. (And when I quit, when Rome was burning, when the empire was in free fall, the number was . . . what? Two? *One?* Wait, was the magazine even publishing fiction at all? For how many more years would the magazine even continue to exist?)

Superficially, "Oblivion" is a self-spiraling interior monologue centered on a marital conflict about snoring, but underneath is a veiled story of sexual abuse. It's a hard, surreal, blackly funny (very Lynchian) piece and is yet another grim assessment of the possibility of human connection. The wife, Hope, seems to believe that her husband's snoring is keeping her awake, but the husband insists that the wife is dreaming the whole thing. The narrator of the story seems to be the husband, Randall, a pedantic, golf-obsessed twit who uses phrases like "a mensa et thoro" and who eye-rollingly sets off words in quotation marks, but the final dialogue seems to suggest that the story has been the *wife's* dream; the character we'd believed was the narrator turns out not to be the narrator at all, and the whole story has been (probably) the wife's unconscious processing of her family trauma through an appropriated voice that may or may not have anything to do with reality.

"Oblivion" wouldn't be scheduled for months, and David and I had a long time to work on edits. We started the editorial process when he was still in Illinois and ended it after he'd moved to California. He told me he'd written the story during a six-month period when he couldn't sleep and believed he was losing his mind.

DAVID WAS SAYING THAT *THE PARIS REVIEW* HAD ASKED HIM TO DO AN interview. He didn't want to do it (but he did want to do it, too), and he was hemming and hawing and making a big dramatic deal out of the whole thing. He *should* do it. He knew he should do it. He'd always wanted to have a *Paris Review* interview someday (what writer doesn't share this dream?), he said, but now here it was, and he just couldn't bring himself to participate. Or was it, he wondered, that he didn't want to *seem* like the kind of person who wanted to participate?

But he *did* want to do it. (Correction: no, he didn't.)

David wondered if, instead of the interview, he could send *The Paris Review* a short-story submission, as a kind of trade. He was big on quid pro quo (QPQ, as he'd have it) exchanges of this sort.

Always looking for an angle, that guy; he always had something up his sleeve.

But then again, he really *should* do the interview. Everyone was telling him he should do the interview.

"Geez, don't do it if you don't want to," I said cavalierly, yet sensibly.

He could have his *Paris Review* interview later. There would be time. David was only forty years old. There would be so much more time.

This was not the response David was hunting around for.

"You *do* know that it's a huge honor to be asked, *don't* you?" he said. "You do know what a *thing* it is for a writer to have one of these, right?"

I assured him that I did understand. The interviews in *The Paris Review* elevated conversation to the highest art; they were always exactly what you wanted in human speech: talk about temples and monuments, talk about why it is that life is so vexed and mysterious. Human voices never provided what you wanted. Instead, conversation was "Is she a 'big' girl?" and "Veal? You *are* veal."

(And David didn't do *The Paris Review* interview.)

At a later date, after he had moved to California, he was asked to film an interview for German TV. As he described it to me, the taping was supposed to take place over *two whole days*. "Do you want to know what will happen?" David asked. "First, I'll start drooling. Second, I'll projectile vomit. Third, my brain will explode."

David was great at talking and great at thinking (or maybe, actually, he was *bad* at thinking, since thinking always became paralysis?), and he *was* the most seasoned of public speakers—so what was the problem exactly? I asked him to explain to me why it was that he hated doing interviews but he enjoyed teaching.

"*You* know the answer to that," he said. "Because with the students, *I* have the power."

Power, yes. Power was always the motivator, for everyone.

I asked him if he could get out of the interview.

He replied that various people in his professional life were insisting he submit to "the Germans" and added a frantic "I'm just trying to be the good little author!"

The stance was as it ever was, a responsibility swerve—he was powerless, a martyr at the hands of the publicity machine. You'd often hear things like "Some *lady* wants to take my picture, and they're saying I have to do it, for reasons I don't understand." He'd been sick during a leg of the tour for the hardcover of *Brief Interviews with Hideous Men* and was forbidden by doctors to fly; hence, he had to drive. There was no small amount of complaining about those individuals who, by dint of their power over him, had made him accede to the automotive tour.

I wasn't the ideal audience for any of his bellyaching about fame and its miseries. Shouldn't he just drop out of the game if he really were such a renegade? Shouldn't he be consistent in his opposition to . . . whatever it was he was opposing? (Said Pindar: "Learn what you are and be such.") It always seemed so clear to me how David should manage life upon the public stage: vanish, like Prospero, into thin air. He'd get more work done that way, and, as an added bonus, he'd have less to complain about. My view (he never listened to me) was always that he gave too much away. Why would someone with so sensitive a psyche want to submit to the rigors, self-chosen though they were, of being perpetually on display? Celebrity seemed too potent an elixir, too full of glittering seductions that corrupted artistic talent. Stay away from it. Protect your gift. You already have all the celebrity anyone could possibly need. You are too comfortable in the temple. Disappear. Become a ghost. I cited the well-worn examples of two of our best literary recluses: Salinger and Harper Lee.

"O-*K*," David said, "but don't you believe there's at least a degree of mental illness involved in both those cases?"

"Yeah, probably," I conceded.

"Adrienne," he said, "can I ask you a question?"

"Yes, David?"

"Has anyone ever told you that you'd be a terrible agent?"

THE PROCESS OF CUTTING "OBLIVION" WAS LIKE SCULPTING WITH A dental tool. The sentences and paragraphs were so long, the language-thickets so dense, that our only real option was to reduce the digressions within the sentences themselves. Issues with that: (1) many of the digressions in early parts of the story foreshadowed what was to come; (2) the foreshadowed material, when it appeared later in the story, couldn't be cut; (3) the narrator's voice becomes more occluded and digressive as the story progresses, and any reduction in the occlusion and digression at the start would have made the occlusion and digression at the end feel unbalanced; (4) the occlusion and digression of the narrator's voice at the end couldn't be reduced because of the convergence of the various plot elements in the later parts of the story.

Over a series of weeks, months, we analyzed the story sentence by sentence, as if hyper-magnifying with a jeweler's loupe. Items: David noted that he was using a backslash (\) instead of the normal virgule for things like "and/or" and wondered why I hadn't queried it. Evidently, he was making a computer systems gag (should I have known this?). And, hello, I espied a consistency error: in an early draft, the Saab makes one appearance as an Audi. ("Please don't tell anyone," David, always the perfectionist, said. "Dead man's talk.") Saffron is mentioned a few times in the story, and when I noted to David that in ancient Rome saffron was associated with prostitutes (a symbol of a character's sexual abuse), he wrote that I was his Fantasy Reader (again with the "fantasy reader," but capitalizing it this time for ironic intent). I told him that he was completely full of it. "But you're my Platonic ideal of everything," he said on a call, charmingly, seductively, jeeringly, because his every utterance always had a converse, of course.

In the lines of dialogue at the very end of the story, the husband seems to be trying to wake the wife, who is disoriented and perhaps still in a lucid dream. There seem to be two separate speakers— husband and wife—but no dialogue tags are given. In my notes on the story, next to each line of dialogue, I jotted which character seemed to be speaking when.

In response, David wrote, throwing me completely off the trail, "Why can't both voices be [the] narrator?" (Similarly, he had suggested to me that the narrator of "Good Old Neon" is perhaps not the apparent speaker, or the character named David Wallace, or the ghost, but all three.)

"Do you think it's too much like the ending of *Dallas*?" David asked. "It's all a dream?"

Oh, but surely this couldn't be right: the story *was* all a dream? Surely David was not going to offer me the actual *solution* to anything. *That* wasn't the David I knew.

"This story is my hate letter to Bloomington," David declared.

Wait, where was Bloomington in "Oblivion"? It's more New Jersey than Illinois, more dream than reality.

"Well, let's *see*," David said. "There's *golf*, there's the *insurance industry . . .*"

He went on to say, with who knows how many different layers of irony, self-mockery, and self-contempt, that he'd been trying to get himself fired from his teaching job (although he had given notice the year before).

His love for teaching was one of the purest and most beautiful things about him (but in truth maybe one of the worst things for his own writing), and I always delighted in hearing him talk about how much time and thought he put into his responses to each student's piece. I was also fascinated by the idiosyncratic high-low nature of the various course syllabi he'd share with me on the phone. What lucky students. He was a mentor to so many people. But by his account to me, he'd again crossed lines he shouldn't have—some pretty bright, sacred lines—and had again taken advantage of various situations and persons he should not have taken advantage of. He was now, he said, close to being tarred, feathered, and run out of town.

For four years I'd been attempting to accept David's paradoxes, his self-contractions, and his darkness—the whole rich Wallace bouquet. I loved David, and I wanted him to be better than he was. I'd try to remind myself that no one is ever clear in moral terms, and so who, really, was I to judge? I was a wayward creature myself—I was haughty (and would grow haughtier still), I had a nasty temper, I was too enticed by material luxuries (David, snooping through my closet: "You've heard of Marx, I presume?"). I was obstinate, solitary, and self-protective, and I could be dismissive of those who did not live up to my own standard of perfection. I knew I was cold. I knew I was inscrutable. I was not a great friend. I waited an unconscionably long time to return David's call when he left a message saying that his grandfather had died. These sins were just the beginning. I didn't have clean hands, either.

One of my most common refrains to David: "How can someone so smart be so *dumb*?" He'd give one of the small, dark chuckles so characteristic of him, say he'd hoped he was becoming more mature but now had to admit that he was not. It was always so baffling. He wanted to change. He tried to change, I guess. And of course people do evolve and grow (even if David's characters do not)—what's the point in believing otherwise? Why even get up in the morning if we're stuck with who we were yesterday? The drive to surpass the self produced, after all, the pyramids, Beethoven's Ninth, the Chartres Cathedral, and *Infinite Jest*. Those are but four examples.

David was laceratingly self-aware, extraterrestrially intelligent, intuitive, empathetic, and sensitive; he was obsessed with the notion of self-improvement and had a deep sense of right and wrong. He knew everything in the world there was to know. But he seemed fundamentally unable to correct his behavior or to manage his anger. Whenever he'd tell me about some bad act he'd committed, whenever David's dark double again escaped its box, I would often reach the following conclusion: he was far crazier than even I knew, or he was actually just a bad guy. I had a copy of my mother's old *DSM-III* and spent a lot of time trying to work out a diagnosis for him, but a clinical manual of mental disorders would never provide any of the answers I needed. David was not summarizable. He was not someone who got "solved."

Questions:

Who looks to the artist's life for moral guidance anyway?

How much of the human condition do the more stringently self-righteous among us believe we're exempt from?

What are we to do with the art of profoundly compromised men?

I've got no answers for you. I do know that Peter Shaffer wrote that "goodness is nothing in the furnace of art." Charles Dickens destroyed the lives of everyone close to him, his family most of all. Same goes for Hemingway, Fitzgerald, Picasso, Beethoven. Mozart and his once beloved sister were estranged at the time of his death. Ingmar Bergman slept with nearly every actress he cast in his movies, and he made a *lot* of movies (most of them exquisite masterpieces). During a rehearsal for G. F. Handel's opera *Ottone,* when a well-known Italian soprano refused to sing her opening aria, Handel screamed, "I know well that you are a real she-devil, but I will have you know that I am Beelzebub!" He picked the soprano up by the waist and threatened to throw her out an open second-story window.

What, you thought creative geniuses were pleasant people? You thought you could be *friends* with them, maybe? Sure, have at it. *Enjoy.*

Famous story, as recounted in Gioachino Rossini's letters: When Rossini, age thirty, visited Beethoven—in his fifties, nearly deaf, and utterly alone—at his squalid apartment in Vienna, Rossini was shocked to encounter such a haunted, desolate figure. (Rossini later wrote that no portraits managed to capture the sadness of Beethoven's face.) The two composers chatted, and Beethoven complimented *The Barber of Seville;* Rossini in turn expressed his profound appreciation and gratitude for Beethoven's superb artistry and genius, for the joy and delight his work had brought to the world.

Beethoven sighed and answered Rossini with these words: *"Oh! Un infelice."*

Oh! Unhappy me.

I'd like to think that I know enough about people to understand that everyone drives you crazy but that you love everyone, too. In the words of Yoko Ono: "It's a wonder that we don't make love to every single person we meet," to which I would add: it's a wonder that we don't also punch every single person we meet. "Is he good?" "Is he bad?" The answer, about pretty much everyone, is: "Yes, he's both."

THE LAST TIME I SAW DAVID, WE HAD LUNCH AT A GREEK RESTAURANT IN midtown. I was running a few minutes late, and he was waiting for me out on the sidewalk, in front of the entrance. (Why hadn't he just gone inside like a normal person? Anyone else would have gone inside.)

I waved to him from across the street and received a flat palm of recognition in response. As I approached, he held his hand out at a stalwart ninety-degree angle for a shake. This was totally unacceptable and I demanded an embrace. We were finally going to put aside our whole complex emotional history and emerge as friends—and as editor and writer. It was going to be easy, so easy, finally. Why *wouldn't* it be easy? Life *was* easy. *Together, we have each other and nature and time. It is as simple as that.*

"You really *are* late," David said. "I thought you weren't going to show up."

How could he not have known that he was one of the most important people in the world to me?

He was wearing a sage-green short-sleeved button-down shirt, white pleated pants, and bright white sneakers. I swear to God, he had the weirdest style of anyone I've ever known. I asked him once why he only rarely shaved (it would have been nice to actually really see that handsome face for once), and he said that if he shaved, the world would know how bad his skin was.

"Do you get taller every time I see you?" he asked as we went through the restaurant.

"Always," I said.

We got seated at the table and David opened the menu immediately. Wordlessly, he started studying the page. I felt an awful dilution in my chest. He did not want to look at me. It was possible that he did not even want to be there.

"Did you know that it's rude to open the menu as soon as you sit down?" I asked lightly.

"It is?" David replied, glancing up at me through his glasses. "I've never heard that. *Why?*"

"Because the other person thinks you're more interested in food than you are in them."

"Oh," he said. "I'm sorry. I apologize."

He closed the menu and pushed it aside.

"You look in no way tubercular," he said. "I was expecting a concentration camp victim."

A few weeks before, I'd been as sick as I'd ever been in my entire life with, somehow, walking pneumonia. David and I had spoken a couple of times when I was out of the office (although I was in bed and had little to contribute to the conversation), and he'd kept going on about how effective zinc was to combat colds.

"I was worried about you," he said.

He was? I wasn't so sure I believed that.

I asked how he was enjoying California. He said he liked his new school, Pomona—the people there were nice, and a nice house had been rented for him. The place wore its insecurities on its sleeve, though: there was a Harvard Avenue, a Columbia Avenue, an Amherst even, if I could believe it. "The best thing," he said, "is that they know I don't show up for any meetings." He offered that he'd been sleeping fairly well lately and had been trying to stick to a 7:30 wake-up schedule. He complained that blurb-hunting publishers had already found him—he had been hoping he'd be able to hide out for at least a year without anyone knowing where he was. He valiantly listed names of various people he felt he had to dodge on this NYC trip. And was he even going to be able to survive the insipid California weather? He'd never even minded winters in the Midwest, as a matter of fact.

"And do you know what happens when your car breaks down in Illinois in February?"

David was one of the few people I've ever known who actually pronounced the first "r" in February: Feb*r*uary.

"Oh, I definitely do," I said. You always feel like a character in a Jack London story in February in the Midwest.

"You *die*," he said. "I miss home."

"Bloomington is home?" I asked.

"It is," he said. "Always will be."

A couple of months before, he'd given me a report about a going-away party: "I will have you know that *eighty people* showed up for it," he'd said. "That's right, *eight-zero*."

"Sounds like quite the party," I'd said.

"I felt like Sally Field—'you like me, you really like me!' I always assume that no one ever likes me," he'd said.

I'd then found myself reassuring him, as you often did, that he was actually a kind, gentle, charming, even sometimes delightful person with an uncommonly sweet nature. These were objective facts, except when they weren't, and you were sure that everything you'd ever believed about him was wrong—when his many paradoxes, self-contractions, and self-involutions twisted into a meta-maze, and somehow *you* were the one trapped in it.

He paused and considered me from across the table.

"So," David said. "That was the Miramax guy?"

That morning, when I was showering, David had called my apartment to confirm lunch. Joe answered the phone. Joe worked then as a director of development at Miramax—and if you want a picture of what it was like to be a director of development at Miramax back in the day, just imagine a boot stomping on a human face forever. That boot was Harvey Weinstein's. (And that face, because I was living the drama right alongside Joe, often, by extension, felt like mine.)

"Yes," I said.

The atmosphere had grown suddenly spiky.

"He sounds like a very nice guy."

"He is," I said.

"Are you going to get married?"

I told David that things were going very well but also that we were both only thirty years old, so who knew. But the truth was that everything was so nice and good—and safe—that Joe and I felt married already.

David regarded me coldly from across the table.

"Are you happy?" he asked.

This was a question David had never thought to ask me before. Had he *ever* thought about my happiness? Was he in fact actually thinking about my happiness now? Multiple motives. There were always multiple motives.

"I am," I said.

"Really," he replied, staring at me with hard eyes.

There are different levels of knowing people, and David's inappropriately penetrating black stare did not fall within the parameters of our present situation.

"I believe you," he said slowly and evenly.

The game was to see who'd look away first.

"How did you meet him?"

"At a party," I said.

"What party?"

"A book party."

I always lost these stare-downs. I often worried if it was because I never quite wanted to look at him directly.

"Fascinating," he said without affect. "And let me guess: you were working the room and he followed you around like a puppy."

There was that awful dilution in my chest again.

"How's your family?" I asked.

"They're about ready to *disown* me because I haven't produced issue yet," David replied.

I thought: *You know what? I'm going to have a glass of wine.* I summoned the server and ordered a Pinot Grigio, although I knew that drinking in front of David was appallingly inconsiderate. He shouldn't have had to be around alcohol. As a recovering addict, the maintenance of his sobriety was the central component of his life.

"Do you know that I've never seen you drink before?" he asked.

"Is that right?"

"Yes," he said. "How long have we been friends? How many years has it been?"

"Four years," I said.

"Yes. Four years. It's been four years."

We were silent for a few moments.

He mentioned that he'd done a reading with Jonathan Franzen a couple of nights before and had been lustily eyeing Franzen's prereading whiskey. My glass of wine arrived, and David asked about the writer I'd been involved with, because he always did that. He talked about this guy at length. We discussed how it's incorrect to say that dogs are color blind, but rather that they have *red-green* color blindness. We talked about Jeffrey Dahmer because why not. David had not known that Dahmer spent the formative years of his childhood in Akron. (It's true that we do try to keep this quiet.) He said that he'd been drinking a lot of carrot juice lately. He said that the Mexican food in L.A. was really good. I asked him how his novel was going. He responded with the international jack-off gesture. I took the hint and pried no more.

I told David a little bit about the novel I was working on. I didn't go on about it too much, or at least I really hope I didn't. (By this point, I'd been around long enough to know that no one wants to hear writers talk about their books, ever.)

"I wonder why you're telling me this," he said acidly.

Of course, David could never bring himself to offer me a token show of support or even display any phony interest in my writing. He was too competitive for that. Power. It was all about power. My role was to be of service to his work. I knew he operated this way, of course, but I guess I'd thought that maybe we had a different sort of relationship now.

I'd recently made the very same mistake, by the way, mentioning to another famous (older male) novelist that I was working on a book. (Safety tip: don't do that.) The old man offered the reply, "Well, even if it's not very good, it's so important that you *write* it."

These comments stung, but at least they served as a reminder that there is only one honest approach to writing, especially if you are a woman: write as if no one will care (most likely no one will); only when you write for yourself will you be freed from the burden of expectation. A Soviet tank of the spirit. That's what I would be.

David asked if I wanted to try his chicken entrée. He slid his plate to me. "Please have some," he said. "It's yummy."

The server asked if I wanted another glass of Pinot Grigio. I declined.

"See, this is so incredible to me," David said, "that you can stop at one glass. I would consume *bottles*. But you, *you* are not an addict."

As we were leaving the restaurant, he asked, "Can you please come with me and drop me off at my hotel, so I don't have to go *all that way* alone?"

His hotel was fifteen blocks from the restaurant, but OK.

Outside, David stayed pliantly back on the curb as I set about the task of hailing a taxi. I glanced back at him for just a fractional moment and was struck by a hesitancy in his bearing—he looked timid almost. He could be so weirdly docile . . . but he could be so very domineering and controlling, too. And he was also, of course, a colossus. David was his own mountain. There was never anyone else like him, and there will never be anyone else like him again. As an artist, whom could you even begin to compare him to? Lewis Carroll? Nikolai Gogol? Flannery O'Connor? Edgar Allan Poe, for God's sake? A freak of nature, a weirdo, an aberration: a genius.

We slid into a taxi and buckled our seat belts.

"You always buckle your seat belt, don't you?" he asked.

"Always," I said. "I'm *very* responsible."

My sunglasses were hooked onto the collar of my shirt and I made a move to unhook them.

"Don't put your sunglasses on," David said.

"Why?" I asked.

"Because I need to be able to see you."

Our eyes met. Slowly, he traced a finger up my arm.

"May I touch your face?" he asked.

My breathing was growing uneven. Did he even notice?

"Yes," I said.

I traced a finger up his arm now. "May I kiss you?" he asked.

"Yes," I said.

The kiss was received, though it should not have been.

What *was* it about this profoundly self-divided, damaged, sweet, cruel, peculiar man, who was so full of need and yearning, yet so utterly lacking hope and trust?

But it was possible that I, too, had inadequate hope and trust.

"What *is* it between us?" David whispered into my hair.

His hotel was on a block of Times Square you'd find yourself on only if you're with someone from out of town. He and I stood facing each other on the sidewalk in front of the entrance. Everything was held in suspension.

"You're welcome to come up," he said.

Harried Times Square dematerialized and dissolved. The silence fell away in heavy beats, and that's all there was in the world: David's eyes and mine.

"I can't," I said.

David's mouth was nearly as expressive as his eyes. That was another thing I always noticed about him.

"OK," he said.

He turned. The automatic doors opened and received him, and as I watched him walk into the hotel lobby, I was as sure as I've ever been about anything that I'd never see him again.

On his flight home, a coffeepot short-circuited and caused a small fire, and he later asked if I'd had something to do with it.

After that, David and I did what we always did: we got back to work. "Oblivion" was still waiting for us. By this point, we'd had quite a lot of practice mentally shoving the eccentricities of the past off to the side and just carrying on. Just proceeding forward. That's how we did it. That's who we were. I would forgive him, and he would forgive me, and we would begin again. Don't even ask me how this was possible. Maybe it shouldn't have been possible. David accepted, by his own accounting, over 70 percent of my suggested cuts on the story and offered others on his own initiative. We were extremely proud of ourselves. We had done the unthinkable and cut "Oblivion" nearly in half. During the process, David helped me understand, more deeply than I had before, that art is about rigor and precision. He was a perfectionist and a visionary and he made art exactly the way he wanted to, and I loved him for it.

A FEW MONTHS LATER, *ESQUIRE* KILLED "OBLIVION." NO REAL EXPLANA-tion was ever given, but I suppose that even at fifteen thousand words, the story was probably still too long. The decision came to me in an email and that was that. I was so enraged that I couldn't even talk to anyone at work about it. I would stay at the magazine for a few more years, but the fate of "Oblivion" was an injustice that latched itself onto me like the vengeful little teeth of a burr.

I told David that they'd killed the story.

"It's possible that you'll take a bigger emotional hit on this than I will," he said.

"What should I do?" I asked. "Should I quit?"

"No," he replied. "I don't know what you'd live on. You've never been poor."

I didn't know what to say. What *could* I possibly say? Sometimes you just have a complete communication breakdown.

"Thank you for being so nice about this whole thing, David," I said.

That was all I could come up with. It wasn't deep enough, of course, and it didn't get to the center of the mystery at all. But words let you down, they did, they did. Words never got at anything real. During communication breakdowns, platitudes and conventional wisdom became your emergency kit. Human voices never provided what you needed.

What I couldn't bring myself to tell him was that I had failed him and failed myself.

"That's the way we are," David said. "We're *nice* to each other."

DAVID AND I WERE IN LESS FREQUENT CONTACT AFTER THAT, AND HE would never publish in *Esquire* again. We spoke a few times, and exchanged some notes—he told me that he was engaged, and later married. As for *Esquire,* let us just say that I reached my career's pinnacle and its rock bottom concurrently. In 2004, we were nominated for another National Magazine Award for Fiction. I hoped that the nomination would help me move beyond the "Oblivion" debacle—or at least mentally shove it to the side. The other contenders for the prize that year were *The New Yorker, The Paris Review, Zoetrope,* and *The Atlantic,* which was nominated for the award twice, for two sets of short stories.

In early May, the ceremony was again held at the Waldorf Astoria. *Esquire,* which was up for seven awards, was given one of the best tables in the grand ballroom. There was no celebrity presenter that year (let's assume the organizers had learned their lesson with Rosie and the staph infection routine), and it was not impossible that everyone at our table drank more dry white wine than was perhaps ideal for an early-afternoon event. *W* won an award for a beautiful and inventive special issue about Kate Moss; the publishing executive (male, fiftyish, now dead) who accepted the prize made a little comment about how Kate, then age thirty, was getting old. The audience laughed, because media professionals were all too often complicit, and the *Esquire* journalist seated next to me, a man whom I had known for a decade, since I was twenty-two, flashed me a look that said, "You're not getting any younger, either." I was just starting to worry about the passage of time. What *was* it that I had been chasing for the past ten years?

Esquire had a great day and won one award, and another, and another. How lucky I was to get to work at such a superb magazine, I thought. The fiction category was one of the last announced. Though the merry wheel of fortune was spinning in *Esquire*'s favor that day, I still didn't believe we had much of a shot with the fiction prize. *The New Yorker* seemed to win the award nearly every year (except for *Zoetrope*'s upset victory in 2001), and *The Atlantic* had those two nominations, and *The Paris Review* was *The Paris Review*.

But *Esquire* won. As Granger climbed the stage to deliver his acceptance speech (it was customary for editors in chief to accept the awards on behalf of the magazine), a fellow editor leaned across the table and said that I ought to have seen my own face. Shockingly, Granger's speech was about *me*. He spoke extemporaneously into the microphone, referring to me as "my literary editor," but then again, he always called me that. He told the room why he had hired me seven years before (in case they had been wondering): I was a good writer, and I had written him a great letter. It was a kind, gracious speech (I was deeply embarrassed to have been made the center of attention, but also appreciative), though he didn't say anything about my abilities as an editor. My assumption, frankly, had always been that he believed I was a better writer than I was an editor. When Granger sat back down at the table, he handed me the trophy.

Everyone at work was thrilled with the award. *I* was thrilled. And for a time, I believed that the prize would be just the thing to spur a renewed excitement in *Esquire*'s fiction program. Yet the following year, despite thousands of fiction submissions, the magazine did not publish even *one* short story. I'd been chasing the mythical Denis Johnson, a frequent *Esquire* contributor from past editorships, and was finally submitted a story. I worked like a little badger to push it through, but I couldn't even get a response. Of course I understood better than anyone that magazine short stories may not have had much practical, bottom-line value, but it was then impossible to imagine *The Atlantic, Harper's,* or, God forbid,

The New Yorker giving up on short fiction with such dispatch. I was no longer an advocate for writers. My only role in the world now was to reject them.

Eventually, I refused to encourage any authors I admired to submit their work. What would the point have been? The magazine, once home to Hemingway and Mailer, Raymond Carver and David Foster Wallace, seemed to have lost all interest in fiction. My novel was published, and I knew it was time for me to be on my way. As Granger had noted during his acceptance speech, my writing had gotten me into this. It would also get me out.

The question: How much could I give up and still be me?

After I quit, the new literary editor had two big early fiction ventures: a commissioned short story about the "death" of Derek Jeter, and the Napkin Project, in which two hundred and fifty fiction writers were sent five-inch-square paper cocktail napkins and asked to write original short stories on those little napkins.

THE NIGHT BEFORE THE CATASTROPHE OF DAVID'S SUICIDE, I HAVE A dream about him. The dream takes place in my bedroom at my parents' house in Ohio, and David is lying on my childhood bed, on his back, dressed entirely in white and wearing his ridiculous white bandanna. His eyes are closed. He doesn't move. My bedroom is flooded with white light, and everything in the scene is still, and lifeless, and silent. I'm standing at the door to the room, but I can't move forward toward him, and I can't move back out; I can't shift my gaze away. There's no other substance to the dream, no other dimension: it is this one still image and only that, and one color: white.

That morning, I had to report to jury duty. In the courthouse, I spent most of my time checking the news on my phone, still flummoxed by the alarming recent entrance of this Sarah Palin person onto the national stage. I'd had such splendid associations with the name "Palin" up until this point (Michael: the best of all Pythons and Palins), and I was having a hard time with this one. The fall of Lehman Brothers and subsequent stock market crash was three days away: Rome was about to go up in flames and the bloated empire about to begin its collapse. We had no idea what we were in store for that particular Friday in September. We never do, I guess.

I'd been in this courthouse before, a decade ago, the last time I'd served on jury duty. Back then I had been a juror on a run-of-the-mill insurance-fraud case. During my lunch breaks, I'd gotten into the habit of calling David from a lobby pay phone—talking to him was a lot more fun than scrounging around Financial District delis for dangerous-looking sushi.

My case had not been interesting, but I had been greatly impressed by the level of seriousness with which my fellow jurors approached it. They actually gave me some sort of hope for democracy. I became friendly with one of the jurors, a club kid who went by the nom de guerre "Justin Thyme" (adjust your opinion: he was actually a very sharp guy), and I ended up getting a ride back from the Hamptons once with another juror for some reason. We were a tight little group for a while there.

One of those lunchtime calls to David on the courthouse pay phone was, I remembered, also on a Friday afternoon. I had a flight to Boston to catch that evening.

"Have fun in Beantown," David had said then. "The people there are *not* nice. They're the worst people on earth, actually."

The purpose of my trip was to visit a friend who was pregnant with her first child.

"Well, just tell her not to watch *Alien,*" David helpfully suggested.

We talked a little about movies—David said he'd never seen *Rosemary's Baby*—and then he was on to his former life in Boston, the place where he really started writing *Infinite Jest,* the book that changed the world. He'd been in a Ph.D. program in philosophy at Harvard because, as it was explained to me, he believed it would help with his work, but he'd had a breakdown. He told me about some of the people who'd cared for him then, when he was, as he put it, in and out of hospitals all the time.

"They were always like, 'Oooh, I love you, Dave, *I love you*,'" he said in an unkind falsetto. That was David for you: always deriding those who loved him. He was also giving me a warning: *Don't love me.* And he added, self-punitively, self-mockingly, "And I'd go, '*Yeah.* There's a *lot* to love.'"

I had not experienced anything like the dimensions of anguish he'd endured and had so harrowingly described—a despair, by his admissions to me, he feared was always still lurking there, lying in wait in the darkest byways of his mind. I would ask him to promise me that his dire predictions for his future not be true. When he was thirty-six, he told me he'd always believed he'd never make it to fifty. He didn't. He would never have a third act. David would never grow old, would never be reduced to irrelevance or self-parody, but would instead reside forever—and forever really is such a very, very long time—as the void he left inside us.

"Boy, I wish *I* had some dark past," I said, attempting, and failing, to be cute.

"No, you *don't*," David replied with unexpected sharpness. "People don't understand what it's *like*." The pronoun "it" was left undefined—was it addiction, mental illness? Was it darkness? Was it the burden of being him? "Stay my French-eyed girl, with blue-birds flying in circles around your head, and forest animals serenading outside your window. You would have been appalled if you'd known me in Boston anyway."

"I think," I said, "I would have liked you fine."

"Well, of course you were a *fetus* at the time," David said, and hesitated. "It's *odd*—I just had this sensation of déjà vu. Do you also feel that we've had this conversation before?"

No, I did not share the feeling.

He said he had a question for me. "Have you ever heard of the theory of eternal recurrence?"

He'd once wondered if I ever felt that he was "testing" me—intellectually, that is. I said then I didn't, but I was never so sure about that. There was a sense in which he was *always* testing me. I told him on the pay phone there in the courthouse lobby that I knew almost nothing about eternal recurrence except for the idea that time is not a straight line but a circle; events in your life repeat themselves infinitely, in the same order. There's no beginning and no end—there's just one thing.

Like everyone else, I'd gone through a little Nietzsche phase, and I knew that his version of eternal recurrence went something vaguely like: if you can't imagine living every second of your life over again, you have not lived well. It's a useful thing to think about—every event takes on a very different intensity and a very different consequence if you imagine you're going to do it all over again, forever. It's probably a good question to ask yourself before you make any decision: *Would I actually want to relive this moment?* If you have any say in the matter, do something only if the answer is yes.

"Do *you* believe in eternal recurrence?" I asked.

Although I knew the answer. I knew of David's interest in simultaneity and in the infinite.

"Of course," David said. "This is why you can never be an asshole to anyone. No one ever really goes away."

AFTER HE SENT HIMSELF OUT INTO ETERNITY, I SPENT YEARS TRYING TO make him go away. I hated him. I wished I'd never met him. I got rid of his books. I couldn't look at his name. I couldn't stand being around writers, or editors, or critics, and I had to make sure I was never in a situation in which he might casually be mentioned. If he, or his final act, did come up in conversation, I stayed silent. It was a grief so hard to speak of. I had to protect myself and build a castle and live inside it. The world of competition and comparison seemed, finally, lethal, and I reached the conclusion that I needed to be free of the place that judges and, in judgment, declares victory. (What I really wanted to do was write manifestos, organize opposition parties, pick fights, scream obscenities into a bullhorn. I wanted to destroy everything and rebuild it better.) When you get thrown into yourself, you'd better have something there. But at least you could say that I found out what I was made of.

Did I even know him at all? I'm quite sure I didn't. You know how it is—as soon as you believe you've declared victory and gotten something solved, that thing collapses and dissolves out of sight, vanishing like a dream. "We are mysteries to each other," I said to him once. "We never get too deep into anyone else." "It's true," he said, "we don't. But we've got to *try*." All we ever have of other people are their shadows. Their truth—who they are—is merely glanced at, groped at. No one ever comes into clear focus.

When I was a little kid, I kept a microscope and a telescope in my bedroom. In the microscope I mostly looked at strands of my hair, blades of grass, or leaves, but when I was feeling ambitious, I'd collect a cup of rainwater from a puddle out in our yard. I'd put a few water drops on a microscope slide and watch the tiny alien life-forms twisting around on the glass, struggling, in this inhospitable new world, for existence. The telescope was trickier, and I had no idea what I was even supposed to be looking for with it. Everything in the sky—the ghost of the moon, the planets, the stars, the satellites, the light left behind by impressions of psychic energy from the dead—always looked the same to me: blackness, and some undifferentiated bits of light. But I did know one thing. When you gaze up into the sky, you're looking into the past. You see the planets and the stars as they were when the light left them thousands—or millions—of years before. I used to think about this a lot, about how time isn't absolute.

The microscope and the telescope, the worlds of the very small and the very large, helped explain something to me early on: the true nature of reality is hidden from us and just out of view.

And so maybe it is true. Maybe all times and events really are happening simultaneously and maybe the past is just as real as the present and the future. Maybe the death of all things is not the ultimate reality, and everything really is happening all at once: all possibilities and realities exist in unison. When you think about it, it makes a lot more sense than any other idea we've ever been able to come up with. Sometimes we'll get a glimpse of this greater reality—that's all we get, though, a glimpse—and then the place again withdraws, out of reach and scattering like fog.

Acknowledgments

Thank you to Denise Oswald, Dan Halpern, Dominique Lear, and the rest of the fabulous team at Ecco. Also to Joe Veltre, Hayley Nusbaum, Joshua, and my parents. My gratitude to *Vogue,* which published an essay about this time in my life, and to Taylor Antrim.

I'm indebted to Carol Polsgrove's excellent history of Harold Hayes's *Esquire, It Wasn't Pretty, Folks, but Didn't We Have Fun?: Esquire in the Sixties.*

And my love to Dean, our joy.